Secrets of Royalty

By Livy Jarmusch

"The knowledge of the *secrets* of the
Kingdom of Heaven
has been given to you."

~Matthew 13:11

Table of Contents:

Daily Devotionals:

Chapter One: The Worthlessness Camp

Once Upon a Time…there was a dirty little camp, fringing on the outskirts of a dusty town. Muddy tent flaps waved in the stale wind. An intoxicating, damp and musty smell spread through the multitudes that lived in this camp. Those who traveled by the muddy camp could hardly stand such a violent stench. The only people used to this foul odor were the poor souls who dwelt there.

The stale smell of death was like a dark shadow that could never be driven away. Perhaps the most peculiar thing about this camp was that it was always raining there. Constant, dreary rain only made things far more depressing and the living conditions much gloomier. Layers of mud in the streets were thick, which attracted swarms of flies, mosquitoes, and other nasty bugs. The depressed campers couldn't remember a day when the sun ever peeked out with a cheerful grin. The idea of leaving this place and finding a new home was unthinkable. In fact, it was impossible, due to the chains on their feet – and in their minds.

A day in the camp consisted of roaming through the streets, scavenging like wild animals, picking up what little scraps of food they could find, with heavy metal chains fastened to their mud-stained feet. The metal chains that clung to them had this word engraved in bold print, "Worthless."

An evil brood of dark rulers patrolled the camp daily, keeping close eye on their prisoners, making sure they were always miserable. These hopeless refugees with such unbearable burdens could scarcely discern night from day. The only way these prisoners knew when evening had come was when the voices came. Voices that were not their own. The voices would taunt, haunt, and leave scars on their seemingly forever broken hearts.

In vain the prisoners would try to catch a few precious

hours of sleep to escape the nightmarish circumstances. But their sleep was fitful and disturbed, and deceptive nightmares blurred the dividing line between awake and asleep. They were tormented. No true rest ever came. In attempting to find sleep they would fail as they did with everything else in their lives. The enemy officers had tormented them, and they were fully convinced, "I am worth nothing."

The tears of the people flooded the streets, but nobody noticed them fall for the heart-wrenching sobs came just as regularly as the heavy raindrops from the gray sky. But where could they find their hope?

Hope was only a phantom, and freedom wasn't even a shadow on the street. How could one ignore the voices, when they persistently wore and tore at the soul? All joy and laughter decayed, and nobody remembered the light of a day. Voices brought messages as though they were straight from Hell; messages of hopelessness saying, "You'll never measure up. Why don't you just give up and die? Nobody cares about you and your life; you're like an orphan who is lost and abandoned. Do you see the mud beneath your feet? Even that is greater than thee."

One day, as the morning sun began to shine on the camp, many still laid on the streets, paralyzed with fear. It was far too depressing to rise to their feet and begin another meaningless day. The prisoners were much too lost inside themselves to hear a new sound that was moving into their dreary atmosphere. For one moment, a beautiful, glorious moment, the rain paused and the clouds parted as they made way for the brilliant morning sunshine. A window was opened from heaven, and a symphony of hope could be heard in the distance. Jubilant sounds of rejoicing, vibrant music, warm laughter, and lots of love echoed through the camp. A new song was sung by these travelers as they came near the outskirts of the camp. The lyrics were like a breath of fresh air offered to the campers who struggled to breathe.

"Arise! Arise, come up from here!" They proclaimed in song, "Wake up you sleepers and arise from your grave, and the King will shine on you!" The choir sang this melody with much joy; the very words the King told them to sing.

Now this King was of course not the King of the Worthlessness Camp, this King was the Ruler of The City of the Chosen. He ruled over a humble people who crowned Him as the King of Kings and Lord of Lords. This King had many names, but most in the Kingdom called Him "Love."

The Faithful King led His citizens around the perimeter of the Worthlessness Camp, like a Shepherd gently guiding His flock. The King's heart ached for the prisoners inside this camp, and it was His burning desire to see each and every one of these captives set free.

"Come and follow me!" He sang, leading the chorus with the loudest and most beautiful voice of all His people, "Come with me to the City of the Chosen!"

"What an offer!" you may say, "I would have gone up and went right away!" But oh how these prisoners had been led astray; and so, in the Worthlessness Camp they stayed. Not a single soul rose to his feet for they could hardly stand the sound of their own heartbeat.

Instead, inside of themselves they said, "I could never go and live in a palace with the King, oh how I despise that song that He sings. I am worth nothing, that's what they tell me, and I don't see how the King could ever truly love me."

Why did these people believe the lie? Could it be that they were wrapped up in pride? How could one feel so trapped inside when the King was offering a brand new life? Had the King asked such a hard thing? Why couldn't they just stand up and leave? Hope was holding out His hand, and His desire was to heal their land, but why, why, did they run away from the One who wanted to remove their chains?

Though this tale wasn't meant to be a tragedy, at this point, it is what it appeared to be. These people hid inside themselves, sold out to the lie that they could never be enough. And they continued hiding all through the day, stuck in the mud of their hopeless ways. It was an apathetic lullaby that got these people believing such lies, the one that's still being sung today; not once upon a time but right now, today, the one that leads so many astray.

"I don't matter. You don't matter. Human life doesn't matter. I don't care about you, and you don't care about me." That was the song that those voices sang, haunting and cursing again and again. Those words were so ingrained in their minds; they were convinced it was the King who lied.

A few days later, a young woman heard the sound of the King's song, and she almost wished she could sing along. She opened her dried and chapped bloody lips, but felt if she sang it would be like a betrayer's kiss. For so many weeks, months, and even years she laid on those streets chained to her fears. But now, something deep inside her heart aroused with such passion that it gave her a start. She would do it. She would just stand up and leave. And the enemy might stop her, but she had to believe.

Wobbly feet led her down the muddy streets. When the guards were not looking, she slipped out the back gate. She ran and ran until she was out of breath. She continued running from her ghosts, her god-forsaken past.

A towering castle sparkled in the distance. Soon she arrived at the city gates. She would ask to step inside and hope she was not too late. Her crystal blue eyes, the same shade as the sky, widened as she stepped closer to the palace. Every stone was overlaid with gold, presenting a dazzling pattern of sparkly diamonds, sapphires, topaz jewels, and rubies. Her eyes had never seen such riches all at once, all in one place. As she approached the palace gate, she felt as though her muddy feet would ruin the beautiful floors.

She took a deep breath and lifted her eyes to look at the enormous giant towering over her. High upon the secured castle wall stood a man who looked like he feared nothing at all. Chiseled muscles, defined and intimidating, lumped upon his chest and arms. He wore a black shirt which read "Security," but his intimidating eye-brows said it all. He was not to be messed around with.

She cleared her throat and clenched her fists, struggling to find some back bone. Perhaps she could somehow appear much braver than she felt. "I have come to have an audience with the King," her voice quivered. Her quiet words were nearly lost with the wind.

She felt a quick shiver run down her spine as the large man set his eagle eyes to inspecting her. From his point of view, this young lady didn't look much like someone who was prepared to feast with the King Himself. The half pint stood hunched over, shivering, and barefoot. Only a piece of smelly cloth filled with holes was wrapped around her boney shoulders as a coat to guard her from the cold. She looked ill, as if she carried some sort of incurable disease. Striking blue eyes stared up at him, but they were as frozen as an icy lake. A strong and vile stench came from the girl, and the Royal Security Guard knew where she had come from, The Worthlessness Camp.

"Madam," he replied, all manners yet firm in his approach, "Do you know this King you speak of?" The guard asked in that loud and rather stern voice of his.

"Well..." The girl glanced down shamefully at her muddy feet. She had already made a mess of the crystal sidewalk where she stood. Someone would have to come along and clean up after her. "Not exactly, your grace. But I have heard of Him. Every day He comes to the outskirts of the camp and invites us to follow Him back to the palace. So this time I did. I grew so tired of the mud and the tears that I decided to escape. I can only hope that His offer still stands. That is why I am here, sir."

The man shook his head, "I'm sorry miss, but I cannot let you in these castle doors. According to Kingdom rules, you're a prisoner. As prisoner of the King's enemy you still belong to the darkness. You are a captive of war and clothed in the wicked schemes of the enemy. I cannot allow you inside the palace."

The girl felt her glass heart fall from her chest and crash onto the sidewalk below. What was he saying? She had come so far, she had risked everything only to be rejected?!

"B-b-but," the girl stuttered, frantically fighting the desperate tears that tugged at her soul, "I only did what the King asked me to do! Please, your grace, I beg you; you must understand my condition. I cannot go back to that dreadful place! If I were to return, I cannot say what my captors would do to me. I escaped against their wishes; and if the rulers discover I have left, they will sentence me to death!" She couldn't stop the tears now, "Please, you must understand!"

"The Light can have no communion with the darkness." The guard firmly spoke the rules, "There are no exceptions. You fall short...your ugly sin separates you from the King."

Losing the will to stand any longer, she let the devastating blow crush her to the ground. She collapsed and held her head in her hands. "What am I to do? Where am I to go?" She finally composed herself, rose with her bottom lip still trembling, and determined to be brave. She left the palace perimeters and took the backstreets into the City of the Chosen. She felt disoriented and lost. She had risked everything for the hope that the King would let her inside. And now what? She would do what she could to survive. But never again would she return to the Worthlessness Camp. *They'll have to kill me first*, she thought with such hatred and disgust for the demons of her past.

Suddenly, a terrible pair of hands grabbed her and tossed her to the ground. She let out a scream, but they were in the back alley far away from anyone who could hear her. One of the Camp security guards grinned wickedly, exposing a rotten tooth smile, as he clasped her hands and feet with those familiar chains.

"I was expecting you," he snarled. "Everyone who leaves to follow that lying and deceitful King always comes crawling back to us. His promises of second chances and life in the palace are just too good to be true. He doesn't mean a word He says. That King is a coward; He is a lying fool! Too bad that you had to learn it the hard way. And now you know for yourself...He doesn't really care about you. You're not worth being cared about."

The girl couldn't argue for everything he said appeared to be true. He dragged her back to the Worthlessness Camp and she had no fight left inside. When they returned, the camp leaders chained her to a post near the entry way, in order to make an example of her.

"Ah, does the miserable girl double as an escape artist? This should teach you to know your place. You worthless wretch, thinking you could run away from us like that without receiving punishment. You have been our slave since birth...your blood is in our hands. We own you and can do with you whatever we please. Tomorrow morning we will sell you on the slave block, in the Town Square...Yes! We will drag you to the slave post and there we shall make a ridicule of you! Why? Because no one will offer a cent to buy you...not one measly little penny." The guard laughed at the idea of such evil fun, "Tomorrow the town will let you know how much you're worth...and you shall know for yourself what a waste of breath you are."

The night offered no comfort as she contemplated her final hours. *Maybe it's better this way,* she thought with a hard heart, as the tears on her face dried with the crusty mud, *Maybe it's better if my life is just ended.*

The morning came. Just as they promised, the leaders brought her downtown and displayed her in the public market on the slave block. She didn't bother to lift her head. She knew how shameful it was to be in such a position. Yes, she had been born into slavery, into the hands of the Worthlessness Camp leaders, and it was their right to do whatever they pleased...but the slave block? How shameful.

She knew what would happen if no one in the town thought of her as somewhat valuable and purchased her...she knew what her fate would be. If she was of no value to the town, they would put her to death. Just like a snake or a rat or some other kind of unwanted vermin...she would be murdered.

"Let the bidding begin!" The auctioneer's voice boomed through the air loud and clear as a crowd of excited townspeople drew near to witness the disgrace.

"What does she do?" one of the men from the crowd hollered.

"She hardly looks strong enough to hold a broom!" another woman shouted among the noise.

"I wouldn't waste a cent on that scum bag," an old man in the front grumbled.

"Me neither," another nodded in full agreement.

"Come on now!" The auctioneer sounded somewhat sympathetic as he studied the boney girl, "Let's look on the bright side." He frowned, not seeing much but skin and bones. "You wouldn't need to feed her much." He shrugged, struggling to see the positive.

"Forget it!" a bossy sounding man in the crowd hollered back. "Get rid of her; let's see what else ya got."

The girl could no longer hold back the dreadful tears that streamed down her face...*It's true,* she thought gravely, *all along...the voices were right. I am worth nothing.* The man tried a little bit longer to sell her, but it was obvious nobody was interested. The auctioneer reached for the rope which was looped around her neck and began to lead her away just like a dumb animal. "I'll give you back to your owners," he spoke quietly. "They can do with you what they please."

Just as a hand reached for the rope around her neck, the subtle sound of hoof beats were heard in the distance. This horse sounded as though it was on a fixed mission, galloping up the cobblestone street. She lifted her head to see who was coming. The sound increased in intensity until both horse and rider appeared. Most of the crowd was taken aback by the man who sat on this white horse. For it was not just any man, but it was the Prince...the Prince of the entire Kingdom. Everyone knew His name, although everyone did not respect Him as they should.

"It's Jesus!" one whispered in awe.

"Oh forget it, He's no extraordinary person," another murmured back, his voice loud enough to be heard above the silence. "Let's get on with the auction..."

The girl could hardly believe this was happening. Here she stood on the slave block, the place reserved for only the lowest of the low, and in rides the Prince of the Kingdom! How disgraceful! She had never seen Him before. She had only heard His voice singing just outside the camp, but it was enough to make her heart ache for whatever He had to offer. But none of that mattered now. She was about to be killed. Everything she had ever known would turn into deepest darkness. Nothing. Worthless. Just like her. The Prince had been rightfully called, "Prince of Peace", the true Light who could not tolerate the kingdom of Darkness.

How shameful! she thought. *I do deserve death...I don't deserve to be standing in His presence.*

Everyone stared at the Prince and few bowed down to acknowledge His royal position. A burning look of anger and fierce fury blazed on the Prince's face as He spoke in a loud and authoritative voice,

"What is this?!" He leaped off His horse and bounded toward the crowd. Several pulled back in fear, clearing a path for Him to make his way to the front of the crowd. "Has My Father not commanded the end of the slave block? It has no place in His Kingdom! We cannot judge others by outward appearances. My Father instead looks at the heart. If we belong to His Kingdom, we should do the same! Such activities as this are degrading, heartless, and disrespectful to our King! His heart would be grieved to know you have continued this forbidden practice in secret."

Mighty Warrior, the girl thought as she fell down to her knees, giving up the will to stand any longer. *And another name they call Him...Savior.*

"Stand up!" the leader of the Worthlessness Camp hissed in her ear. "On your feet! He is not worthy to be worshiped for He is the one who lied to you! I told you nobody wanted you and it is true. Not a penny was offered for you, so now your life must be destroyed. But I can't kill you here...not now...or else that blasted Prince may see me and tell His Father...come and I shall kill you at the Camp. Come."

Savior! the girl thought frantically, *If they call Him savior, He must save. But would He reach out His hand to rescue me? Would He even want to set me free?*

The enemy's fingernails dug into her arms as he grabbed her and began to pull her away. Suddenly she let out a scream: "Jesus!" she cried with utter desperation, "Save me!"

Horror swept over the enemy's face as Jesus turned to look at him. The Light confronted the Darkness with three simple words, "Let her go." He commanded it, drawing out each word with passion and intensity.

"Never!" the devil hissed as he only pulled her chains tighter. "She is mine, a disgusting daughter of Eve, property of darkness and captive prisoner of the Worthlessness Camp. Her blood belongs to me, her last breath belongs to me, and I can do with her whatever I please. Even *You* know that."

Jesus took a step closer and spoke with much determination as He lifted himself onto the slave stage which had been raised so everyone in the town could see the slave block, "Then I will buy her back."

"It's too late for You to save the day," he argued, knowing the Kingdom Rules by heart. "If only You would have ridden in on your white horse a few moments sooner...we were in the middle of an auction. You might have wasted your money on her then. But lucky for You, I'm saving You the great trouble of teaching a rat like her to be a princess...I'll simply give her what she deserves, death!"

"If it is death you are so thirsty for," Jesus spoke as He took off his outer cloak, "If it is bloodshed that you crave, if it's the sight of raging torture and misery on a face, and blood spilled on the ground, then that is what I shall give you. Her life in exchange for Mine."

The enemy was completely astounded by the Prince's offer. Everyone in the crowd gasped. The enemy leapt back in dramatic fright and astonishment, "You do not mean it!" he shouted. "You would never do such a thing! Lay down your life like a helpless little sheep...preparing Yourself for the slaughter?! You would be slain! Your Father's Kingdom would be destroyed...and I...I...." The enemy gasped, "I would win!"

The girl could not believe what her ears were hearing. Her mind raced in absolute fear. *Why would the Prince offer to do such a thing?* She panicked, *For....for me? Worthless, horrible, wretched...me?*

The Prince made eye contact with her as if He somehow understood what she was thinking. He set down His sword and held out His hands. That one act said it all. In His silence the Prince had spoken so many words. His love was heard in all languages, but the girl couldn't even begin to interpret everything He was saying to her.

As the devil took the chains off of her feet and hands, and strapped them onto the Prince's, the girl could do nothing but stand in amazement. *Who is this man"* she thought, *that He would die...for me?*

The young girl returned to the palace gates, wondering how she possibly escaped. She didn't have to run, she didn't have to die; all she did now was ask the question, *Why?*

~*~

She found herself standing by the Palace once again, hoping that someone might let her in. That old, familiar security guard scowled from above, and the girl was tempted to turn around and run. But where would she go, where would she live? She had seen what the Prince had to give. His very self, His life, His Kingdom, His pride...all crushed in one second, because of her life. Her wrists were still scarred from the grip of those chains, her hair greasy, her body smelly, and her feet were still grossly muddy. She shivered like she had the first time, but something was different and she didn't quite know why.

"S-s-sir" she stuttered, "I-I-have come to offer my deepest sympathy to the King about the death of His son. I know...I know that last time I was not allowed inside, but may I perhaps see Him to offer my apologies, just this once?"

The whole Kingdom had been mourning because their beloved Prince died. Three days now, and His faithful people still continued to mourn in the streets. They wore black and covered themselves in ashes. The girl knew a terrible secret that nobody else did: it was all her fault. The future King had been snuffed out like a burning candle wick long before His time. He was so young and handsome, and so full of potential. He had been predestined to rule, and now there was no heir to the throne.

What would happen to the Kingdom? What would happen to the City of the Chosen? She felt the guilt weigh heavy on her chest. She needed to see the King. *She should've been the one that died!* She was the one who was a slave to pride. She had never known this kind of love before. Why would a stranger, nevertheless a Prince, do something so selfless? These questions had stirred in her soul for the past three days, keeping her awake as she hid in the alleyways. Would the rest of the Kingdom desire to kill her if they knew she was the reason why He had died?

The guard studied her with those intimidating eyes of his and wondered why the young lady had come so late. Nearly every other citizen offered their sympathies days ago, weeping openly and tossing beautiful roses on the gravesite of His Royal Majesty. A stream of people had been flooding the palace gates, which meant that security risks had increased.

"Miss, I'm going to need to do a thorough security and background check."

"Ummm....yes sir." Her tiny hands were trembling so she placed them behind her back. He pulled out a clip-board and appeared as though he was searching for something.

"Name?" He asked the first of a series of questions.

"I do not know" she replied quietly, "I never had one. I'm from the Worthlessness Camp."

The man frowned, feeling as though he had already had this conversation, "I cannot let anyone from that place inside these palace gates. For light can have no communion with darkness."

The tears came once more, as the girl clung desperately to the tiny sliver of hope that remained. "Please, sir!" She slipped to her knees, "I beg you! I must speak with the King!"

At that very moment, she heard the palace gate open and quiet footsteps followed. She did not look up for she was so distraught.

A strong voice asked, "What seems to be the problem?"

Finally, her quivering chin arose and she looked at him through blurry tears. She did a double take. The Man that she saw standing before her looked much like…no, it couldn't possibly be. Perhaps she was hallucinating. Yes, that had to be it.

"This is none of your concern, Your Majesty" the security guard spoke, "Just another no-namer from the Worthlessness Camp. We will discard her and remove her from the premises immediately."

"No." The Man's voice was firm, yet held a gentleness inside as he looked at her with compassionate eyes. "You'll let her stay."

"Forgive me Your Highness," the guard replied, "but we must abide by the Kingdom Rules. For even a king cannot forsake what he once said. A royal decree is in effect for all time."

He nodded, and the young girl felt her breath catch. She was kneeling in the presence of the King Himself! "That is so." The King continued, "But have you forgotten the new rule? The rule which I put into effect just this morning as we received news that my Son is no longer dead, but alive?" A smile radiated from the depths of his eyes, as He spoke, "Love is a far more powerful force than death. My Son offered Himself as a ransom. He laid down His life for every captive in the Worthlessness Camp. It's true that Light can have no communion with the darkness…that rule shall always stand firm. But the new rule has been put into effect, signed and sealed by the blood of My Son. This is a royal declaration to endure for all time: 'Yet to all who receive Me, to those who believe in My name, I give them the right to become Children of the King - children born not of natural decent nor of human decision or a husband's will, but born of God.'"

The young woman couldn't believe it. Her mouth hung open in shock and wonderment. How could this be true?! The Prince was alive?! She was allowed to enter the palace gates?!

"This young maiden has traveled afar to get here." The King grinned, looking right at her, "We shall not leave her waiting outside My gates any longer. Step inside My daughter, Welcome Home!"

Chapter 2: The Banquet Table

Everything happened so fast. She scarcely had time to choke down the news that the Prince was no longer dead, but alive! She wished she knew what to say to the King; something, anything as He gently reached for her grubby hand and led her through the palace gates. He spoke to her as they stepped inside the palace, but she didn't hear a word He said. Her eyes were much too distracted by the dazzling scenery.

The Armory was entirely breathtaking. Marble floors glistened below, reflecting the sunshine which beamed in from the full-wall windows on either side. She was so worried that her feet were making a terrible mess on the flawless floor. The long hallway was lined with the palace guard; sturdy knights on duty, who stood tall in their royal attire. The sunshine sparkled like diamonds, glittering on their swords and suits of armor.

The King was saying something about a grand feast to be held in the honor of the Prince that evening, and that she was invited to attend. She tried to listen, but the scenery around her captivated her attention. It was too much to soak in. She had never seen such extravagant riches displayed all at once.

She gasped out loud as they stepped into the Ballroom. Nearly a hundred crystal chandeliers sparkled above, reflecting the sun and dancing around, making the floor appear to be painted with rainbows of every color. The room was larger than anything she had ever seen and she wished that she could explore each breathtaking detail, from the golden flower pots to the silver furniture. She glanced down at her feet and saw rubies embedded into the very ground she walked on!

She was quickly introduced to the Royal Tailor, a slim woman with a pointy noise who whisked her up a twisting marble staircase onto another floor. She was told that this woman would be in charge of making her ready for the ball tonight. But the girl felt as though she could never be ready. Her stomach lurched at the realization that she would be meeting the Prince tonight. The very One who saved her life. What was she doing here anyway? Didn't she belong in the Worthlessness Camp?

The tall woman's uppity high-heels clicked on the floor as she pushed through the double doors, and into the Royal Fitting Rooms. The large room which stretched out before the girl's eyes could be compared to the size of a modern-day retail store such as *Forever 21*. Hundreds of dresses adorned the room, and suits and ties of every color imaginable hung on racks. Bolts of material decorated the walls, and lifeless mannequins styled the Kingdom's latest original designs.

"...the King's servants are drawing your bath." The Royal Tailor had been speaking to her the entire time, but only now did she start listening to the words. "Here at the Palace our attire ranges from evening gowns, party dresses, blue jeans and casual wear, to tennis outfits and preppy sun dresses. The accessories corner located in the back of the room is filled with shoes, purses, clutch bags, sunglasses, and the finest collection of tiaras. A large runway is the centerpiece of our fashion studio where our models display our newest Kingdom designs. Along the left wall are vanity sets with bright lights and comfortable chairs where you may sit to have your makeup and hair done by the Kingdom's styling staff."

The girl was pretty sure that this would be her favorite room in the castle. Like appeasing eye candy, there was always something marvelous to look at. She felt like a wide-eyed little girl staring in the glass windows at a shopping mall. It was all so delightful! Her eyes were not accustomed to seeing such bright colors.

"Alright my dear, let's get right to work and not waste any time. First we must take a step into the wardrobe of your heart. What are you styling these days? In Romans, Chapter Thirteen, Verse Twelve in the Royal Handbook, the King instructs us on our first Royal Fashion Tip; one that we subscribe to faithfully and never waver from here at the palace. That rule is:
'The night is nearly over; the day is almost here. So let us put aside the deeds of darkness and put on the armor of light.'" The Royal Tailor spoke as if she had the words memorized by heart. "It's true that this world is dark all around us, but you no longer belong to the Kingdom of darkness. The Prince woke you up from that apathetic lullaby just before dawn, but you must know that you are still in danger of falling back asleep if you don't change. So choose a dressing room my dear, and strip away those awful, smelly clothes."

The young girl did as she was told, and pulled a scarlet curtain across the changing area to allow her privacy. Mirrors on every side of the dressing chamber echoed what she was wearing. She had been in these clothes for so long…how would it feel to be rid of them? A strange thought came over her, and for a moment she didn't even wish to take them off. They had been comfortable for it was all that she had ever known.

The woman outside must've been reading her mind… "Just because Wendy styled her blue night gown all the way to Never Never Land doesn't mean that is at all acceptable in the Royal fashion world!" She giggled, as if amused with her own little joke. "You've got to strip off these comfy cozy PJ's and get your head up off the pillowcase of yesterday! You cannot, my dear, continue to sing the same song that this world is singing. Just because you left that nasty old camp does not mean that you won't be tempted to switch back to humming that same old dreary and lifeless tune. Those old clothes have to go!"

The girl obeyed and wiggled out of her dirty rags. She tossed them on the floor never to see them again. Then, she tiptoed into the hot bath that was waiting for her. Steam rolled out of the golden tub. Royal maids scurried around her as they soaked and scrubbed every part of her, as the Royal Tailor continued speaking.

"It's going to take a lifelong transformation of switching your mind from thinking like you used to, and instead thinking like a citizen of the City of the Chosen. Our motto here at the palace is: 'Do not conform any longer to the pattern of this world, but be transformed by the renewing of your mind. Then you will be able to test and approve what the King's will is. His good pleasing and perfect will.' That means that no guest at the Ball can have clothes in the closet of her heart patterned after the same way this world puts their outfits together. It can't even be made from the same material as them! This season, the kingdom of darkness is styling some frightening fashions. Make sure that you never have anything to do with them.

In the Royal Handbook, Romans 2:29-32, it clearly tells us what not to wear. The material of their hearts is patterned out of wickedness, evil, greed, and depravity. They wear outfits of envy, murder, strife, deceit, and malice. They wear sparkly jewels of gossip and slander. On their hats are written the words, 'God Hater,' 'Insolent,' 'Arrogant,' 'Boastful.' Their trendy tee's read, 'We invent ways of doing evil,' and 'We disobey our parents.' Their shoes are made of senseless, faithless, heartless and ruthless patterns. And although they know the King's righteous decree, which states that those who have such hearts deserve death, not only do they continue to do these things, but they approve, encourage, and pat their friends on the back for wearing the same exact things. Do you have any of this junk in your closet? If you do, I'd suggest you throw it out now! Alright ladies, make her smell good as new, dry her off, and get ready for phase two!"

The young girl was soon wrapped in a soft towel and sent back to the wardrobe area. The Royal Tailor clasped her hands together with excitement, "now it's time for phase two of your royal makeover: what to wear. When exploring what not to wear, we looked at this world as our example. But when looking at what to wear in the Kingdom, we are always inspired by the beautiful heart fashion icon Himself, The King! 2 Corinthians 13:4-8 tells us what He's always wearing as the King of Love. It also gives us a great place to begin with your new outfits! Or rather, should I call them in-fits?" She laughed again at her own joke before gesturing the girl to sit down on the round, purple ottoman. The young woman had the feeling she was in for a lecture. This lady *loved* to talk.

"Now, tonight the King will be wearing a long, white robe of patience. The King wears silk slippers made from kindness. None of his clothes are patterned from anything envious, boastful, or self-seeking. He wears a glorious crown that is not easily angered. On the tablet of his heart, He keeps no record of sin or wrongdoings. He does not wear anything created by evil, but instead everything is patterned after truth. The King gives His shield of protection to anyone who asks, and His eyes purely hold trust and peace. His laughter is full of hope, and on His right hand He wears perseverance. Our King never fails.

So if that's what our King looks like, I think I have the perfect in-fit in mind for you! How about...a cream colored, floor length dress of patience, and glass slippers made from kindness. From your lips, you will try not to speak anything envious, boastful, or self-seeking. Your small, yet quaint and lovely tiara will remind you that your King is not easily angered...and neither should you be. On the tablet of your heart, you will try not to keep records of wrong about people who have hurt you in the past. You won't endorse anything evil, but instead boldly confirm all truth in love. You will remember the King's shield of protection around you and learn to trust Him with peace in your heart. You shall wear a silver necklace of hope, and a matching bracelet of perseverance. You will remember that our King never fails. Ladies, bring in the dress!"

Several servants hustled inside, bringing a rack on wheels. There the gown hung beneath a dress-bag. The contents were hidden, and the girl couldn't wait to see what was inside. "The King himself chose these garments for you," the Royal Tailor spoke as she slowly unzipped the bag. "Now close your eyes and we shall dress you."

The girl did as she was told. She could feel the soft, velvety material tumble over her and cover all her nakedness and shame. She had never felt so clean or lovely in her entire life.

"Ah, I do believe I see the makings of a Princess," the Royal Tailor smiled. "Now open your eyes, and look in the mirror."

The girl slowly opened her eyes and twirled around. The flawless material was free of wrinkles or blemishes of any kind. She had never seen anything quite so splendorous. The bodice of the cream-colored dress had silver sparkles all over it; they were tiny diamonds embedded into the dress. Surely it would sparkle in the Ballroom tonight. She felt warm tears come to her eyes, and she wondered what she could've done to deserve all this. Had the King really handpicked the dress? My, it was regal enough for a queen to wear! The full skirt proofed out as if she were wearing a hoop beneath it and gently tumbled onto the floor. Several servants came and began to flock about her, busying themselves with her preparation. One brought her silver slippers and the other her diamond necklace. Several servants began curling her hair and one applied a light layer of makeup.

"I believe you won't need much makeup at all," the Royal Tailor sounded pleased, "due to your lovely features. Your scarlet lips, blue sparkling eyes, and pale skin make you by far, the fairest young beauty in the land."

~*~

The moment had arrived. Every guest in the City of the Chosen appeared in their fancy horse-drawn carriages. Our frail heroine paced back and forth across her bedroom floor. She was to wait here until she was ushered downstairs. From her vantage point, she could see flocks of carriages prancing up the drive, with laughing men and women inside. They all wore magnificent gowns and stunning tuxes as they escorted one another through the palace doors.

"Are you ready miss?" the Royal Tailor asked. Her voice slightly surprised the girl who peered out the window. She was finally going to meet the Prince who had died for her! But what on earth would she say? Her stomach was in knots and she felt like she was going to trip in her heels. She nodded nonetheless. "The Town Crier is going to announce your entrance as you descend down the staircase. Everyone is eager to see the young maiden that the Prince offered his life for."

Her eyes widened, "You mean...they know? Everyone will know that I was the girl who..."

Her voice trailed off and the Royal Tailor beckoned her, "Come along now dear, we don't have much time. You will be waiting on top of the stairs, just hidden from the audience until you are announced. Simply follow the crimson carpet down the stairs and into the Banquet Hall where the Prince will be waiting. Don't worry, everything will be fine. And don't forget to smile!"

The Royal Tailor shimmied down the stairway in a glamorous silver party dress of her own, leaving the young girl standing by herself. She thought about bolting. But where would she go? Perhaps she would dart back to the wardrobe room and lock herself in the closet.

"Ladies and Gentlemen!" A voice boomed through the Ballroom from below. The excited murmurs hushed, and a blanket of silence filled the room. "Citizens of the House of God, and the City of the Chosen, may we all stand and cheer in honor of the Prince's beloved as she graces us with her presence. She is one of a chosen generation, a royal priesthood, a holy nation, His own special people! She has been called out of the kingdom of darkness and redeemed by the blood of her Prince Jesus, that she may declare His praises among the congregation of God's people in the Kingdom of Light! She is anointed, established and sealed by The King. She is the apple of His Majesty's eye, and He calls her His Beautiful One." A roar of applause thundered below and she didn't know how she did it, but suddenly she was descending down the staircase.

I've never been one to feel very comfortable in front of crowds. She felt her face turn a beet red as all those eyes stared at her. *What if I trip and make an absolute fool out of myself? I'll be utterly humiliated! Am I even ready for this? Just this morning I was wallowing around in the Worthlessness Camp...and now I stand inside these palace walls?* Her head felt dizzy as she clung to the railing, and the bottom step couldn't come fast enough. She followed the red carpet as people on the sidelines clapped and smiled and snapped a few pictures.

"You're not worth it," a chilling voice whispered in the depths of her mind, "You could never live up to the King's expectations." She suddenly stopped, dead in her tracks. She whipped around to see who had spoken, but there was nothing but air. Surely no one from the crowd had shouted that!

"Once the Prince realizes what a loser you are, He'll regret that He even tried to rescue you." She recognized the voice. It was the same voice from the Worthlessness Camp.

But how had it followed her here?! She thought she would be safe inside these fortress walls, but now she wasn't so sure. She took another small step forward, but the voice was still following her.

"You make one pathetic little princess. Even if you were pretty enough to be someone important, you and I both know that your heart is ugly enough to last you and the rest of this kingdom an eternity of disappointment. Disappointment caused by you and your fatal attempts to make the King happy."

No! She argued with the epic battle that was forming in her mind. *That can't be true! I don't belong to the worthlessness camp any longer! Darkness you don't have a hold on me! Lies I don't have to believe you.*

"Ugly," the voice whispered as he sent another fiery dart into her soul, "Ugly and you know it! Admit it. Surrender and put down that shield...say these words because you know they're true. 'I'm just not worth it.'"

His lies made her cringe as she quickened her pace. She had to reach the Banquet Hall. She had to know, finally, the truth for herself. Did the Prince really care for her? Or was it all just a big, fat mistake?

Suddenly, she saw it. A magnificent table spread out before her. Every food imaginable was present. Savory meats, sweet sauces and mouthwatering desserts mingled and flirted with one another, creating a most enticing smell. The decorations were by far the grandest display of material items she had ever seen. Dimmed lights made the entire room feel lit up with love and romance as candles flickered, reflecting on the dishes. Pure golden goblets, silver diamond- studded plates, and glorious napkin rings with rubies in them! Was this a dream?

An orchestra played in the background, violins carrying out a soft and entrancing tune. She feasted on the scene with her eyes, running them down the long table until she reached the end where something far more grand caught her eye.

There, seated at the other end of the room, was the Prince of the Kingdom of Light. His handsome features were lit up in the candle light, and the golden crown proudly proclaimed his royal position. A soft smile played on His lips, and she felt herself go suddenly shy. She could scarcely even look Him in those beautiful eyes.

The royal orchestra etched out a beautiful song upon their stringed instruments, and the regal choir lifted their voices to sing from the Book of Psalms, Chapter 45:

"Beautiful words stir my heart.
I will recite a lovely poem about the king,
for my tongue is like the pen of a skillful poet.
You are the most handsome of all.
Gracious words stream from Your lips.
God himself has blessed You forever.
Put on your sword, O mighty warrior!
You are so glorious, so majestic!
In Your majesty, ride out to victory,
defending truth, humility, and justice.
Go forth to perform awe-inspiring deeds!
Your arrows are sharp, piercing your enemies' hearts.
The nations fall beneath your feet.
Your throne, O God, endures forever and ever.
You rule with a scepter of justice.
You love justice and hate evil.
Therefore God, your God, has anointed You,
pouring out the oil of joy on You more than on anyone else.
Myrrh, aloes, and cassia perfume your robes.
In ivory palaces the music of strings entertains you.
Kings' daughters are among your noble women.
At your right side stands the queen,
wearing jewelry of finest gold from Ophir!

Listen to me, O royal daughter; take to heart what I say.
Forget your people and your family far away.
For your royal husband delights in your beauty;
honor him, for he is your lord.
The princess of Tyre will shower you with gifts.
The wealthy will beg your favor.
The bride, a princess, looks glorious
in her golden gown.
In her beautiful robes, she is led to the king,
accompanied by her bridesmaids.
What a joyful and enthusiastic procession
as they enter the king's palace!
Your sons will become kings like their father.
You will make them rulers over many lands.
I will bring honor to your name in every generation.
Therefore, the nations will praise You forever and ever."

She was speechless. What would she possibly say to this
Man…a complete stranger, who had gone to such great
lengths for her? She felt shy and uncomfortable as all the
servants buzzed around bringing out foreign dishes, foods
that were steaming and making her mouth water. She had
never seen such delicacies, but her stomach was so nervous
she couldn't possibly think about eating them.

"I'm so delighted that you came," the Prince started
slowly, a sweet smile creasing His lips upward, "Welcome to
my Kingdom. I expect that you have found everything quite
satisfactory…the service, the dress, the jewelry?"

"Oh yes!" she nodded, feeling overwhelmed by it all. The
violins in the background were distracting as were the
sparkly dishes and the servants buzzing like bees. "It's…it's
more than I ever could have asked for. I never dreamed that
someone would do this much for me."

His smile didn't disappear, and the girl wasn't sure that
it was possible, but it was almost as if His smile grew.

"These gifts I have bestowed upon you this evening are the finest I have to offer. Every element of this night; your gown, the meal, the music has all been given much thought and planned especially for you. I'm glad that you have taken a fancy to them. But these are only material items. It's true that I love to give gifts, but I would like to offer you something of far greater value."

She was listening as she reached for a golden goblet, bedazzled with small rubies and emeralds. She lifted the goblet to her lips to taste what was inside.

"I would like to offer you My very self."

The words made her suddenly drop the goblet, slipping out from beneath her fingers. With a great crash the goblet slammed down, knocking all the inner contents out of the cup. The red liquid bled into the table cloth and she lifted frightened hands up to her face. "Oh, forgive me your Majesty, I did not mean to-"

He let out a small chuckle as servants bustled about, cleaning up the mess, "No worries, please don't let it trouble you. There is plenty more where that came from." He cleared his throat, as if trying to block the comical memory out of his brain. "Moreover, as I was saying, I would like to offer you something more than all these temporary, material gifts." He reached for something in his pocket and placed it on the table. The small box caught her eye. "I would like to offer you a marriage covenant."

He slowly opened the box, and the light from the ring nearly blinded her. Either that or it was his soft-spoken words. "I desire to make you My Princess, to share My Kingdom and My love with you."

At that very moment a man dressed in a tuxedo, who looked slightly more like a penguin than a person, handed her a slim menu. "Here you are Miss," he bowed as he presented it to her, "The Royal Banquet Menu."

Her careful eyes scanned over what was written. Her

mind raced as she pretended to be distracted by the menu. What just happened!? Did he just?! She tried to buy herself time as she scanned over the words.

"So?" the waiter asked eagerly, "what will it be?"

The girl gently refused the menu, "Thank you, but I don't have much of an appetite at the
moment." She glanced at the Prince, "Um, may I be excused?"

He looked disappointed as he nodded slowly, like a complete gentleman would, never holding a maiden against anything she wouldn't wish to do.

The young girl who had been the center of attention slipped out of the Banquet Hall, the Ball Room, then finally out the backdoor of the palace. The familiar cold air greeted her as she hugged her shoulders to keep warm.

What was she doing here? Didn't the Prince know who she was – a captive from the Worthlessness Camp? It was one thing for him to offer kind gifts, a warm meal, and a place to stay. But marriage?! That was an entirely different ordeal! Those voices from the Worthlessness Camp were right. She couldn't possibly ever fit in here. She didn't deserve any of this. She could never be the kind of Princess that the Prince wanted to pretend that she was. She would have to fake to be someone that she was not…every single day of her life, just to make him happy.

As she begin running down the cobblestone pathway, she couldn't help but notice the flowers in the garden that had turned cold and desolate. The cheery faces that shared their smiles and brightly colored petals in the summertime had closed up. No longer could the bees gain wealth from the nectar that was so richly stored up inside. A large rose bush alongside the path that usually blossomed so beautifully in the summertime had withered up and died. As the girl ran by, a thorny branch from the bush reached out to grab her, and her cream colored dress was torn from the wild branch. She sighed, looking down at the small rip in her new gown. It wasn't the rose bush's fault nor the wind that caused the branch to blow in her direction, but still the tear dug into her patience, and a seemingly small mistake had upset her.

With that, she continued running down the path, and through the Palace Garden. She wanted to escape so swiftly, that in the process of doing so, she ran right out of her slippers. She didn't care. Her stomach ached with hunger as confused tears burned in her eyes. There was an aching desire inside of her that needed to be filled, and her stomach cried out in hunger pains. As did her heart. It had all been there, right in front of her. The whole meal. Everything she could have dreamed...the warm coffee, the mouthwatering appetizers, the garden fresh salad, the steamy soup, and everything that was exceedingly abundant and above all she could ask, imagine, or think! So why did she not take part in the celebration and eat? Why did she not sit down with the rest and enjoy the Prince's sweet company?

The glaring image of that ring was now plastered to the front of her mind. The diamond was lovely. Yes, even the Prince was lovely. He was just so perfect. Too perfect. Falling in love with him would be an effortless task. He made it far too easy; rescuing her, bringing her to this glorious place, adoring her with gifts, and saying all the right things. There was no way that every dream she never knew she had could be coming true, all at once, all in one place.

Absolutely free. What was the catch? What did this Prince want from her in exchange for everything He was giving? Was she to be a servant destined to scrub palace floors and clean out golden bathrooms the rest of her life? Wouldn't freedom be better than having to report to someone daily? It seemed so simple, yet so extremely difficult. How could she just sit down and receive it? How could she possibly say "yes" to his offer? She had not earned any of it, and she knew in her heart-of-hearts that she didn't deserve it. How could she simply sit and eat?

The girl continued thinking about these things as she sat down on the stone wall of a wishing well that was no longer working. The fountain that usually teemed with water was all dried up. "I wish," she sighed as her shoulders hung low and desperation started to sink in, "I wish I had something to eat."

"Well then," a strange voice replied, "it must be your lucky day."

She whirled her head around, hair flipping wildly in the wind, only to see three people approaching her. They looked about her age, perhaps a few years older. A young man accompanied by two beautiful women dressed in nice, well-to-do clothes. As they drew closer, she couldn't help but notice the sparkly jewels the girls were wearing. Very striking. One wore gossip around her neck, and the other slander. The man wore a hat that read "Arrogant" as he offered his seemingly humble invitation, "We were just getting ready to have a little feast of our own. Would you care to join us?"

Their clothes. Wasn't that what the Royal Tailor had been talking about? Outfits fashioned by the pattern of this world? The Royal Tailor warned her about such people...the King's decree was not even to eat with people like this. But her desperate appetite drove her to stand up and quietly introduce herself.

The three strangers returned the favor, and each spoke their names in turn. "I am Self Seeking," the first girl spoke, "and this is my sister, Envy Seeking."

The girl couldn't help but wince. Self and Envy. What horrible names. What terrible things to be!

"And I," the man removed his hat as he took a slight bow, his eyes dancing with a playful charm, "am Boastful, but my friends call me Boast. My last name is of course Arrogant, but you already read that on my hat. Pride is my Uncle. Perhaps you've heard of him?"

The girl felt her eyes grow wide as she realized where she was standing. She knew of Pride, and how he was the King's worst enemy. Pride was the leader of the Worthlessness Camp. These were obviously agents from that dark place. Could she dare trust them after everything the enemy had done to her? The girl was going to live up to her reputation and take off running, but for some strange reason her feet remained planted in place. Something about Boast, Self, and Envy had captivated her, and she wasn't quite sure why they felt so alluring.

Soon Boast, Self, and Envy had led the girl to a different part of the garden. Boast used his keys to unlock a garden wall, as he bragged about a most magical place. "Something you will not believe," he spoke with wide eyes, darting every which way as he spoke, "Until you see it for yourself."

He pushed open the cold, stone door and she followed the shady characters inside. She couldn't believe what was happening. It was almost as if she had stepped into another world, for in the dead of winter a vibrant garden bloomed all around her. Pretty fruits and flowers colored the scene. She attempted to wipe the look of awe off her face as she stepped into a seemingly secret garden, but she could not hide her surprise from Boast.

"What," he raised bushy eye brows, "have you never been here before? Don't tell me the Prince didn't tell you this place existed. Come on now, aren't you that girl that he died for? Supposedly He gave everything just so His Father could adopt you as his daughter and make you his Princess? Everybody knows this place."

"What is it?" the girl asked, truly not knowing this place she had gotten herself into.

Boast burst out laughing, and Self chuckled along. "Oh

how naive we are!" Boast continued with his obnoxious laughter, "Didn't you read the Teenage Survival Manual issued by my uncle, Pride? It tells you all about this lot of open property, entirely free to anyone who claims it."

"So you're saying..." she started slowly, obviously impressed, "the fruit on these trees are free?" She echoed, unable to wipe the look of astonishment and wonder from her eyes, "and anyone can eat them anytime they want? And they blossom all year long? I don't understand...this doesn't seem possible. Wouldn't the Prince have told me about this place?"

Boast straightened his hat and spoke, "You'd have to be a fool to follow a Prince like him so blindly. I never believed in all that nonsense the King was dishing out about whosoever believed in His Son could have everlasting life with Him if they repented and blah, blah, blah...it's a whole bunch of who-hash if you ask me."

Self shot the naive girl a "how-could-you-be-so-stupid-look" as she spoke, "Don't you get it? Take a look around, everything you need is right here. No duh the Prince didn't tell you about this place! He hid this from you because He knew once you came here you'd never want to go back to Him and His stuffy old ways. Besides, when you live the life that we do you in this garden you don't answer to anyone but yourself. No rules, no regulations, nothing except what you wanna do when you wanna do it." Self reached up and grabbed a juicy, chocolate candy covered apple off the tree and took a bite.

"What is this place called?" the girl asked quietly.

"Sin," Self smiled with much pleasure. "Your twenty-four-seven access to everything you ever wanted."

She felt her conscience begin to warn her as something inside her heart exploded like a siren. She knew that she had to leave. "Sin..." she whispered quietly, "Isn't that what killed the Prince?" She raised her voice, "This is the Prince's

37

forbidden garden! I-I can't be here!"

"Want one?" Envy held out a candy-coated apple. Despite all the obvious warning signs of how her accepting sin would betray her loyalties to the Prince, she couldn't control the reflex. She wanted to resist, but found herself slowly extending her hand forward.

Why are you doing this?! Her conscience screamed at her, *The Prince has forbidden this!*

Yeah, well maybe that's why I need to do this! She screamed back silently at her conscience as she held the tempting, tasty fruit in her hand. *Maybe Self is right...I don't need anyone to tell me what to do, and this will prove it. Just once, I'm going to do what I want to do. And oh, I want this so badly.* She could feel her mouth begin to water as she drew the poison close to her tongue.

"Wait!" Boast suddenly interrupted, "What about that tiara of yours? You can't actually expect that you can leave that on your head as you do this. That metal piece of junk declares your loyalties to the Kingdom of Light! You'll look like a hypocrite if you leave that on. Go ahead, just rip it off your head. You don't need that any more. You've got us. "

She reached for the tiara and felt the small and precious jewels that adorned her head. "But..." she argued with herself out loud, "The Prince gave this to me. He is the One who actually chose everything that I would wear tonight. I can't just throw it onto the ground and watch it shatter into a thousand tiny pieces."

"Wow!" Envy shook her head, rolling her eyes in disgust. "Look at her. She's having second thoughts. I never thought she was strong enough to do it in the first place. She doesn't want our life badly enough."

"My sister is right," Self shook her head disappointingly. "You just don't have it in you to rebel. You just don't have the guts."

"I do too!" she fiercely argued, hating the fact that they

might be right, "I just...."

"Just what?" Boast had the last words in the matter. He stood in front of her, and looked her square in the eyes, "There are no excuses. There is no middle ground. Either you're with the King or you're with us. Take it or leave it."

~*~

She slipped into the Ballroom, desperately hoping no one would see her. In the past she could have achieved this task quite flawlessly, as back in the Worthlessness Camp she was used to being invisible. But not this time. As she stepped foot into the Ballroom where the King's grand banquet was taking place, it seemed as though every eye looked her way. She wasn't sure if it was because of the tear in her dress, or the mud streaked on her face, but they saw her indeed. Maybe it was because her bare toes were filthy, or her hair had been blown in too many directions at once. She tried to enter unnoticed, but the task was impossible. Everything changes when you're a Princess.

"My daughter!" The King greeted her at once, embracing her in a strong, Fatherly hug. The warmth of his arms surged through her like a comforting cup of tea. Why had He sent His Son to rescue her...just so that He could love her like only a Father can?

"I'm sorry," she whispered, as regret-filled tears begin to stream down her face. "I don't know why I left the party or why I ran away. May I speak with the Prince? I have so much to say."

"I know," He whispered back, "and it's alright. You're here now, and that's all that matters. My Son has been waiting for you and will be more than eager to talk. But first, I think we should see the Royal Tailor about a quick bath and a wardrobe change. Besides," He spoke with a playful twinkle in his eye, "you wouldn't want to miss the dancing."

The girl wasn't so sure. Honestly, she wouldn't have minded at all going straight to bed at once. She preferred that the whole kingdom didn't know she had two left feet. She was sure that she would be as graceful on the dance floor as a walrus!

After her quick change, when she returned to the Ballroom, her ears were greeted by the angelic tone of harmonic whispers, pouring out of a symphony of violins. Black boots shuffled around on the marble floor, as high heels clicked around in perfect step. The dancers who took the stage looked flawless. As the women moved about in their beautiful dresses, skirts rustled against one another, following the graceful lead of the young men who had been partnered with the maidens. She began to feel that familiar apprehensive spirit of fear take her over. *I can't do it,* she shook her head. *The King would be dreadfully embarrassed.*

She stood awkwardly on the sidelines, eyeing the snack table with caution. Maybe she could manage to scoop a cup of punch without spilling it all over her dress. The Prince's tall figure began to make His way across the room, and she had second thoughts about trying to drink punch. His white-gloved hand reached out to touch her arm,

"I am delighted to see you that you decided to join us once more."

The words sliced like a knife across her guilty heart. "Oh, please forgive me," she lowered her head in shame, "I never should've run like that. You've been so good to me...too good. I don't know what I was thinking, really. I suppose I've just been so overwhelmed that I...well, it's a bit much to take in."

"I want you to know that it doesn't matter how many times you may choose to run from me; my offer of engagement and unwavering love still stands. It is my deepest hope that you will accept it."

At that moment, she wished that she could disappear

beneath the floor. Fear desired to keep her mouth locked up tight, but she had to say what she felt inside. "Your Majesty, I feel like a despicable worm that has spit upon Your very face. You have offered such extravagant messages that tell me how much You care. But I must admit that I am afraid for I have never been loved before. I'm not sure that I would even know how to love You in return. You deserve the very best, and I fail to understand why you would choose someone, well...someone like me. I would only hope that I could make you proud, but I cannot promise that I will ever reach the perfection of a bride You might desire. I can only accept your ring if You promise to be patient with me. Promise that You will not cast me out because I am displeasing to You. If you must, punish me to working in the cellar or the kitchen with your other maids. But please, never send me back to the place where I have come from."

The words spilled out of her mouth much more fervently than she thought they would. Her acceptance speech now sounded like a desperate plea to be cared for. Would He now change His mind? Would He wonder what on earth He had gotten himself into? She wasn't sure what she expected His response to be; maybe a frown or a look of disappointment. Instead, a deliriously happy grin lit up His entire face as he reached for the ring in His pocket.

"This engagement promises all the things that you have asked for. This ring, which I pledge to you is merely a symbol, a deposit guaranteeing all the things which are yet to come. Cherish it in faith. Know that I am never giving up on you, and I will never leave you. The road ahead will not always be easy but my faithfulness will see you through it."

The hands which formed the Universe reached around hers, slipping the delicate ring onto her finger. It was official. They had both given their pledges, their hearts and their lives to one another. The girl knew, as she stared at that ring, that from this moment on, nothing would ever be the same.

Suddenly, the music stopped. A silence evaporated every noise in the room. The Town Crier lifted his voice, "Attention, ladies and gentlemen! Citizens of the city of the King! May I present to you the Prince and His Princess as they perform the Dance of the Ages." A burst of applause filled the room, and the Princess felt like her stomach was falling down a bottomless pit.

"May I have this dance?" The Prince asked as He reached out His hand, waiting for His partner to accept it. She studied His eyes, and it was almost as if His warm gaze was whispering, *trust Me*.

But she wasn't so sure of herself. Fear gripped her heart again, and she wanted nothing more than to run. She was quite sure some miracle took place inside because amazingly her feet remained firmly planted right in place.

Just look at Me, His eyes continued speaking mysteries to her heart. *Forget about everyone else in the room. Just take My hand.*

This was too much. She felt her head start spinning and could only nod a yes. Next thing she knew, in a burst of blind faith, He grabbed her hand and swept her to the center of the Ballroom. A large open space on the floor displayed the royal crest. She couldn't believe she was standing upon it. She was well aware of the risk. The fear of falling flat on her face pressed in, and she wasn't even sure if she'd be able to tell her feet which direction to move.

A grand symphony rose from the orchestra. The music began instructing His Majesty's feet through steps He knew by heart, gently leading his brand new Princess through the uncharted waters. Though she had no formal ballroom dance training, she caught on quickly, and wished that she wouldn't trip. They were spinning so rapidly, she wondered if the dizziness was coming from the circles they made around the floor or the utter shock of what was happening. She had never intended for this to happen. Why He had chosen her, she hadn't the slightest idea. Scared of what might happen if she looked away again, she determined to look nowhere else but His eyes. It was a bold decision, but something about the genuine purity of the ocean-like blue pouring out of His eyes set her heart at ease. They held a smile somewhere deep inside, and she couldn't help but smile as well. It didn't take long for her to forget about the lingering crowds, and soon it felt as though all the spectators had vanished.

The music was rising and falling throughout the room, like tidal waves, in perfect unity with the lights. A soft glow lit up the entire ballroom, as the regal red curtains were drawn, the chandeliers were lit, and the sparkling lights began dancing as well.

The orchestra climbed and built with great intensity as they reached the climax of their number, when suddenly they released a note which seemed to penetrate the very atmosphere. The noise instructed the fountains to light up, and caused a large, six-foot-tall model of Cinderella's Glass Slipper to sparkle and shimmer as a small firework burst from the shoe. An invisible circle around the Prince and Princess, surrounding the royal crest, suddenly shot up with water fountains of various colors; pinks, blues, and purples. The water and fireworks display danced right along with them causing everyone in the audience to gasp in wonder. Like a scene straight from Cinderella or Beauty and the Beast, this real life fairytale enchanted everyone in the room.

She looked like a delicate flower growing taller and taller, as her skirt spun around every which way. She was spinning like a top or a figure skater moving elegantly on the ice. She no longer felt like she was dancing...no, she felt as though Someone had picked her up, and she was flying on eagle's wings! The transformation was unthinkable. Clumsy old her...now flawless as a ballerina!

Bubbling up like water in a tea kettle, joy began to swell

inside her heart, and she couldn't help but laugh. And for a moment it felt as though the whole world was laughing along with her! She was entirely weightless in the arms of her Prince. And as she continued to stare deeply into His eyes, she saw something she never noticed before; passion, burning bright and intense like a fire, as though the flames were coming from the depths of His soul. She had known that the Prince cared for her. After all, He laid down his life for her and provided her with a home in this palace, new garments of beauty, and a grand feast. But maybe there was more. Maybe he saw her as something more than a charity project or a good deed. Just maybe.

The dancing couple made one more sweeping round of circles about the room, and then met once more in the center of the royal crest. The Princesses breath was short with exhilaration, excitement, and wonderment. The orchestra punctuated their final notes, and without warning a spiral of fireworks sparkled from around the royal crest, and the Princess was awestruck to find herself in the middle of them. Applause reminded the Princess of where she was, and He clenched her hand, bowing to the adoring audience. She quickly caught on, and curtsied gratefully. He led her to the sidelines, where an explosion of "Hooray! He has chosen His Princess!" and excited pats on the back greeted the Prince.

As she watched Him, the gentle way He had with His people, and the spark that lit up in His eyes every time He laughed, she couldn't help but think, *I've never been in love before, but I think it must feel something like this.*

That same evening, long after the last note had been played, and the final goodbyes were said, nothing remained in the Ballroom but empty furniture sitting in the dark. The Princess lay upstairs in her bed chamber, safe and content, reliving the events of the day in her mind. She already knew sleep was something she would have to do without. At least for tonight. Her heart was still spinning, spinning, spinning.

He's so good to me, she thought, still dancing with the memory in her mind, *He's so...so... perfect.*

The bed she lay in was nothing like she'd ever experienced before...nothing like the Worthlessness Camp. Her bedchamber was larger than she could've dreamed it would be and her closet almost twice the size of her room! And as if that wasn't grand enough, on the side of her room lay a set of double French doors with a balcony overlooking the entire Kingdom! The view was breathtaking.

He must love me, she thought as she rolled over and sighed, *no I mean really, truly love me. More than I could imagine.* She imagined the Prince's love for her being like an ocean. No, it had to be bigger than that. What about the entire galaxy of stars strung across the midnight sky, as far as her eyes could see? No, still bigger. It was unfathomable.

Chapter 3: Mr. Adorable

The next morning breakfast was indescribable. The King had entirely outdone Himself. As soon as the dishes were cleared, the Princess and Prince sat in silence as the King excused Himself to go about His work. The King was so jolly and joyous, making jokes and saying witty things that made her smile all throughout the meal. She had almost felt as though she knew the King her entire life. He had made life at the Palace feel so comfortable. She now knew that it wouldn't take long for her to get used to it. Last night, the Princess rehearsed what she was going to say to her Prince Jesus that morning. How she was going to express her deepest gratitude, and how she was eternally indebted to His great kindness. But she could not find the words. They all seemed to come up empty. How could she express how she really felt?

"Breakfast was…divine, your Highness." The Princess squeaked. But even as the words slipped out of her mouth, she wished she could stuff them back in. Trying to speak with the Prince was harder than she'd thought it would be.

He smiled, as though He understood what she was thinking.

After another short stint of silence He spoke, "My Beautiful One, you are like a delicate rose with beauty inside that has been surrounded by thorns. You might still feel like the prisoner in the Worthlessness Camp, but that is not the girl that I see. Whenever I look at you, I see the makings of a Queen. I have provided much for you. I have delighted in bringing you into my Kingdom! Although you have much to learn, you will grow very beautiful and rise to be royalty. You must know that my Father's enemy, Pride, leader of the Worthlessness Camp, has not given up on you. He still desires to hold you captive, and snatch you from my hand. As you are learning to be a Princess, you are very vulnerable to his attacks. You must be on your guard, my Beautiful One. Your enemy walks around like a roaring lion and desires to devour you. He has come to steal, kill, and destroy, but I have come to give you life and give it to you abundantly, to overflowing! This morning, I am riding into war against him with My army."

"Oh may I go with you, my Prince?" the Princess offered her services, "I may be of some assistance. Perhaps I could…" she thought long and hard about what she could possibly do, "Polish your armor or care for your horse?"

"Not today" the Prince shook His head, "you will stay here. Someday you will fight with us on the battlefield, but until then you have much to learn."

"So you're leaving?" The Princess frowned, "Without me? Whatever am I supposed to do here at the palace? Iron Your socks, learn to serve tea, just sit around and knit? If I am to be Your bride, I have to spend every moment of my waking hours with You. I must, as You said, learn and that means I must learn what You do, what You fight for and what you are passionate about. I do not desire to be betrothed to a stranger. I would like to know You. Please, take me with you. I'm sure I could learn to fight your battles alongside You! Do I not hate the enemy, Pride, as much as you do? For He was the one that lied to me, and I will do anything I can to see that he is destroyed."

He laughed, setting down his golden goblet, "I admire your passion and fervor, and believe Me we will have plenty of time to get to know one another. But you have to trust that I know what I'm saying is best. You're not ready for the battlefield yet. I will always be with you, my dear one. If you love Me, obey My command and stay at the palace until I return. You will be safe here. The enemy cannot torment you if you are hiding in the secret place that I will take you to. I leave my peace with you."

After breakfast He carried her up the staircase and into

the highest room of the tower, just like a husband would lift His bride over the threshold of their new home. The room in the tower was small, but cozy, and the Princess didn't think she'd mind waiting here for a while. She smiled at Him, feeling something like a starry-eyed school girl forming a butterfly crush. He was so strong and brave.

"Wait here," He commanded. "Wait faithfully for I will return."

"When?" she asked, hating with everything inside her to see Him leave.

"Soon" He replied "I wish I could bring you with me, but as long as there is war in the Kingdom, you are safe nowhere but here in the Secret Place. This is the tower of My love, and you must not leave it. Do you understand that?"

"Of course I do!" The Princess suddenly embraced Him as she cried out, "I'd wait for you forever."

The hug was over all too soon. "Goodbye, my lovely one."

The Princess watched as He rode off on His white horse down the cobblestone road that led to the battlefield. A whole army of men and women went with him. They were all citizens of the Kingdom of the Chosen and decked from head to toe with armor that stated that they were not kidding around. They were driving their war horses toward a bloody battle scene, and the Princess could only hope that He would be safe.

Several long hours had past, and darkness begin to fall. She sat up waiting for Him to return, her eyes faithfully set out the front window, scanning the horizon for the returning of His white horse. In her mind she replayed over and over again how beautiful the evening before had been. Dancing, twirling, and rejoicing. It was like a repeating record in her mind. She felt so thankful, blessed, and loved. She wanted to dance around the room and sing a song! But she didn't dare leave the window. She wanted to be ready for His return.

The Princess waited even after darkness had long settled in. The anticipation of seeing her Prince again kept her fully awake. Soon the sun peeked up from behind a mountaintop. She had waited all night. Soon she had waited a full twenty-four hours. A full day and night had passed. Then it was two days…and then three days…and then four. By the fourth day, the Princess was beyond exhausted, and she felt the vision of dancing with her Prince grow fuzzier, and fuzzier. She fought the lie inside her mind which whispered, "He's never coming back. Surely he's abandoned you."

Her eyes grew tired waiting for his return. She could keep them open no longer. She let out a yawn as she crawled into the fluffy, queen-sized bed in the corner of the tower. The pillows were perfectly comfortable, and it wasn't long until she drifted off to sleep. She slept for hours, possibly even days, and when she awoke again, there was still no sign of the Prince. She stood up and wandered about the room. Why was the Prince taking so long? He hadn't forgotten about her, had He?

Suddenly, she heard a pebble hit the back windowsill. She felt her heart skip a beat and went running. But as she looked out the window all she saw was a young man standing in the field. It was not her Prince.

"Whatever are you doing up there?" He called up. "I beg your pardon ma'am, but I do not think someone as beautiful as you should be confined and hidden from society!"

"It's not safe down there!" She called back "Don't you know the kingdom is at war? The Prince has ridden away to fight against the enemy. I have been given orders to stay put."

The young man raised his eyebrows, "Really now? That is peculiar. You must be confused fair one, the war is long over."

"Excuse me?" The Princess called back. The distance they were shouting was so far. Had she heard him wrong?

"See?!" The man stooped down as he picked up a flower, "The war is over in our land. The bitter winter has past. The rains are over and gone! Flowers appear on the earth, the season of singing has come, and the cooing of doves is heard in our land. All the earth is celebrating! Just look at the beauty of this flower and its delicate petals? There is no war! Something as beautiful as this flower couldn't grow in a war. Why don't you come down from there? Join the celebration of life!"

The Princess almost smiled. She admired his theatrical excitement when he spoke waving his arms about. The young man seemed sweet and kind. But she had orders. "No thank you," she replied gracefully, "I will wait for my Prince to return."

The man shrugged and continued on his way down the road. As she left the window, a doubt hung in her heart. Was this man speaking the truth? Was the war really over? Why hadn't the Prince returned yet? The ring which sat so sweetly on her finger reminded her that everything would be okay. He promised his faithfulness to her. He would return.

Another day passed, and pebbles were heard on her window again. She peered out, seeing the same man who visited yesterday. "Are you going to stay up there forever?" The young man asked again. "It must be awfully lonely."

"It is," the Princess admitted with a sigh, "but I must wait."

"Well...as long as you're waiting," the young man bent to pick a daisy, then tossed it up the tower. The flower suddenly landed in her lap, "Shall I keep you company?"

Something inside strongly urged her to say no. But the Prince hadn't told her she wasn't to speak to anyone outside the tower; He only commanded that she didn't leave it. Right?

"If you insist," she replied, with the hint of a smile

twinkling in her eyes, "I suppose I wouldn't mind."

And so it was settled. Every day the young man came by the tower, and they would talk and laugh for hours. He gave her news of what was happening in the world; and to be honest, the Princess quite enjoyed his company. Waiting was lonely.

"What is your name?" the Princess inquired to know. It had been a full week since the Prince had left her.

"Adorable," he replied, "what's yours?"

Adorable. She could see that. He was very charismatic, likeable, and not to mention cute! She found that Mr. Adorable was consuming more and more of her thought life which meant the space in her heart that the Prince occupied was slowly growing smaller and smaller. She scarcely remembered the joy of dancing with Him. It all seemed so distant and faded now, like it was nearly a lifetime ago.

"I am...was...the lost Princess," she replied, slightly confused with her identity. *I'm still His Princess, right?* she thought.

Adorable laughed (quite adorably I might add), "You're lost alright. You know you can't wait up there forever."

~*~

Another week passed, and the only joy the Princess found in her days now was when Adorable came to visit.

"I just don't understand," Adorable kicked around a few pebbles before resting his arm on the tower wall. "Why would someone you say cares about you so much do this to you? Why would He forbid you from living your life?"

"It's not safe down there," the Princess replied for what felt like the hundredth time. But she wasn't so sure she believed those words anymore.

"What could be so dangerous about this life, when everyday miracles are happening down here? Flowers are blooming, birds are singing, and all of nature is rejoicing! Didn't the Prince create all this anyway? If He really is the Author of Love, why would He deny you the pleasure of it?" His words worked like rocks, slowly knocking down the walls which she had built around her heart. *Wasn't Adorable right? Didn't she deserve more than being left alone in a tower to rot?*

"Princess, you have stolen my heart," Adorable told her. "I've never loved anyone like you. Never have I felt this way before. But you are like a garden locked up, a door to which I don't have the keys! Hidden away and out of my reach. But would you trust me and come? Would you come down from that tower? I love you Princess. Isn't that enough? Doesn't love conquer all? I desire to be with you. Come, escape with me! We will go to our own secret place, and I will show you the world as you've never seen it before! You will be my Princess, and I will love you forever and always."

The Princess bit her tongue trying to decide what she must do. Life in the tower had grown devastatingly lonely, and Mr. Adorable was her only chance of escape. She longed to experience life, love, and adventure. But what about the Prince's words? Would He really return for her?

The brush traveled through her hair, untangling the knots, leaving every path it traveled as smooth as silk. The reflection in her mirror, staring back at the young Princess, was nearly unrecognizable. So much had changed since she'd been waiting here in the tower. She wasn't sure how long the Prince had been gone now, but she eagerly awaited his return. There was a time when Mr. Adorable was a dazzling temptation. But the Princess had made up her mind, refused Mr. Adorable, and had to believe the Prince would come back for her. She clung to His words daily as she brushed her hair, and prayed that He might return quickly.

Suddenly, all at once, the creaking sound of an old oak

door broke through her atmosphere. It let out a sleepy sounding yawn, and the eyes of the Princess shot up to see who was coming.

Alas, there He stood. Even more beautiful than she remembered. An unspeakable joy swelled up inside her heart, as she beheld the Lover of Her Soul. Dressed in glory, a victorious look was stamped across his entire face. Unable to speak, the Princess ran toward him and did the only thing she knew to do...embrace Him.

"My Lovely One," He spoke gently, "I am pleased with your patience. You loved me enough to obey what I commanded you. I know it was hard, but you endured the refining fire of trusting Me blindly, even when you couldn't feel my love anymore. But I never stopped loving you, Beautiful One. I am so very proud of you. The faithfulness of your heart has been proven like gold. I will never leave you in this tower all alone again. Next time, you will join me on the battlefield."

The Princess couldn't have been happier. "Oh, Your Majesty!" She clasped her hands together, "Do you really mean that?"

"Do not doubt my words for they are faithful and true. You will fight with me by my side as a warrior in the next great battle."

"So, the war is not over yet?" Her words came out confused and somewhat terrified. She thought, by the look on his face, that everything would have been accomplished.

"My dear, the war has already been won. I've defeated the enemy. His days are numbered. But he has deceived himself into thinking he can get away with lying to, stealing from, and killing my Chosen people. We must continue to fight battles for the captives until the final hour of victory is unleashed at my Father's command."

"Oh yes!" she nodded, not totally understanding, but eager to please him she pretended that she did. "I would be honored to fight by Your side."

His sweet smile sang love songs to her heart, "I am pleased with your enthusiasm!" He lowered onto a cedar bench by the window, "but the battlefield is an ugly place. Now my dear, you are as soft as a rose and gentle as a dove. You are patient and gentle and kind. Those are all wonderful things, but you wouldn't survive a second on the battlefield. In order to fight with me, you must undergo strict training. This isn't going to be just a leisurely walk through a garden of roses. I cannot promise that this will be easy. But I can promise that I will protect you with my life and be by your side every step of the way."

She sighed, elated with the fact that He had returned. He was even more wonderful than she remembered! How did he do it? The Prince made something like going to war sound like a dream. "I understand," the Princess nodded gingerly, not having a clue about what was ahead, "I trust you completely and will do whatever you tell me."

Chapter 4: The Apron of Humility

The Princess arose the next morning far before the sun did. She danced across her bedroom and into the closet where a colorful arrangement of new summer dresses sat stylishly on life-sized mannequins. She tried on several before choosing the perfect one - a bright yellow, floral-print, with gold thread embroidered on the hem. Of course, her outfit would not be complete without the proper accessories. She chose a straw sun hat and a pair of brown leather boots. Glass slippers simply wouldn't do for Battlefield Training. She left the closet, feeling cheery and content, ready for whatever plans the Prince had for her today. She was so looking forward to spending time with Him and wondered how long until breakfast would be served. She gently rested her elbows on the window sill as she looked across the balcony and towards the city. The whole town appeared to be in a deep slumber. *I must be the only person awake in this entire sleepy Kingdom*, the Princess thought. Just then, a songbird appeared on the window sill.

The blue bird began to sing a tune. The Princess smiled, wondering why this bird was awake before all the rest. *He must be singing his pre-dawn song*, she thought, *wake up world! Even the birds know that the Prince's faithfulness is new every morning.*

The Princess then heard a tap on her door. "Come in!" she called, stepping away from the window. Her voice frightened the bird, and it fluttered its little wings, off to find another place to sit and sing. Jesus walked in, and she offered a little curtsy.

"Good morning," He grinned as if he had something delightfully sweet up his sleeve.

"Finally!" she burst out, "It's so good to see you. I've been awake for hours. I'm ready to begin training!"

His Majesty laughed, "I see that. You are dressed in

garments of Joy this morning."

She knew he was referring to the dress. She twirled around slowly so that he could get the full effect. "You like it?"

"Very much so. But I believe you're missing something."

"Oh," she drew her hand up to her right ear, "I was going to try on jewelry, but I thought earrings might get in the way a bit."

He smiled again. "You're correct. This isn't the occasion for earrings. But that isn't what I was referring to." He pulled a box dressed in silver wrapping paper from behind his back and handed it to her.

The Princess' smile ate up her entire face. "Oh! Thank-" as she pulled out what was hidden inside, she suddenly stopped. The gift was an apron. It wasn't a luscious purple, scarlet, ocean blue, pearl white, or gold. Instead it was grey; an ugly, eye sore type of grey. As she opened up the fabric to get a better look, she couldn't believe the Prince would give her such a thing. There was nothing special about this raggedy old piece of cloth. It looked like a blanket a dog might sleep on. The Princess tried to act impressed, but she was not very successful. "How ehh…lovely…I mean, the thought of it….yes, it's nice. Um, thanks." She quickly stuffed the rag back in the box.

"I want you to wear it." He instructed.

Her ears stung with the uncomfortable command. She quickly thought of an excuse, "Oh, but I really don't want to get it dirty, being brand new and everything…." Her voice trailed off.

"It's not new," Jesus picked up the box, "it is Mine."

The Princess didn't know what to say. Something about this didn't compute. Why would He save a dirty old rag? And He never would have actually worn such a thing in public, would He? And why on earth did He want her to cover up the magnificent dress she had chosen this morning?!

"I'll wear it later" she excused the ugly old garment, "if you don't mind, I'd really like to keep it as a, uh...special keepsake. In the box."

"It's your choice," the Prince almost sounded disappointed. "I will not force you to wear it."

"Good," she breathed a sigh of relief, glad the issue had been settled, "some other time then."

Once outside, she and Jesus walked across the paddock and she took a deep breath of fresh air. The sweet scent of summer was near and riding on the wind. As they stepped into the cool barn, the sweet scent disappeared entirely as a whole new smell arose. A heavy mix of horse hair, grain, oats, fresh hay, and manure monopolized the air. She resisted the temptation to plug her nose.

Why would Jesus lead me in here? Couldn't he have just asked one of the servants to bring the horse outside? Why would the King of kings have to go and fetch His own horse? Surely there are people for that.

The hired stable hands rushed around hauling bales of hay and gallons of water for the horses that lived there. They all greeted the King like He was a close friend, and Jesus' replies were just as warm. After walking down several aisles, the Prince stopped at a stall. "The first thing you must learn to do is ride."

She warily eyed the gentle giant. The horse was rather large. But He wasted no time in properly introducing them, "This is Quitina. She is a chestnut mare, standing 18 hands high; one of the strongest, able-bodied thoroughbred horses in our barn."

"Remind me why must I learn to ride again?"

"Every warrior must know how to skillfully ride a horse."

She bit her lip with uncertainty, "Oh."

Several hours later, and the Princess knew the mud on

her dress was unsightly. Every puddle Quitina pranced through sent a whole new splash of dirt desiring to cling to her petticoat. Her beautiful brown riding boots were now defiled with thick crusts of mud and horse manure. Her beautiful dress was practically ruined. But training had only just begun. The Prince was a kind, patient teacher and didn't grow upset the first time she fell off Quitina. But He was also very focused and liked to stay on task.

"May we please take a break?" she asked, her leg muscles growing sore, and giving up the will to hang on.

"Not yet."

She tried not to roll her eyes with disgust at the way He was pushing her through such uncomfortableness. She was a Princess for goodness sake, not a solider!

Later that evening the Princess wanted nothing more than to soak in a hot bath and head straight to bed.

"We will be training again first thing tomorrow morning," the Prince told her before he said goodnight. She was relieved when the door closed behind Him, and she had a break from His commands.

As she looked in the mirror, she was absolutely horrified. "Look at me!" She gasped, "I look like I'm made of mud!" She remembered the past mud of the Worthlessness Camp and felt sorry for herself that she was covered head to toe in ugliness once again. *Why is He making me do this?* she thought bitterly, as she kicked off her leather boots. *It'll be months before I'm ready to ride out to war with him...maybe even years. I'm so weak; I can hardly stay up on the big, stupid horse. I'll never be able to ride and fight like He does.*

She wandered over to her bed where the silver box lay uncovered. She pulled out the wretched grey apron and sighed. *This just doesn't make any sense.* As she lay the garment across her bed, something caught her eye. A small tag on the back read, "Apron of Humility."
Suddenly it hit her. The apron of humility! "He wanted me

to wear that this morning because He knew I would be getting mud and dirt all over my dress. If I would have worn this, my dress beneath wouldn't have been covered in filth. I fell off my high horse and pride splattered all over me. Whatever was I thinking? Why didn't I do as He said?"

~*~

After slipping on His worn out apron, He knocked on the door and entered, "I see you are properly dressed this morning."

The Princess felt a tad bit of shame. The Apron of Humility was tied firmly to her waist now. "I'm sorry."

The Prince smiled as He grabbed her soft and small hand, "Nobody wants to wear humility. My Dear, there are times when Royalty is to wear their finest and be dressed in glory. There are times to be praised and honored and dressed in splendor. But much more importantly there are times to humble yourself and become a servant of others. Yesterday you learned that the apron of humility will protect you, but it's not just for you. It's for others. In my Kingdom, the first shall be last, and the last shall be first. As the Royal Family, we set an example for all the rest. That means we shall be the very last."

"I suppose I thought," she began slowly, "that I was above wearing weakness. And this apron...well? It's ugly. I want to be beautiful. For you."

"Humility is beautiful," He smiled, "just wait and see. Now that you're dressed in the foundation of humility, we can finish your outfit. Here." Jesus reached around His waist, and his fingers quickly untied his leather belt. The belt had pouches of money, gold, treasures, and hidden provisions. It also had a sheath with a sword tucked inside. He took his belt and placed it around her waist.

"This is now yours." He said as he fastened it tightly.

"Everything I have is yours. This is the belt of truth."

The Princess couldn't help but notice how heavy the sword was. Next, he gave her a breastplate as a piece of armor. To the Princess, it just felt like an extra weight. "The stronger you become, the lighter it will become. This armor declares your identity and is absolutely vital for the battles ahead."

"When will I fight my first real battle?" she asked quietly, trying to adjust to the new weight.

"The first real enemy you will fight is the one inside of you, and the voices that keep telling you to quit. But I declare that you will finish the race, and you will fight the good fight, and you will stand strong."

That night, the Princess penned these words in her leather journal:

Dear Diary,

I am so exhausted, I find it a struggle to keep this pen straight in my hand, but I must record what has been happening. The Prince finally said I was ready to go on the Battlefield with Him. Can you believe it?! Me, fighting by His Majesty's side! When He first told me, I was absolutely elated. He told me I must undergo strict training, but I really didn't think I would mind. Anything to spend more time with Him made my heart begin to dance simply at the thought of it. But I didn't quite understand how much I had gotten myself into when I eagerly told Him "Yes." My petticoats have been getting dirty lately, and I can't seem to keep the mud off my riding boots. The romance of living in this palace as a Royal One is beginning to fade as the Prince teaches me how to fight. I must say that I prefer dancing over sword fighting.

The Prince has taught me to put on my riding boots and ride horseback. I learned to shoot a bow and arrow and jump off my horse while it's still cantering. I learned to jump over obstacles on horseback and fight with my sword. I learned to defend myself with the shield of faith and protect my mind with the helmet of salvation, just in case I take a fall. I am learning to stand firm. I am learning to be a warrior. Oh, I still have a long way to go before my first real battle. But I am growing stronger. I can feel it.

Chapter 5: Slaying Fear

As the long, dark shadows cast their frowns, the Princess felt as though she were riding her horse straight into a nightmare. She eyed the Prince, who confidently led the way down this dark path. The One who redeemed her, was leading her back to the very place this had all began. The Worthlessness Camp.

She had not remembered it being quite so dark, nor dreary. Despite the fact they stood yards away from the cold iron gates, she could already hear the desperate cries. The Prince told her they were going to set captives free and break the heavy chains that ensnared them. But she knew all too well how it felt to be in a cage. And as Quitina tiptoed closer and closer to the outskirts of the place where they were to wage war, she felt a dark feeling of dread and despair run down her spine.

"Woah!" the Prince held up a hand, and everyone pulled their horses to a sudden halt. Hundreds of Citizens from the City of the Chosen rode behind them, swords tucked perfectly in place, ready to fight for the rights of these victims.

The Prince gave his commands, ordering a troop to spread out to the left, one to the right, one to march through the main gate, and one to come in behind. They would ambush their unsuspecting enemy from every direction. As the Prince spoke, revealing the strategy of war, the Princess wished she had never come.

Why didn't I just stay in the palace? She thought. *Who am I to attack and devour like a roaring lioness and shed blood as a warrior?* The idea of shoving a sword into someone's heart made her feel queasy. *Am I strong enough to kill? Moreover, how I do know that I myself will not be killed? It would be such a tragic ending to a most beautiful story. To return to the place I was born, after all the Prince has done for me, only to be slaughtered by my own fears.*

Suddenly, she felt a new fear creep up. *What if I disappoint my Savior? What if I fail and bring shame to His name? What if I'm not strong enough to be everything He's always wanted me to be? What if-*

But the Princess had no more time to worry. The Prince was now ordering to move forward. She signaled Quitina with her heels and they trotted along, nearing closer and closer to the Camp. Then the Prince ordered that they leave their horses behind. At the sound of His command, they were to run on foot and charge into the camp.

The Princess wasn't sure if she would remember how to run. She felt fear clinging to her ankles like an invisible weight tying her down. What if she couldn't move?

"Remember who you are," the Prince looked at her as though He understood her every thought. "Remember all that I have done for you. I will never leave you nor forsake you. This will not end in death, but will end in the Glory of God."

The princess nodded, choosing to believe His words. "I can do this," she whispered to herself, "I am His." She took a deep breath and prepared to move in one accord with the rest of the army. Only in complete unity would they succeed. Running and fighting as one body with the Prince at the Head. The moment was now. She could not turn back.

And then it happened. The Prince let out a terrifying battle cry. With a deafening lion's roar, He sounded the trumpet, and every Citizen echoed his call.

The Princess felt empowered as she let out a shout of her own. The war cry rumbled and churned from the deepest place of her soul releasing a terrible noise. Suddenly, her feet were running full speed ahead, like an arrow rushing to its target. She no longer had time to think. It was happening! A wave of adrenalin and energy washed over her as they flooded through the gates of the Worthlessness Camp. Following the Prince's lead, she pulled out her sword and ran straight ahead.

The unsuspecting demons watched in horror as the kingdom of darkness was flooded with light. The Chosen Citizens poured over the gates like ants rushing to an apple pie. Terrified, the demons grabbed iron clubs, leather whips, and anything else they could reach for in haste. Some of the enemy's warriors had bows which shot fiery darts at the invading Children of the King. Of course, they knew the Truth and held up their shields which were able to extinguish every arrow that flew their way.

The Warrior Princess dashed her enemies in half with the sword. She tore off limbs, sliced them apart strategically, and did not feel at all guilty about it. As she remembered the pain and lies from this camp, she desired that no one be locked up inside of it! A passion that burned like fire fiercely flickered in her eyes as she cut her enemies to pieces with the Sword of the Spirit.

"Release their chains!" The Prince shouted to the Princess as he fought off many demons who were trying to kill her. Of course, they could not get past His strong arms which protected her like a Tower of Refuge.
She ran down the muddy streets where captives sat chained, sleepy-eyed and lifeless. As she broke the chains off their hands and feet, they didn't move. Their eyes stared at her in wonderment, yet too discouraged to get up.

"Get up, go!" She called to them. "You're free! You're free! Go! The Prince has set you free! You're no longer captive; see your chains are gone!"

A few stood up slowly, but most sat in place. Paralyzed.

The Princess did not understand. "We've come to fight for you, go! Go!" She felt burning hot tears surface, and she tried to hold them back as she carefully sliced away more chains. Why weren't they leaving? Didn't they see what was happening?

"Worthless," a girl her age muttered as the Princess

64

slipped the cold metal off her scarred hands.

"No, no you're not worthless! The King loves you! He sent His Son here to rescue you!"

Another sat beside her, a knife in his hand. He was cutting his arms, even though he was free.

"Stop!" she cried. "Don't hurt yourself! The King loves you! You're valuable!"

But the captives couldn't seem to hear her. She looked helplessly at the Prince, who was still fighting for her. Couldn't they see the love and loyalty of her Prince? Couldn't they see the purity and devotion of His heart? If only they could see how beautiful He was, she was sure they would get up and follow Him! He had so much more to offer! He was everything she'd ever dreamed of. He truly was her fairytale.

In that moment, as she watched Him protect her and keep every enemy at bay, she stared at him with such great passion and admiration. She knew in that moment that she would fight for him always. He had given everything for her. She was now determined to give everything for Him. In the heat of the battle, the Princess ran into a brown tent where more captives were hidden. The moment she stepped inside, she came to a sudden halt. There, sitting in a chair, wearing the most disgusting, crooked smile was her nightmare. Her worst enemy. It was Fear himself.

"Well, well, well," he grinned, showing a mouth full of decaying yellow teeth, "If it isn't my favorite little good-for-nothing loser."

The Princess held up her sword, but her hand was shaking. "Shut up!" she ordered, "I don't belong to you anymore."

Fear stood up, "Ohh, nice sword you've got there. So the Prince gives you a stick with a pointy edge on it, and suddenly you think you've got nothing to be afraid of. That's just another one of his lies…"

"He is not a man that he would lie!" she argued, "unlike you, who is the father of all lies."

He shook his head sadly, "I don't understand why you're trying. You and I both know who you really are. We both know what you've really done. Doesn't this place bring back any memories?"

Suddenly the Princess dashed forward in one motion, "ARGGG!" She cried, pointing the sword in his direction, desiring to slay him once and for all. But she missed. And the power of the jolt pushed her into the back of the tent. Fear was now guarding the entry way, and as he closed in on her, she had no way of escape.

He stepped closer and closer, suddenly knocking the sword out of her hand. Soon he was close enough for her to smell his foul breath. "Don't you remember what happened last time you were in this tent?" He grabbed her wrists.

"I'm not the same person anymore!" she screamed, struggling to escape his tight grasp. "I've been forgiven! You don't own me anymore! Jesus, help me!"

Suddenly, the Prince was standing in the doorway. "Let her go." He demanded.

Fear whirled around, "So we meet again. Last time we talked, if my memory serves me correctly, we talked about me taking this little wretch off your hands. But you, stubborn as always, wanted to do a little experiment and turn her into a 'princess'. Well, how's that workin' for ya?"

"Pick up your sword" He ordered, ignoring the obnoxious taunts of Fear, speaking directly to the Princess.

She glanced at her sword, now crusted in blood and mud, and stooped down to grab it.

"So he rides in to save the day again," Fear sat down sighing discontentedly as he plopped into his chair, "Big surprise ending! If it wasn't for Him," he eyed her with his beady yellow eyes, "I would've had you."

"She *will* fight you, Fear," the Prince told his enemy, "and she will win. But not here. Not now. She challenges you to a duel, and my Warrior Princess will destroy you."

The Princess could not believe her ears. The Prince wanted her to fight Fear…all by herself!?

~*~

"Warrior Princess," she spoke slowly as she studied her image in the mirror. "How can that be?" What she saw today was a girl covered with dirt and mud and battle blood.

The last battle had stretched several hours long and though her arms ached, her back screamed at her, and she had a slight scar on her face where the enemy's sword nicked her, she needed to count her blessings. She was still alive and had all her limbs. Several of the Chosen ones on the frontlines had been injured. This evening, the Prince would be visiting all his troops and anointing them with healing oil.

The Princess felt her muscles shake as she took off her armor and sat down on the floor. She was lodging in a tent in the wilderness with the rest of the troops, spending the night hundreds of miles away from the castle.

"Send out your Princess!" The voice suddenly cracked through the night like a whip, "Let her fight me now! Your Prince challenged her to a duel! I want to fight, right here, right now!"

She recognized the voice. It belonged to Fear. His words unnerved her as she nearly lost her breath. Why had he come so soon? And this late at night, just when darkness began to sink in?

She could hear the commotion going on outside her tent as several officers argued with the man. The Princess shuddered and hoped they would send Fear away. Soon she heard the voice of her Prince. He had joined the scene. She couldn't hear what he said, but she didn't dare step outside.

She was too terrified.

"I gave you my word," the Prince replied, "she will fight you."

"Now!" Fear hollered. "I don't believe you! Bring her out here at this moment! How do I know that you won't just whisk her away to the safety of your palace tomorrow? Let her fight me now or else I'll attack her on my own!"

More mumbled conversation. Then silence.

Suddenly the Prince opened her tent curtain and said, "Come. Put your armor back on, My Dear One. I know you are tired, but your work is not yet finished."

"Oh please," the Princess ran up to him and begged, "don't let him fight me! I-I-" she fought back tears, "I don't think I can! He hates me so terribly, and he is so much stronger than I and-" She couldn't finish speaking because of the tears.

He placed a gentle hand on her shoulder and held her close, drawing her into his chest, "Shhhh," His voice sounded like healing balm to her wounds, "you can. You have all the training you need in order to defeat this enemy in your life. I believe in you. You must also have faith. Come now, put on your armor."

The Princess couldn't believe he was making her do this! She wanted nothing more than to stay hiding in the tent, but she loved her Prince, so she obeyed his command.

Several moments later she was standing on the edge of the battlefield. There was no time to think. The Prince was right. She had to believe in herself. The Warrior Princess stood firmly in position. Now was the time. Fear flipped his sword up in the air, and caught it without even flinching.

"Ready to die?" he sneered, standing far off, at the other end of the fighting ring. "Say 'goodbye' to your precious Prince because you're never going to see him again."

The Prince had instructed that they duel it out on a barren battlefield several miles away from both camps. The

Princess thought their surroundings looked much like a boxing ring. It was in a large circle upon a high plateau with steep edges. Falling down the side would be like tumbling down a mountain. The Prince watched from the sidelines, reassuring the Princess with a confident gaze of his eyes.

She wanted to make him proud. Oh how she did! She desired nothing less than to knock Fear on his rear end and send him tumbling down the steep slope never to return. Never to see the light of day again! But as she stood there, facing her enemy, she knew he desired the same thing of her. The hatred in his eyes was real. If he had the chance, he would kill her. The Princess only hoped she could beat him to it.

Without warning, Fear lurched forward with a terrifying lunge of his sword. The Princess blocked his blow as their swords clashed together. The duel was on! The sound of clanking metal filled the air as each fighter was responsible for both defense and offense. Fear pushed her closer and closer to the edge, and just when he thought he may have finally defeated her, she sprang forward and pushed his back closer to the edge. It went on like that for hours. The Princess had lost track of all time, and as the evening dragged on, she felt her muscles growing weaker and weaker. Her arm was tired, and her feet felt as though they might slip at any moment. But she had to stand up. She had to keep fighting. To give up now would mean total loss. She refused to forfeit to her enemy. Complete darkness had settled in and the Princess was beyond exhausted. I *have to finish him off*, she thought determinedly, *once and for all*! She made a hasty move and jumped forward in a desperate attempt to slay fear. Suddenly, he knocked her right foot from under her with the edge of his sword. Stumbling, she slipped onto the ground.

"Ugh!" she cried, meeting the floor with a hard crash. Her head throbbed from hitting the ground, and she realized that the sword had bounced out of her hands. She struggled to regain her footing, but Fear kicked her with a hard blow from his boot, right into her stomach. She winced as she fell onto the ground again, this time on her back. Her fingers fumbled around in the dark, reaching for the sword that couldn't be found.

Fear hopped on top of her and lunged his weight upon her with a crushing blow. Her chest collapsed under the weight of her enemy. She fought to breathe beneath the heaviness. She gasped for air and reached in desperation for her sword. She was just about to lift up a cry for rescue to her Prince when, with a terrifying cackle, the enemy shoved his sword into her heart.

~*~

The kiss, which rested upon her scarlet lips, was gentle, yet powerful enough to awaken her. This sleeping beauty fluttered her eyes open, as the fuzzy face in front of hers soon came into sharp focus. The Princess smiled as he took her hand. Her Prince faithfully kneeled beside her bed, "Awake," he spoke, "clothe yourself with strength."

Suddenly the Princess realized what had taken place. She was no longer dead. She was not sure how long the darkness had enveloped her, but she remembered how it happened. She remembered the sharp, miserable pain of the sword twisting into her heart. She had tried to breathe, but she couldn't. Her heart began to swell with pain simply at the thought of it. It was a pain she had never experienced before. She felt as though she wanted to release a scream from the mere memory of the trauma, but she couldn't. Nothing came out. While she was dead, bitterness had wrapped its way like a tangled vine around her heart. She did not view her Prince in the same perfect light she had before. Something was tainted. This could not be the same one who so lovingly cared for her. The one who rescued her, dressed her in beautiful garments, and danced with her. No, this couldn't be. For he had not stopped the enemy from slaying her! He had stood by and watched as this happened. How could he allow such a terrible thing to happen to her?! Her eyes stung with tears as she fought them back. Had he looked away for only a moment? Had he forgotten about her? Surely he did not stand there helplessly as Fear destroyed her! Why didn't He stand up and fight!? The Princess could not understand. She was alive, but she didn't feel like the royal beauty she was before her death. No, now she felt like a failure. A miserable, wretched failure.

"Stand up," He spoke, calling her out of bed. "Follow me."

The Princess didn't dare look him in the eyes. She ignored his voice and turned her head the other way.

He kept calling her, but she pretended not to hear. This was outrageous! How dare he ask her to stand up and follow Him! Who knew what He would have her do next! For all she knew, he might command that she march straight out to that battlefield and fight her enemy again! Ha! Like that was gonna happen! She tightly clutched her chest as her heart ached so badly. She was bleeding inside and didn't know how to stop the pain. The one she trusted most had deceived her and abandoned her in her greatest time of need. She wasn't sure if she could ever love again. Suddenly, the pain welled up so greatly inside that she had to release the pressure.

"You hurt me!" she screamed. "You hurt me! You watched him shove that knife into my soul! You let him do it! It might as well have been Your hand!" She screamed until she could not holler any longer. All words were gone. She began to cry terrible, heart-wrenching sobs.

The Prince only stood there. He listened. He understood. He watched her shake as she held herself and caught every tear that fell. He placed each tear in his pocket, and shed some of his own. Of course the Princess did not see this happening because she was too caught up in the spirit of sorrow. She was unaware of the comforting lullaby that He was singing to her. He had never stopped loving her, and he never would. In this time of pain and confusion, He would be there to comfort her. He was not offended by her grief and anger. He simply understood.

~*~

The Princess skipped breakfast. She turned down the Prince's invitation for afternoon tea and excused herself from dance lessons. She spent the next day cooped up in her bedroom, flipping through magazines and staring out her windows at the world outside. *What am I doing here?* she asked herself. *Why did I seriously think that he could change me? Turn me into some great hero? I will always be the girl I have been...*

For the next week the Princess was quite lonely, avoiding the Prince whenever she could. She asked that meals be delivered to her bedroom and all of their "dates" be rescheduled. It's true that she was lonely, but why would she want to spend time with the Prince? He had proved to be crazy, dishonest, and just plain insane! She could have avoided him for the rest of her life if it wasn't for the fact that He kept showing up doing all these incredibly sweet things for her.

The Prince left her notes, chocolates and roses on her pillow, and sent love letters to her bedroom which sat on her desk unopened. He just happened to walk by her window every day, humming a gloriously sweet song. As much as she desired to avoid Him, it proved to be an impossible task. He was determined to draw her to himself. Well, it wasn't going to work. Not this time.

She considered calling off the engagement entirely, but couldn't bring herself to do such a thing. So she just lived under his roof, ate his food, and wore the clothes that he provided for her. She felt like a worm, but she couldn't bring herself to leave.

One lonely afternoon, another letter arrived. A maid added it to the mountain of letters that had stacked up on her bedside table. She wasn't sure why, but she decided to read this one. It beckoned her to meet him that afternoon for a horseback ride at three o'clock. She argued with herself, then finally decided to go. They had to talk about what happened.

"WHY?" the Princess asked, arms folded tightly across her chest. He was waiting for her beside the stables.

A grin slipped across his face as he kissed her on the cheek, "It's nice to see you too."

"Don't try to play all coy and sweet with me!" she snapped. It had taken her a long time to get there, but she was here now, and she wanted answers. "Why did you let me die?"

The conversation that followed was a personal one. A dialogue between two lovers. Their conversation revealed secrets from the Prince's heart. Secrets which you probably shouldn't incline your ear to listen in---unless of course you love eavesdropping. On second thought, perhaps you should peek into that room and listen, just for a minute. For you just might have a conversation like this with your Prince one day too.

The Prince looked at her lovingly as He replied, "Because My Dear, Sweet One, you were ready to die." The words sounded strange to her ears. Like foreign enemies, they did not sit peacefully with her. A look of confusion cast over her face as her eyebrows rose up in anger.

"I know your heart," He explained gently. "I see it all. I know your every thought. You have come a long way, my Princess. This journey has brought you from the depths of the darkness of the Worthlessness Camp and into my courts.

You have been brought into the Kingdom of Light, and your transformation has been beautiful! But it is not complete. Fear still whispers to your heart and mind. And those who fear have not been made perfect in love. The purifying process is still taking place. You have not "arrived" yet. And though this death looked like a major setback, it is for your good and for My glory. Trust me with the things that you do not understand. I promise you, 'This will not end in death, but in the glory of God.'"

The Princess fought back tears as she shifted her footing, "But," she sniffed, "can't you see it? It's over. Fear won."

The Prince shook his head, "He has not won. The battle isn't over yet. You will defeat him."

"You-you mean," her voice began to shudder at the thought of it, "I must fight him again?"

The Prince nodded with a calm confidence that frustrated her, "Yes."

Every part of the Princess ached with dread. "No!" she cried, "I cannot! That wicked grin of his victory is like a picture playing in my mind over and over! I shall not give him the satisfaction of watching me fall again!"

Jesus gently persuaded her, "My love, there are many captives in the Worthlessness Camp, and all of them are chained by fear. If you destroy this enemy in your life, you can help set others free into the glorious liberty that you have experienced."

She stomped down a stubborn foot, "Well, maybe I don't want to set others free. Maybe I don't want to be part of this stupid marriage anyway! Have you ever thought about that?" She huffed in frustration, "Come on, let's just go for our horseback ride."

They rode in silence for several miles until they reached a part of the wilderness the Princess had never been. They arrived at a picnic in the middle of nowhere. They dismounted from their horses near the peaceful stream of water. The picnic blanket was spread along the top of a grassy knoll. A sweet summer breeze was blowing around as the two sat down for a meal. The Prince served her favorite foods, told her jokes, sang a little song that he wrote just for her, and picked a bouquet of wild flowers to give to her. He wooed and charmed her with all of his goodness, eyes beckoning her to simply trust him once more.

The Princess sighed. It was just too much to bear. He was clearly too good to refuse. But why was he asking her to do such a hard thing? She could not go back and fight Fear. She could not stand the pain of that knife again or listen to his evil cackle.

"The captives," she slowly spoke, "at the Worthlessness Camp, they didn't even want to be set free. I told them of the freedom that had arrived, and they only sat there and wouldn't budge! Why didn't they get up and follow you?"

"They have the gift of choice," He replied sorrowfully, "and many abuse that gift. They choose things that tear my Father's heart apart. But it is all part of this mysterious, miraculous thing called love. Some choose to embrace it and some stick their nose in the air in pride and reject it."

The Princess cried out again, "But I don't know if I can handle so much pain!" She paused for a moment before continuing, "Say that I do fight Fear again. And say that I win. Then what? How can I watch those captives not accept the truth that I give them? And after working so hard for it! After pouring out my heart in blood, with sweat and tears, would they dare turn me away? I don't know if my heart could bear it!"

This time, the Prince placed His hand on her shoulder as he spoke, "To share in my sufferings is to share my heart. As Prince, My heart is like a wailing wall, where the desperate cries of my people are lifted up to me every day. The pain of their words stings my nose like a terrible smell that makes it hard to breathe. At times, my tears are so distraught that they turn to blood. To know love is to know pain. Never forget that, my dear one."

"In that case," she replied, "I'm not so sure that I ever want to love, ever again."

"But to know love is also to know the greatest joy," He smiled this time as he spoke. "Though there are many who turn away and reject my gifts, there are a few, the called and the chosen, who embrace me just as you did. Those who respond to my invitation, who come running to me and fall into my arms. And my dear Princess, those moments make it all worth it! If you were the only one who accepted me, my teachings, and my love, it would have been worth it. Ah yes, all the rejections in the world pale in comparison to your one, exuberant 'YES'!"

"If you love me so," she replied thoughtfully, "and if I bring so much joy to your heart, why do you allow me to be hurt?"

The answer to this question I cannot write, for how the Prince replied is not to be spoken in words. He replied in a very mysterious way. He placed his hands upon her head and prayed. He prayed in a language that the earth does not understand. He prayed for a knowledge that only the heart can know. What He spoke, He bypassed all words and met the Princess straight in the depths of her soul. Later that evening, she wrote to the Lord and replied to His many love letters that had been collecting dust.

My Precious Prince,

You love me so much that You'll destroy me so that the real me may come alive. Jesus, You kill me so that You may live in me. Every time You look at me, You see who I'm going to be. To share in Christ's sufferings is to become nothing. To go lower, lower, and lower, so that You may be lifted higher, higher and higher.

Lord, You can only use me if I am broken and crushed to powder. You desire a pure bride. The word pure means to be "emptied of sin." Everything beautiful happens in purity. When I am pure, I can see you. I can come close to You, and You will come close to me.

Oh what a mystery! A mystery which I fear will take a whole lifetime for my heart to understand. And so I echo very vulnerably with words of Job, with my lips trembling and my hands uplifted in surrender, 'Though He slay me, yet I will trust in Him." Do what you must do inside of me to create the Bride that you desire. A girl who one day you may be proud to call your Bride.

Love Always,
Your Princess

Chapter 6: Tears Turn into Diamonds

The Princess never wanted to return here. And several months before, she would've done anything in her power to avoid it. But in the weeks that followed her death and resurrection, her Prince proved to be all that He said He was. He was slow to anger and compassionate, and even though she found it frightening to trust Him again, she slowly came to the realization that there was no safer place than with Him.

Where else could she run to? Who else would accept her when she was a weak and fearful coward? He had been very patient with her, and just like a gentle shepherd, he brought the Princess to a grassy plain, a wilderness where she camped beside a healing stream, which brought peace and restoration to her soul. Slowly, she regained strength, but this time it was not her own. She knew she could not slay Fear, for she had already proved that. But she wanted His strength to be perfected in her shamefully weak place. When camping in the wilderness she did not train for battle. His perfect love strengthened her heart, and together in the wilderness He did nothing but court her. He sang to her, danced with her, and reminded her of all the reasons that he was everything lovely! During those starry-eyed months, she fell head over heels in love with the One who called her beautiful. She could do nothing to catch herself, but there was no need to. For He promised to catch her this time.

After this short season of refreshing, the Prince brought her back to the battlefield. The very place where she had been defeated. And now, she heard the familiar voice of failure and fear whisper words of defeat. But she refused to believe them.

"Jesus," she spoke, "I cannot do this. My heart is like wax, and my hands are shaking so violently that I cannot tell one end of my sword from the other. But I believe the words You spoke. That this will not end in death, but in the glory of God. I cannot do this. It's going to have to be you completely."

The enemy took his place across from her, showing off his intimidating moves. "Are we really here again?" he sighed, looking ridiculously bored and over-confident. "This feels like a bad rerun of a lame TV show. Oh well, release the so-called-warrior so I can kill her just as I did before."

This time Jesus didn't have to say anything to calm her raging fears. He simply gave her a gaze of total confidence and she responded with a look of trust. He could totally handle whatever happened next.

And so, this time, the Princess plunged her sword into the enemy's stomach. Before he had the chance to intimidate her, lie to her, and make her afraid, she took him down. In the blink of an eye, Fear was standing and then he was not.

Just like that the victory had come. The Princess had not performed a strategic swing or growled at him or talked smack to her enemy. No, she simply trusted with a faith that rose from the depth of her heart. And from that trust came her victory.

She blinked in surprise as she realized that he was on the floor. She glanced at the Prince who pumped victorious fists into the air, "Woo hoo! That's the way you do it, My Lady!"

The Princess laughed, totally overtaken with joy and surprise as she clapped her hands together and did a little dance. "Yes!" she cried back, "We did it!"

She reached down and tore free a ring of keys from around the dead man's belt, clenching them tightly in her fist. The Prince had told her about these keys. They held everything that had been stolen from her. Every door he had locked. Every lie that shackled her with invisible chains. She now held the keys in her hands!

With the new prize of her first real victory, the Princess ran to her Prince and he gave her a warm hug. "What do I do next?" she asked, elated and breathless.

He grabbed her hand and smiled, a look of triumphant victory stamped across His face, "We ride!"

~*~

The Princess gripped these keys close to her heart. Though they were rusty and not something lovely for eyes to behold, she understood the power of these keys.

She had now entered the enemy's territory and began to quickly ascend the steps of his castle. He too had a kingdom. But his castle was not dressed in the glory and splendor like the one she was used to living in. Now accustomed to the pure gold foundation, walls made of sapphire, and battlements sculpted out of rubies, it was such stark contrast to the ugliness of the enemy's kingdom. Words could not describe the thick darkness that smothered the air, and the cold stone walls which towered before her. She had been sent here on a mission by the Prince. She was to come and release prisoners from their chains.

"Because you defeated this enemy of fear in your life," the Prince had told her earlier, "you have rightfully gained the keys that the enemy stole from you. My dear, you must understand that warfare, though as unpleasant and uncomfortable as it is, is a must. What you hold in your hands will bless and touch the lives of others more than you could ever know. Now go! Only be strong and very courageous as my Spirit goes with you."

The Princess meditated on these words as she hastened to ride her horse Quitina to this dark place. A certain excitement began to stir inside her as she realized the reality of the Prince's words. *If I fight another enemy,* she thought slowly, *and if I defeat him, I can bring others into the Kingdom of light. I can use my battle experience and heartaches to teach and share with others.*

These joyful thoughts were still in the forefront of her mind as the Princess finished climbing the staircase. Soon she reached the top step and began to keep a keen eye out for enemy spies. They would desire to ambush her as she entered their territory. Despite the frightening surroundings, the spirit of Fear had not gripped her heart this time. It was the first mission the Princess had embarked on that she felt certain she would succeed. Her faith in the King's love was in action, and his love had bound the spirit of Fear far from her. Though the enemy was near, so were His love and His angels. She sensed the secret service of the Lord's angels very near, and her heart soared with trust in the One who had brought her this far.

Her eyes scanned the scene in front of her, and quickly found the answer to her puzzling scenario. The rickety, old, wooden draw bridge was up, and a canal of crocodiles, snakes, and other nasty creatures slithered below. She didn't dare look down as she took one great leap across it. Landing on both feet on the other side, she saw her next hurdle that needed to be overcome – getting inside the castle. Iron doors were bolted tightly in front of her, and she knew there was no choice but to scale the wall. She reached for the rope tucked inside her leather bag of provisions from the Prince and tied a quick lasso. She tossed the rope up the wall and hooked it over a secure stone at the top. Taking a deep breath, she quoted Psalm 18:29, "With Your help I can advance a troop, with my God I can scale a wall."

Those words proved true, and before she knew it she was standing atop the lookout tower. She had yet to see her enemies, and interpreted their absence as the Prince saying, "It's time to move forward." Her combat boots quietly thumped on the stone wall below her as she found an entrance into the dark castle. Descending down a series of pitch black staircases, the only light she had was that which came from within her. Descending lower, lower, and lower, the air felt colder the further down she went. Soon her body shivered, feeling as though she were being covered in ice. She had arrived at the lowest part of the castle – the wet, chilly, freezing-cold dungeon.

Placing her key in the rusty lock, she gained access into the first cell. And there, shivering in the corner, wrapped in nothing less than a thin-threaded shell, was a little girl. The girl turned to look at the stranger who opened her cell, and the Princess saw the saddest pair of blue eyes she had ever seen. Her heart was stung with compassion as this girl spoke a string of frightened words, "W-ho are y-y-yo-you?"

The Princess knelt down beside her and spoke slowly, "I am a daughter of the King, of the City of the Chosen. I've come to take you home with me."

"This is my home," the bony little girl quickly retorted

The Princess thought it looked like she hadn't eaten in days. Her fear-stricken eyes were in such contrast to her pale complexion, chapped and bleeding lower lip, mud-encrusted face, and wrists bleeding from the tight chains by which she was ensnared. As the Princess looked at the little girl, she saw a picture of herself. It was not so long ago when she was this girl; lost, abandoned, and entirely unloved. The Princess wanted nothing less than to get her to the Prince immediately.

How did He do it? she thought in awe. *It's just like looking in a mirror. This used be me. Doubtful, terrified, afraid, wretched, and ugly. But now...*the Princess had not realized what a magnificent transformation she had experienced until this moment. She was an entirely new creature.

What a powerful love He has! she thought in amazement, *That His pure and loving eyes can look at a girl like this, a girl like me, and somehow see a Princess in there. And then with such great skill, romantic love, tremendous patience, and terrifying trials He uncovers the girl that he always knew was there.*

The Princess used her key to unlock the chains from her hands and feet, and with a smile grabbed her cold, bony

82

hand. "Come. The Prince has invited you to a magnificent banquet. And I expect He'll want you there as soon as possible."

~*~

The Princess recognized those wonder-filled eyes. She was seated at the Ball with the Prince and the newest addition to His kingdom; the lost orphan whom He had rescued from the depths of hell and seated in heavenly places beside Him. The little girl was starry-eyed as she stared at the magnificent banquet table which spread out before them. The Princess also recognized that condemning spirit which whispered in her new friend's ear.
The Princess reached across the table and grabbed the freshly manicured hand, offering a squeeze. "Don't listen to the lies," she leaned over and whispered. "You will make a stunning Princess and a much needed addition to His kingdom." The used-to-be-but-no-longer orphan offered a shaky smile in her direction.

After the evening of festivities was through, the Princess escorted her new roommate upstairs and conducted a lively tour of their newly-shared closet. "All these lovely garments are yours now!" The Princess was overjoyed to be sharing all these wonders with another. "Our feet are the same size, and we can take turns with all these shoes!"

~*~

The next morning the Princess arose early and quickly wrapped the Apron of Humility around her waist. She hadn't a clue what this day held in store for her, but she wanted to be ready.

As soon as her apron was in place, the Princess ventured into the Throne Room, which had become her favorite place to talk with the Prince before beginning her busy day. She had gained access into this grand and holy room only by His grace. She was so grateful to be standing in His presence whenever she pleased. She stood before His glorious throne with a bowed head and bended knee, honoring His Royal Majesty.

"Good morning, my Prince" she smiled.

His right hand reached out to lift up her chin, and she was greeted with a wonderful smile. "Good morning, my Beautiful One. Where is your new friend?"

"She's still sleeping," the Princess replied. "I suppose this is the first time she's been able to sleep in such peace and comfort. Oh Jesus, it's such a magnificent thing you've done. The fact that you would use me to bring others into Your Kingdom, it's more exhilarating and fulfilling than anything I could imagine! To see You crown her with your lovingkindness and teach her how to dance with You, only makes my heart stare at you in wonderment all the more. This unfathomable love makes me want to serve You with my whole heart. But what can I do for you, my Lord? You have it all."

Jesus only smiled in return, understanding her heart's cry to give all of herself to Him. The joy and pleasure which radiated from His face was so bright that the Princess felt nearly blinded as she looked at Him. She stared at His feet, which were also shinning with glory. She desired to do something for Him; fix His breakfast, clean His palace, or wash His feet, but He was so holy and self-sufficient, she couldn't think of one thing she could possibly do for him. But then, it came to her.

"Excuse me," she excused herself and quickly exited the room, running down the hall and into the Maid's Closet. She fetched for herself a bucket of water and a rag. As quickly as she had disappeared, she reappeared once again. Kneeling down, pouring out her heart just like the water in this bucket, she completely dumped herself out in service, and began washing the floors of the throne room. It was not because they were dingy. No, quite the contrary! These floors were made of sparkling sapphire, emeralds, diamonds, and jewels. Her heart began to sing a song of love to her Prince. Just like Cinderella, gaily washing the floors, she sounded like a sweet bird, and she happily offered her service. She continued for hours; humming, rejoicing, and perfectly content to be in the Prince's presence, washing the floor around His beautiful, holy, nail-scarred feet.

Any other on-looker casually passing by would not recognize the Princess who scrubbed on hands and knees, dressed in the apron of Humility. They would have mistaken her for a servant girl or a maid. She was not dressed in a breathtaking beautiful ball grown, nor a sparkling tiara, or sweet glass slippers. Instead she wore that ugly, old rag which the Lord had given her to wear. The Princess no longer cared about her appearance or getting dirty. Her heart had been crushed, destroyed, killed, and brought back to life again. Now, there were no longer traces of pride, vain conceit, or false ideas of self-sufficiency. Love had transformed a despicable, wretched, repulsive, dark-hearted, sinful orphan into a humble, kind, beautiful-hearted Princess. The Princess was now convinced that there was no stronger power or force in the universe than Love. Love which chastened, rebuked, corrected, destroyed; then healed and strengthened, turning something ugly into something beautiful.

"My sweet girl," the Prince spoke, drawing the Princess' attention away from the thoughts which enraptured her mind, "come." The Princess ceased from her serving and stood before Him. "I have something to give you," He stated.

"Oh, please, Your Majesty," the Princess objected, "You have already given me more than enough! I was just meditating on the love that you've shown me, and I couldn't possibly ask for anything more!"

"I only want to give you something which already belongs to you," He replied. "Do you remember your tears? Do you remember when I allowed Fear to destroy you? Do you remember the bitterness and pain you felt that day you died?"

The Princess shamefully glanced down at her feet, memories slowly resurfacing, "Yes. I remember. I was so angry with you. I almost wished you had just left me alone in the Worthlessness Camp to die on my own. I didn't trust You anymore. You had hurt me so deeply; I couldn't possibly understand what any of that had to do with love." As the Princess recalled the past journey, the memories stung. He had hurt her more than anyone ever had. "You ripped a hole in my heart," she whispered, "a terrible, gaping, paralyzing hole." She remembered the jagged stab of that crooked knife, and the "So-Called-Loving" God who just sat by and watched at all happen. She thought of the fight which He let her lose, and for a moment nearly despised Him for it. She considered running. One last time, her old character flared up and she wanted nothing more than to vanish from his presence. *Perhaps He is a hypocrite. Why did I let Him do that to me?* The thoughts whispered one last time, *Are you really going to let Him treat you this way? You deserve better. Now's your chance, make a run for it!*

"But," the Princess spoke, staring hard into His eyes, "it was good for me that I was afflicted." She remembered all the goodness of His character. She remembered the second victory; the keys that were hers and the captive that had been set free. It was only one soul. But somehow the Princess knew that all this pain she had been through was worth it. It was worth the one. "I will not pretend to understand why You allowed my enemy to defeat me in my first big battle. And I will not fool myself in thinking that the purifying fire of deathly pain will never plague my heart again; but whatever You do and wherever You take me, You have proved your character of Faithfulness, and I can say with full confidence that I have placed my Hope in You and You alone! Oh, where would I be without you? Who would I run to if I didn't have you? What human being would ever dare to love me like You do? There is no One who compares to You my King and Prince, not even one! Though You slay me My Lord, I will trust in You."

The Prince's smile was a fixed feature on his face, and the proud love in His eyes was indescribable. "I believe this belongs to you." He reached out and handed her a glass jar with the Princess' name engraved upon it. She let out a small gasp as she stared at the dazzling jewels. It was a jar full of diamonds.

"Why, I-"

"These are the angry and bitter tears which you cried the day I brought you back to life. I caught every last one from your face, kept them in a jar, and they have been transformed into diamonds."

As the Princess stared at this beautiful gift, she felt new tears begin to surface. But these were tears of joy.

"I love you my Princess," He whispered, "will you dance with me?"

It was nearly unbearable. The joyful weight of it all was coming down, and the Princess found it almost impossible to stand in such glory. Here she was dressed in a raggedy old apron with a runny nose and messy tears of joy pouring from her eyes, an unkempt mane of hair, bare feet, and a helpless heart growing more and more aware of how undeserving she really was. Yet despite it all she wanted to dance. Oh, how she wanted to dance! Her awkward feet wanted to leap and spin and laugh and twirl; and her racing heart desired to express the love for Him that was pressing inside her chest.

His blazing eyes of passion and understanding burned for her, radiated from his entire face with a flame of fiery glory. Every inch of him was beautiful. His strong chest and muscular arms were eager to fight for her, eager to embrace her, and his gentle fingertips were quick to wipe away the messy tears that fell. His legs stood firm, supported by his beautiful, nail-scarred feet which were so perfectly clean. The Princess now realized how silly it was that she was thinking about washing His feet just moments earlier. But the most beautiful of all his handsome features was His heart. His heart was an expression of his love, and that is the reason the angels never stop singing, "Holy, holy, holy; worthy, worthy, worthy!" Such love cannot be comprehended, even if one was given all eternity to do so. His heart, His love, His purity, His selfless motives always abounding in love for His beloved Bride.

"I cannot dance with You," she choked and sniffled. "Why, I'm not even dressed properly."

The Prince only laughed, and his laughter released a force of magic that would put Tinkerbell's pixie dust to shame. Even Cinderella's Fairy Godmother would stand in awe as his laughter worked more miracles than "Bibbity Bobbity Boo!"

All at once, those ugly garments of humility were transformed into a pure, white ball gown; beginning with a form-fitting bodice which led down to a full, floor-length skirt. This caterpillar to butterfly metamorphosis was nearly complete.

"Why, I..." the Princess stuttered and gasped, and smiled and laughed, and twirled around slowly in amazement, "It's so...it's so...beautiful."

"Indeed you are. But we must give you some shoes." Then, Love spoke into existence the most darling pair of glass slippers ever invented. He instructed her to sit on her throne, then He knelt down, and slowly slipped each slipper onto her feet.

"There," He spoke at last. The Prince offered a hand, and helped her to her feet. "Now, we may dance."

"But Your Majesty," the Princess only had one last thing she wished to say, "what happened to the apron You gave me?"

"Don't you see your dress? Humility has been transformed into the same, beautiful garment that you are wearing now! I told you Darling, 'humility is *Royalty.*'"

And *that* was something to dance about.

Introduction to the "Secrets of Royalty" Daily Devotionals

Some people may call it a story. Some might think of it as a parable. Others might even label it as a whimsical fairytale. But the tale you just read isn't a product of my overactive imagination. Every word in that story and every scribble from my pen was entirely true. I would know, because that was *my* story. The orphaned girl from the Worthlessness Camp? That was me. I was the criminal standing on the slave-block. The girl whom nobody wanted, nobody loved, and nobody knew. I had broken so many of the Kingdom rules that the dreadful threat of an eternal punishment of hell and torment lingered like a dark storm cloud hanging over my head. I was utterly hopeless. My pitch black surroundings and hidden sins clung to me like a heavy fog, until the day a glorious light broke in!

The day I heard the song that the Prince of Heaven was singing just on the outskirts of the camp, "Come and follow me!" He sang, leading the chorus with the loudest and most beautiful voice of all His people. "Come with me to the City of the Chosen!"

Jesus Christ rode into my life and transported me into His Kingdom of Love. "Wait" I hear you say, "Let me get this straight. You used to live in a muddy camp where it always rained and evil voices tormented you at night?"

Okay, so the Worthlessness Camp isn't a geographical location on the map, but it's not a fictional place in my imagination either. The Worthlessness Camp is vividly real in so many of our human hearts. It can be seen as a mental, spiritual, or emotional place where we are bombarded with dark thoughts that confuse us and attack us with lies. That place of shame is trapping, tight, and constricting. It is a place of condemnation where you're constantly reminded of past mistakes and wounds that make you feel sick and depressed. The Worthlessness Camp is simply this: thoughts that beat you up and make you feel as if you're not good enough. It is thoughts that torment you, wishing you could change something about your life, but feeling utterly powerless to do so.

If you've ever experienced days when it feels like the walls are closing in on you and you're struggling to breathe, you're not alone. I could share depressing statistics about young girls who daily dwell in this camp, who struggle to find their self-worth and can't bear to love themselves, let alone even *like* themselves.

So many young ladies in this generation believe they are un-beautiful, unworthy, and unloved. Living in the Worthlessness Camp can manifest in so many different ways, such as battling with insecurity, eating disorders, or even physically hurting themselves. We all know the staggering statistics of young adults who attempt suicide – this is the Worthlessness Camp performing its darkest evil. The statistics of young women who come from broken homes, have suffered abuse, or have deep wounds from memories of abandonment or rejection are overwhelming. But statistics are only stale numbers on a chart. They don't live or breathe, or tell stories.

Through my ministry with *Crown of Beauty Magazine*, I have heard many stories from young women all around the world. I've received emails from girls in India, Africa, the United Kingdom, and the United States; all sharing their struggles about living in the Worthlessness Camp. Proverbs 23:7 says, "For as a man thinketh in his heart, so is he..." Everything we perceive to be true about ourselves, our world, and the people around us come from our thoughts and the way we think. The Worthlessness Camp is a mental place we hang out in when we listen to the enemy's lies.

Some of you who are reading this left the Worthlessness Camp a long time ago, the day you repented of sin and crowned Jesus Christ as the Lord of your life. You packed your bags and moved into the Palace of His Love choosing to daily dwell in the City of the Kingdom of the Chosen. Others have moved into the Palace of the King as well, but your mind is still tormented by memories and thought patterns from that camp. You might be living in the palace, but still thinking like a pauper. Many of us would be afraid to admit that demons and monsters have followed us from our past right into the palace. Even though we're born again Christians, lies daily attempt to drag us back into the muddy Worthlessness Camp.

One of my favorite movies is *The Princess Diaries*. (If you've never seen the movie, I would recommend watching it because I'll be referencing it throughout this book. Plus, it's the perfect chick flick for your next slumber party; super girly and totally fun! Don't forget to rent the sequel too!) Princess Mia grew up with royal blood coursing through her veins, yet her mind hadn't been raised in an environment that would teach her to think like the true princess that she was. She was raised just like the rest of us, smack dab in the middle of American pop-culture and didn't have a clue what it meant for her to be royalty. The princess mindset was something that she had to be taught by her Grandmother through daily Princess Lessons. Mia was insecure and lacked confidence, faith, and vision for the future. She grew up thinking just like everyone else around her even though she was called to live and *think* entirely differently.

Romans 12:2 says, "Do not be conformed to the pattern of this world, but be transformed by the renewing of your mind. Then you will be able to test and approve what God's will is, His good, pleasing and perfect will."

We are *just* like Mia. We have royal blood pumping through us, and we are the most legitimate royal ones on this earth. You are a real life Princess! This reality is so much sweeter than any Disney tale. We're not just talking plastic magic wands and pathetic pumpkin carriages. We're talking the real deal. Royalty. Being a Daughter of the King and an heir to a real Kingdom! Yet, despite our unwavering, eternal, royal identity that has been declared by the King of all creation, there are days when we as God's Daughters struggle to feel royal, let alone loved and valued.

93

There is a massive disconnect between who God actually created us to be and who we are in our own eyes.

Mia had to embark on a journey to discover what it meant for her Daddy to be King. She had to abandon her own twisted self-perception and believe that what her Grandmother said about her could be true.

It is difficult for us to imagine what living and thinking like a princess would look like because we have nothing to emulate or relate with. How are we supposed to think like royalty when we've grown up as paupers?

Just like the Princess in the story you just read, you are about to embark on an unforgettable adventure. Over the course of these next few weeks (and hopefully, the rest of your life!) you will be daily transformed by the truth of God's Word. These daily devotionals will teach you more about your royal identity in Christ, help you to think less like a pauper and more like the glorious princess that you are!

Day 1
Heavenly Princess Training

The closest thing we have to modern day royalty in the United States are the "Pop Princesses" who rule over the media and our Hollywood-saturated culture. These powerful women on magazine covers carry the weighty influence that is similar to that of a princess. Although some of these "stars" massively lack the understanding and worthy execution of being a "Princess Role-Model," strangely enough, Hollywood is the closest thing our brain can use to connect with what life might be as a Royal.

All we know is what we've seen on the silver screen and what Disney has told us about princess life. How scary is that?! Are you beginning to see why it's so important for our minds to be renewed through daily *Heavenly Princess Training*? So much of our thinking is based on what we see in the world, what we've learned from our culture, and what we've heard from the Worthlessness Camp. So how do we escape from the Worthlessness Camp in our minds, and the life-sucking thoughts that have followed us into the City of the Kingdom of the Chosen?

The more energetic girls in the crowd might bounce off their seats and say, "Ohh, ohh, I know! I define myself! I just need to be more confident and believe in myself!" Hmm, interesting answer. Sounds similar to something Disney Channel would suggest! Add a measuring cup of confidence and a spoonful of self-love, and we'll be good to go, right?

The world has given us girls lots of "Seven Step Recipes for Instant Happiness." In fact, every time I glance at a popular magazine cover while standing in the checkout line at Walmart, I see catchy recipe titles like, "Ten steps for the Bikini Body of your dreams!" or "Twelve Ways to Capture His Heart." And my personal favorite, "One Hundred and One Ways to Be Blissfully

Happy for the Rest of Your Teenage Life!"

I've tried many of the recipes suggested in magazines, movies, or catchy pop-anthems, and my cake of inner bliss always seems to flop. The world suggests that we can escape the Worthlessness Camp by "looking within," "embracing ourselves," and "developing our own self-confidence." I love that so many magazines and teen idols are trying to help us out in our pursuit of freedom. I find it a little ironic, though, how the cover appears like it really wants to help you out; but by the time you flip to the confidence-boosting article, you feel even more terrible about yourself, thanks to the ten pages of beauty product ads reminding you how much you *don't* measure up! It seems a little counter-productive, am I right?

As much as Hollywood might think they want to help us out, we have to realize that they do **not** have the answer. If we want to be set free from captive, life-stealing mindsets and lies, we need to have an encounter with the One who created us. We need to have an experience with God's burning bush of love. We need to hear the voice of God speaking to our hearts, declaring who He is, "I AM, THAT I AM." (Exodus 3:4.)

It's easy to want to set ourselves free and try to do so in our own fleshly zeal, but our determination and self-will can only carry us so far. Have you ever tried a fad diet or made a New Year's Resolution, telling yourself, "I'm not going to watch Netflix for a whole week," then find yourself on Friday night eating a tub of ice cream and devouring a whole season of *Doctor Who?* Yeah, our own strength can definitely fail us.

When Moses felt the passion for deliverance rising up inside of him, and the desire to throw off the chains of injustice, he wanted to rescue his people from the oppressive Egyptian rule. And what did he do? He murdered somebody. Moses was predestined to be a deliverer, he just didn't know what to do with all that inner zeal, yet! When his flesh took over, it turned out ugly. Just like the way

Hollywood has attempted to tell us that "Girl power, loving yourself, and believing in yourself is the way to go!" Yet, the media's actions speak louder than their words. Next to their positive messages of "self-fulfillment," we find messages that we need to change in order to be beautiful. Like Moses, attempting to change something in the flesh without the empowerment of God's Holy Spirit, is utterly pointless. Until Hollywood and the media has a major burning bush experience with Jesus, their efforts to help us girls feel "beautiful" will be in vain.

When Moses had that burning bush experience and encountered the One who made Him, everything changed. Why was that? Because encountering the King of Kings begins to put us back into alignment with who we were originally created to be. The Bible says we were made in the image of God (Gen 1:27.) If we don't see God for who He really is, how on earth will we *ever* see ourselves for who we really are, when we were designed with the purpose to be a glorious reflection of Him? The world cannot tell us who we are or how to be free, because the world did not create us. It's not fair to ask our family, friends, the media, or even ourselves to define who we are because they do not know our true purpose or our value.

The ONLY way that we can know our true value and be set free from the demons of the Worthlessness Camp is to ask the One who created us, "What do you see when you look at me?" and, "What am I worth to You?" Have you ever asked God either of these questions?

Dear sister, we must understand our value in Christ. To Jesus, you were worth it all. You are the *treasure* of His heart. When Satan, the enemy of our souls, separated us from God and stole us away through sin, God was robbed of His greatest treasure. The devil thought he was in a pretty good position, that we would be eternally hopeless. He knew the Kingdom rules. He knew that sin would be our deadly snare, and that once we forfeited our crowns to him, no man could ever purchase us back from the dead.

"The ransom for a life is costly, no payment is ever enough." (Psalm 49:8) According to this verse, there was nothing that could purchase us back from the kingdom of darkness. There was no amount of money or gold...not even the wealth of the world would be enough to meet the lofty price-tag of *one* soul! One of the greatest lies Satan has ever whispered into the ears of humanity is that human life is worthless; because every demon of Hell knows exactly how priceless *one* human soul is. The enemy doesn't want you to ask the Lord, "God, what am I worth? What do you see when you look at me? What were your thoughts when You created me? How do you feel about me? How much do you love me?" Because the enemy knows that if you hear God's answers and choose to *believe* what He says about you, his lies will be rendered powerless and you will be utterly unstoppable!

In the Bible, Jesus talked a lot about the value of a human heart. In Mark 8:36 he asked, "What does it profit a man to gain the whole world and yet lose his soul?" In other words, Jesus was saying that if a man were to trade his soul for all the money in the world, he would make a devastatingly terrible trade. That is a little bit mind-blowing because there is a *lot* of money in this world. Even if you traded your heart for the income of the richest man in the world, you would be getting majorly ripped off. You are worth more than billions of dollars. When God created you in His image, the price tag on your soul was so lofty it made the angels in heaven gasp. "How is God going to pay for *her*?" they might have whispered among themselves. "She's the most gloriously expensive thing I have ever seen!" Sister, not even the Kardashian's could afford you! The only thing that could match the startling fee for your redemption was the blood of the Son of God.

When I was standing on the slave bock, I didn't think anyone was going to purchase me. Why would they? The Worthlessness Camp had convinced me that I was a waste. Little did I know, I was a treasure worth fighting for.

When the Father, Son, and Holy Spirit discussed among themselves what a lofty price it would be to create you, redeem you, and bring you into the Kingdom, Jesus didn't roll His eyes and say, "Ughh, do I really have to go and die for her? I mean, she's okay and I love her, but I don't really think she's worth *My life*. I'm the Prince of Heaven, the most amazing and valuable treasure ever! I am priceless. Father, why have you placed such a lofty tag on her? Isn't that a bit much?"

1 Peter 1:18-19 says, "knowing that you were not redeemed with corruptible things, like silver or gold, from your aimless conduct received by tradition from your fathers, but with the precious blood of Christ, as of a lamb without blemish and without spot." Not even silver, gold, or billions of dollars could redeem you. The price was too high; nothing on this earth could match it. There was only one thing precious enough that could match that price: the blood of Jesus Christ.

Wow, have you ever seen yourself as *this* valuable before? In God's mind, everything about you is more than worth His time, love, attention, energy, patience, and sacrifice. God would have *never* made a bad investment. I mean, He is God! He has all wisdom, and knows what is worth spending His time and effort on and what is not. Your price tag was ridiculously high, but God saw you as an *absolute necessity* to His Kingdom.

To dive even deeper into the truth of how valuable you are, read Isaiah 54. That's right, close this book, open your Bible, and read chapter 54 nice and slow. And read it out loud. Let these life changing words sink into your heart.

Now that you've read it, let's zoom in on verses 10 and 11: "Yet it pleased the Lord to bruise Him; He has put Him to grief. When You make His soul an offering for sin, He shall see His seed, He shall prolong His days, and the pleasure of the Lord shall prosper in His hand. He shall see the labor of His soul, and be satisfied. By His knowledge My righteous Servant shall justify many, For He shall bear their iniquities."

There are some puzzling words in these verses. "It *pleased* the Lord to crush Him." Does that sound as bizarre to you as it does to me? How could God the Father possibly get pleasure out of seeing His son crucified, tortured, and destroyed on a cross?!

That passage continues with, "The *pleasure* of the Lord will prosper." What does this mean? Isaiah was prophesying that Jesus would see the labor of His soul, look back at those moments of sheer agony on the cross, and be satisfied, saying, "Oh yeah, that was pretty bad, but she was TOTALLY worth it!" This truth is so staggering! The Father was pleased to crush His Son, because He knew that it would bring forth His beautiful daughter…you! Jesus wasn't just willing to die for you, He was actually joyful, excited, expectant, longing, and looking forward to paying the price for you.

Hebrews 12:2 confirms that truth by stating, "For the joy set before Him, He endured the cross." Joy. What joy could He possibly find in that old rugged cross? There was only one thing that kept Jesus hanging there, enduring the nails, the crown of thorns, the mocking, the spitting, and the cruel suffocation and collapsing of His lungs. There was only one thing that kept Jesus from crying out to the Father, shouting, "It's off! Forget it! Plan OVER." He could have had a band of angels swoop in and rescue him, strike all the losers below with fire from heaven, and in a split second Jesus would be back in comfy old paradise! So what on earth kept Him hanging there? What caused Him to endure? What kind of radical joy set before Him enabled Jesus to endure that suffering?

It was the sheer joy of seeing YOU come into the Kingdom! The joy of embracing YOU and winning your heart back from the kingdom of darkness! Many fathers promise their sons dazzling things, such as armloads of money and vast properties, as an inheritance. But do you know what Jesus' inheritance is? The one thing that God the Father promised Jesus long before the beginning of time? YOU. The only prize worth giving a Prince is a Princess. To Jesus, you're worth more than anything else in this world.

And I must say if the King of Heaven wants you more than anything, and if He thought the price-tag of who you are was worth the equivalent of His precious Son, then you are pretty special. I just might dare and venture out to say, that you are *totally priceless.*

"The eyes of your understanding being enlightened; that you may know what is the hope of His calling, and what are the riches of the glory of *His inheritance* in the saints," (Eph. 1:18). You are Jesus' glorious inheritance. Remember, God would never make a bad investment. If He was willing to spend so much on you, you must have been designed for a most noble and glorious purpose. I encourage you to pray what Paul prayed in Ephesians, Chapter 1. Pray that the eyes of your heart may be enlightened, that you may know the hope of Jesus' calling and what are the riches of His inheritance in His people!

Meaning, to know what we are truly worth. It's not prideful to ask the Lord, "What do you see when You look at me? What did you create me for? What is my glorious purpose? What am I good at? Why am I special?" These are questions God is longing for us to ask Him! He desires to reveal the great worth of who we are in Him. Understanding the worth of each human soul shifts us to begin thinking from God's perspective. That will change the way we see and value ourselves, as well as the people around us.

Day 2
The Forbidden Spinning Wheel

One of my favorite questions to ask when I interview people at *Crown of Beauty Magazine* is, "Who is your favorite Disney Princess?" I love hearing the colorful variety of answers; as artists, musicians, authors, TV personalities, and band members explain why they relate to their favorite Disney Darling. Another question just as fun to throw out there is, "Who is your favorite Disney Prince?" The most popular answer is usually Flynn Rider from *Tangled* (or shall we call him Eugene?). But my favorite Disney Dude is the heroic Prince Philip from *Sleeping Beauty*.

There's just something so exciting about the idea of a valiant prince who would ride his horse onto the scene and slay dragons for me! I used to think that princesses could only be locked up in towers in fairytales. But over the years I have learned that so many are trapped in real-life prisons. A whole generation of princesses is locked up inside something stronger than themselves, fortified castle walls that can be scaled by no man.

Just like Sleeping Beauty, most in this world are captive to darkness but do not know they need to be rescued. It's like the thick overgrowth of weeds and thorns that spiral up the tower, coiling around the chamber that holds the young girl in its tight grip. The unwelcome weeds have choked every flower to death. The vines slowly crawl into the shattered windows, finding their way through each tiny crack in the wall. The suffocating weeds subtly entangle the girls' wrists, wrapping themselves around her hands and feet like chains. In the midst of her deep and fitful sleep, she is in grave danger. The ancient walls begin to crack and the evil spell which controls where she sleeps desires to destroy her. Purposing to choke the life from her lungs, it's only a matter of time before she is suffocated. She is entirely helpless. And though she dreams of a life in another place, the visions of happiness deceive her for she does not know that death is crouching at the door.

The colorful description above is an image of what happens when sin overtakes our lives. When sin is swallowed in small doses, it's easy to believe we have the whole thing under control. Lying to our parents, sneaking out with our boyfriends, getting drunk at parties, or watching movies that make us feel dirty...it's only a matter of time until the wild weeds overtake our lives. Evil is a deceptive thing. It convinces us that our rebellious behavior and selfish attitudes won't hurt anyone, when suddenly, a few months later, we find ourselves chained to *mindsets*, *behaviors*, and toxic *emotions* that choke the very life out of us.

God knew how detrimental it would be for a girl to listen to the deceptive voice of sin and crown herself as self-indulgent queen. Choosing to daily satisfy our own selfish, fleshly urges and ignoring the commandments God has given us for the purpose of making our lives amazing, will leave us in an ugly, desperate place. Just like Eve in the Garden of Eden, we have allowed a cunning serpent to strip us of all splendor, dignity, and the glory of heaven. Like a fair and lovely Princess who demoted herself to a prostitute, an entire generation of captive Sleeping Beauties lies in an apathetic slumber of darkness.

Yet, a most miraculous thing has happened. While you were in that tower completely oblivious to what was happening in the spiritual realm, a valiant Prince fought to rescue you.

This humble Prince has given Himself as a ransom for the terrible curse which distorted our beauty, innocence, and perfection. He has set us free from the consequences of sin. Sin is the selfish heartbeat that consumes like a fire, sucks like a leech, and steals like a barren womb. *Our* sin is that selfish voice that whispers to our minds and tells us to do things that we later deeply regret. It's the voice that suggests we are our own God, and that we have the right to trample all over others to get what we want.

That *same* sin was allowed to crush the Lamb of God on behalf of every captured, tormented Sleeping Beauty. Jesus has slayed dragons for you, conquered your biggest fears, and defeated your worst enemy! He desires to scale those tower walls and sweep you into His arms. He desires to whisk you out of this nightmare and transplant you in the middle of an exhilarating, high-action, never-ending fairytale!

In our classic Disney film, Princess Aurora is in a hopeless state. Cursed upon her entrance into this world, she's told that at age sixteen she will prick her finger on a spinning wheel. Even though her parents try their best to keep this from happening by burning every spinning wheel in town, the curse has been spoken into motion and nothing can be done to stop it. So at sixteen, curiosity and rebellion get the best of her, and she touches the forbidden spindle. A deep sleep creeps upon her, and there is nothing she can do to rescue herself. Meanwhile, Philip embarks on his mission with nothing more than a sword in his sheath and a relentless heart of love! Refusing to give up long before adversity shows its ugly face; Prince Philip has already won the battle in his heart. His faithfulness to complete his task is established long before given the opportunity to turn back.

What I love about Philip is that he faced evil Maleficent and that creepy dragon *head on*. He is a true hero; and rescues Aurora at a time when she doesn't even know she needs to be rescued! Jesus has done the same for us.

"Let this mind be in you, which was also in Christ Jesus: who, though he was in the form of God, did not count equality with God a thing to be grasped," (Philippians 2:5-6). Think of that! The King of kings who dwelt in holy and unapproachable light, who is adored day and night by angels who never stop singing, "Holy, Holy, Holy," did not consider equality with God something to be used for his own advantage. Jesus, just like Prince Philip, didn't shrug and say, "Eh, let someone else do it. I'm kind of too amazing for that." Instead he leaped out of his chair, hopped onto his horse and said, "I'll do it! Send me!"

Verses 7-8 continue, "But made Himself nothing, taking the form of a servant, being born in the likeness of men. And being found in human form, He humbled himself by becoming obedient to the point of death, even death on a cross." Jesus fought and defeated the dragon. He slayed the evil one and came out victorious with the ultimate blow to the enemy's evil plan. What a breathtaking, awe-invoking story! Jesus didn't get the victory by doing the obvious, prideful, heroic thing; instead he took a back road, found a loop hole, and used the secret weapon of humility to save the day. Who would have expected the King of kings to come in human form, be born of a virgin teenage girl, step into his hometown totally UNNOTICED and UNAPPRECIATED, and then obey His Father every step of the way even to the point of death on a CROSS!?

Verses 8 and 9 declare triumphantly, "Therefore God has highly exalted Him and bestowed on Him the name that is above every name, so that at the name of Jesus every knee should bow, in heaven and on earth and under the earth, and every tongue confess that Jesus Christ is Lord, to the glory of God the Father." Jesus showed us that *humility* is true royalty. His ways are much higher than ours. Even though darkness and evil flooded the earth, making it appear as though things were hopeless, Jesus still had a plan to overcome! God still had a good and perfect gift to give to His children. He gave us Himself!

Just like Princess Aurora, we were all cursed at our birth. Because of the sinful choice that our father Adam made, all of humanity has been caught up in a deadly sin cycle. We were told on the day we were born, "You will touch the spindle of sin!" And we each did. The Bible says there is no one without sin, and the punishment of sin is death (Romans 6:33). So while we were sleeping in sin and apathy, something amazing happened. "While we were still yet sinners, Christ died for us". (Romans 5:8) Jesus came, while we were still asleep in sin, when we didn't care, when we didn't love Him; when we ignored Him, mocked Him, and believed we were totally self-sufficient. He came and slayed the dragon anyway. Why? Because of love! Because He wanted a Princess!

If you've never taken time to thank Jesus for what He did for you personally on the cross, why haven't you? His love for you was proclaimed *so* loudly as he hung and bled so that you didn't have to. Choosing to surrender your life to Jesus will indeed be a sacrifice. You'll have to abandon selfish thoughts and anything that doesn't line up with the commands of the King. (To find out what His Ten Holy Commandments are, check out Exodus 20:1-17.) These commandments of holiness and righteous living were never meant to depress and detain us from freedom, instead they were given for just the opposite purpose: for our freedom! Following His Kingdom ways is the key to living amazing, totally fulfilling lives!

In the presence of One who gave up *everything*, how could we possibly respond in any other way than giving Him our everything? Jesus died on the cross then rose from the dead three days later because His love for you was even stronger than the power of death. I know that this sounds like a radical fairytale or a fabricated dream, but history confirms the events of Christ's life, which were recorded in the Bible to be true. Witnesses recorded seeing Christ *after* He rose from the dead and before he resurrected to heaven!

In the same way, riding on the clouds, He will be coming back someday for all who believe in Him. Those who reject this free gift of love and salvation will be eternally punished in a place of torment called Hell. Jesus doesn't want anyone to be thrown into the lake of fire other than the enemy, that fallen angel who deceived Eve and twisted truth into lies. He wants *you*, your friends, and your family to spend eternity with Him in His sweet presence.

He is worthy to be trusted as King of your life...so will you let Him? Why not ask Him *right now* to forgive you of your sinful past, thank Him for His amazing love, and ask Him to be King over every part of your heart? All you have to do is ask; His salvation and love are a free gift. And trust me my friend, when you take the crown off your head and place it at His feet, you will *never* be the same.

"Though your sins are like scarlet, He will wash you *white as snow*." (Isaiah 1:18) Don't you desire to feel *truly* beautiful again? Doesn't your soul long to be washed with the pure water of heaven; dressed in garments of white, radiating with a brilliant beauty that shines from the inside out?

The harsh, ugly truth is that there is NOTHING attractive about sin. Jesus says if you're in sin, you're disgusting to Him, and He will vomit you out of His mouth. (Revelation 3:16) True beauty cannot be applied with makeup, designer jeans, or fancy airbrushing. If sin is hanging around your soul, it smells as bad as a repulsive garbage dump, and the King of Heaven does not want to hang around that mess.

The Evil Queen in *Snow White* daily asked her mirror for approval. She wanted to know she was beautiful and loved. "Mirror, mirror on the wall, who is the fairest of them all?" The answer was *never* her. She never got the answer she wanted! As many times as we can ask the world, our parents, our friends, or the media, we will always get the same answer. Like the Evil Queen, our hearts often ask these questions, frantic with insecurity: "Am I beautiful and brave? Am I worth being loved? Am I attractive to guys? Do my friends like me? Am I enough?" Even Princess Mia struggled to believe she could be everything she was called to be. When she looked into the mirror, she would sigh with disgust and say, "Well, as usual, this is as good as it's gonna get."

This world will always tell us that we're less than enough. The answer is always a big, fat, negative "NO!" It's a loud door slam, a slap in the face, partnered by the painful memory of the last time we were deeply hurt. Someone else is always better. Someone else is always more beautiful. According to the mirror, we are *not* the fairest in the land.

Perky, fun-loving, girl-power pop-anthems might suggest that we can be confident if we muster up enough self-esteem, slap on our high heels, embrace our beauty, and define ourselves. But that doesn't work. Trust, me, I've tried. Any "copy and paste" beauty that I've tried to apply to myself has failed miserably. We can only find beauty, peace, and restoration for our souls from the One who is brilliant and shining in radiant glory. Jesus is the only answer. He is the only TRUE mirror who speaks words of truth. He cannot lie. Jesus shows us our *real reflection*, not a deceptive, hazy one held up by Satan. When we look into the eyes of Jesus, we see who we were created to be. We see love, second chances, and the wild and raging possibility that maybe, just maybe, we were created to be *like* Him. Shining and beautiful. Confident, pure and lovely.

Sister, your moment is now. Choose to make an eternal, life-changing decision. Repent of sin, renounce the enemy, abandon his lies, and shake out of the grip he's had on your life. Don't believe the haunting lies that say you're not good enough, or that you're not worth what Jesus did for you. Jesus said you were worth it. He spent His very own blood. God gave His Son's life in exchange for *yours*! Allow the overwhelming truth to sink in, and come join us in the City of the Chosen!

~*~

Going Deeper (Bonus Study)

Do you remember a young man in the Bible named

Mephibosheth? Maybe not. His story isn't a very popular one, but it should be because it's so beautiful. He was the son of Jonathan, grandson of King Saul. King Saul was a guy who had a lot of potential, but made some terrible, terrible choices. Just like Adam, his choices affected his family for generations to come.

Mephibosheth had a rough life. He was supposed to be king. He knew in his heart that he was destined to be royalty and to live in the palace, but his Grandfather Saul totally messed things up for him. As a young child, he was dropped and his legs became crippled. This gave him a seemingly huge disadvantage in life. Many of us were "dropped" by those we trusted and have crippling memories that have scarred us and hardened our faith from believing in childhood dreams. So many of us have been abused, deeply hurt, and have even been "cursed," so to speak, with lameness. So many of us feel like the orphan. We're so broken and raw that we build up walls, and it's much easier to trust ourselves rather than trust in and rely on God.

But just like Sleeping Beauty, in our own efforts of self-sufficiency, we've touched the evil spinning wheel of sin and it has left us in a deep and fitful sleep. It is my prayer, sweet sister, that you remember your dreams. Return to the carefree visions you had long before your faith was stolen. You've had dreams and visions of what it could be like to be loved by a glorious Prince; you long for it and ache for it to be true. Aurora dreamed of her prince before he appeared. When she met him in the forest, she knew that it was right as she sang, "I know you, I walked with you once upon a dream!"

We're like Mephibosheth in the way that we know what we were created for. We were made for love. In the depths of our souls we know what we want, but there is something that separates us from it. Maybe it's pride, fear, or sin, but there's a reason that we feel fatherless and broken. It's because we haven't run into His presence and thrown ourselves onto His lap crying, "Daddy, I need you!" We all know God's righteous decree against sin and how much He hates it, yet we mess up time after time after time! The question lingers, "How can we simply come to Him as His children and know for sure that we will be forever cherished and loved?" We're broken, tainted, and inadequate. It seems so unjust and so wrong that the Prince would choose us as His bride when we're so...well...*lame*. Just like Mephibosheth, we have major imperfections that keep us out the King's presence.

"On that day," David said, "anyone who conquers the Jebusites will have to use the water shaft to reach those 'lame and blind' who are David's enemies." That is why they say, "The 'blind and lame' will not enter the palace." (2 Samuel 5:8) This royal decree meant that Mephibosheth could never enter the palace.

We can't seem to understand how God could love us despite our sin and like Mephibosheth, we steer clear of the royal court because of the law. But do you want to know what David said to Mephibosheth? This is perhaps the most amazing, tender-loving thing ever spoken by a king! "Don't be afraid," David said to him, "for I will surely show you kindness for the sake of your father Jonathan. I will restore to you all the land that belonged to your Grandfather Saul, and you will always eat at my table." (2 Samuel 9:7)

Wow! Long before Mephibosheth was born, David and Jonathan made a covenant which was a binding, legal agreement. When Jesus died on the cross for our sin, a new covenant was made, which trumped the curse of sin and the heaviness of the law. Colossians 2:14-15 says, "Having canceled and blotted out and wiped away the handwriting of the note (bond) with its legal decrees and demands which was in force and stood against us (hostile to us). This [note with its regulations, decrees and demands] He set aside and cleared completely out of our way by nailing it to [His] cross. God disarmed the principalities and powers that were ranged against us and made a bold display and public example of them, in triumphing over them..." [AMP]

David excused his kingdom rules (no lame person shall enter his palace) on behalf of Jonathan. Now, because of Jesus' sacrifice, the Father is *legally obliged* to let us into the King's presence because of His new covenant! Our sin is removed as far as the east is from the west, our dirty orphan rags have been replaced with robes of righteousness, and our lameness is totally excused!
You are Jesus' Princess, His beloved bride, and He wants you hanging out with Him, inside His palace, sitting with Him! We are seated in heavenly places with Christ! Now we can sit down, rule, reign, and eat at the King's table in total freedom and fearless faith, because of Jesus' sacrifice.

Sister, this is only the miraculous beginning of what God has in store for us. I encourage you to continue this journey through *Secrets of Royalty* because there are many more adventures ahead. We have royal beauty treatments awaiting us, princess lessons that will transform the way we think, wars to wage, weapons to wield, and a world that is waiting for us to arrive on the scene as the brave heroines we were created to be!

Day 3
Chosen Cinderella

There's nothing quite as special as seeing the Cinderella Castle lit up with a warm glow, as fireworks explode and send bursts of light shooting across the sky. I'll never forget that moment. For a five-year-old, there was nothing like it. I stared in wonderment at the dazzling home of my favorite Disney Princess, as twinkling lights which looked like fairies danced around the castle. It had been a spectacular day at the park, complete with chicken nuggets, a regal carousel ride, and performances on the castle stage. I sighed contentedly and smiled at the big purple and pink sky where God slowly dimmed the day into the evening starlight. In that moment, I felt a little bit like Cinderella myself. I felt blessed, beautiful, and radically loved.

Cinderella's story has always enchanted me in the most lovely sort of way. The obsession started in preschool. When I was three years old, I watched Cinderella's movie too many times to count. I sang along with musical mice and bounced with excitement through her Bibbibty Bobbity Boo, rags-to-riches makeover. I still remember the way Cinderella's tale started. On the screen her fairytale book opened slowly, and big, loopy letters formed printed words I could not yet read. As the tale unfolded, I had no need to worry about reading...that's what the narrator was for. The introduction went something like this:

"Once upon a time in a faraway land there was a tiny kingdom, peaceful, prosperous, and rich in romance and tradition. Here in a stately chateau, there lived a widowed gentleman and his little daughter, Cinderella. Although he was a kind and devoted father and gave his beloved child every luxury and comfort, he felt she needed a mother's care. And so he married again, choosing for his second wife a woman of good family with two daughters just Cinderella's age; by name, Anastasia and Drisella. It was upon the untimely death of this good man, however, that the stepmother's true nature was revealed. Cold, cruel, and bitterly jealous of Cinderella's charm and beauty, she was grimly determined to forward the interests of her own two awkward daughters. Thus as time went by, the chateau fell into disrepair for the family fortunes were squandered upon the vain and selfish stepsisters, while Cinderella was abused, humiliated, and finally forced to become a servant in her own house. And yet, through it all, Cinderella remained ever gentle and kind, for with each dawn she found new hope that someday her dreams of happiness would come true."

Following this grand introduction, Cinderella woke up with a song on her lips. Hugging her pillow, and looking much too cheerful for any normal teenager waking up in the morning, she sang. The lyrics were planted deep inside of my little soul, like seeds of hope for the future. "A dream is a wish your heart makes when you're fast asleep. In dreams you will lose your heart ache, whatever you wish for, you'll keep. Have faith in your dreams, and someday, your rainbow will come smiling through. No matter how your heart is grieving, if you keep on believing, a dream that you wish will come true."

When I was young, I merely thought this story was about a kind, pretty girl who took care of her animals, believed in impossible dreams, and danced her way to a happily ever after. It wasn't until a few years ago when Jesus sweetly led my mind back to this movie, and my heart returned to the story of Cinderella, that I discovered so many hidden treasures and nuggets of golden wisdom as I studied this story.

My favorite scene in this fantasy is near the end, the morning after the ball. Prince Charming enters Cinderella's house, slipper in his hand, determined to find his missing love. (If you've never watched the 1997 production of Cinderella, starring Brandi and Whitney Huston, it is a must see! It's a beautiful retelling of the tale. I think you should watch this movie as soon as possible! Time for another sleepover party!) In the Rogers and Hammerstein musical version of this story, two eager stepsisters kick their feet into the air and try in a tireless effort to jam their size ten-and-a-half feet into the tiny size-six shoe. The scene is comical because the girls are so desperate. It's obviously not fitting, but the sisters don't give up. Meanwhile the shrewd step mother slips a key into the lock where Cinderella is kept tucked away.

The Prince's face has grown tired and weary in this great search. "Are you *certain* there is no one else here?"

The stepsisters giggle and snort their infectiously obnoxious laughter and deny any such thing as they make their way over to stand in front of the locked kitchen door, flinging their arms out in every direction. It's obvious now there is someone hidden behind that door.

This search reminds me of when Samuel the priest was sent out to anoint the new King of Israel. The Lord sent him to Jesse's household where he scanned over a fine-looking bunch of young men. Samuel spotted the eldest son who was tall, handsome, and hardworking, and he knew he was the one. But then the Lord said, "Don't judge by his appearance or height, for I have rejected him. The Lord doesn't see things the way you see them. People judge by outward appearance, but the Lord looks at the heart."

Just like Prince Charming, Samuel asked, "Are these all the sons you have?"

The brothers tossed uneasy glances at one another, eyes visiting their toes, fidgety hands rubbing the back of their necks. "There is one more," Jesse spoke slowly, "but he's the youngest. And he's out in the fields with the sheep."

You can almost hear the disappointment in Jesse's voice. Jesse did all he could to hide little-old David in the same way Mrs. Evil Step Mom locked Cinderella away. Both Cinderella and David could have grown highly offended at the lack of attention and gross mistreatment, but instead they each allowed the season of suffering to soften their hearts and prepare them to someday rule.

Cinderella's evil stepmother daily discouraged, lied to, and attempted to convince Cinderella that she was a total loser. Her words were ruthless, "You'll never capture the heart of a prince. You're just our dirty-little-servant girl. You're ugly, weak, and pathetic."

These fiery words were shot at poor Cinderella every day as she was confronted with demons from the Worthlessness Camp. (I think Taylor Swift's song *Mean* would describe Evil Step Mom perfectly. "All you are is mean, and a liar, and pathetic, and alone in life and mean!")

I think we've all been in Cinderella's shoes. And no, I'm not talking about her glass slippers. I'm talking about her muddy-old servant shoes. We know what it feels like to hear harsh words of discouragement. We've all heard the chorus of noisome critics from the Worthlessness Camp, telling us to give up, reminding us of past failures, and causing us to believe the future will look just as dreary as the past. But amidst the voices, we hear the stark contrast of the song Jesus is singing.

When we first hear our Lord's beautiful voice, it can be quite shocking to the system, because it's so different than what we've ever heard before! He is singing, "You did not choose me, but I chose you." (John 15:16) "I want to be with you. I want to hang out with you. I think you're fabulously amazing!"

I like to believe that Cinderella heard this song ringing in her spirit much louder than any dirty-old words her step mom was speaking. Cinderella arose each morning with such hope as she gazed toward the castle outside her window, singing songs of promise that had been whispered into her heart while she was sleeping.

The Lord is singing a song over all of His daughters. It's a song of destiny, hope and delight. Can you hear it? Zephaniah 3:17 says: "The Lord your God in your midst, The Mighty One, will save; He will rejoice over you with gladness, He will quiet *you* with His love, He will rejoice over you with singing."

When the Almighty God has got someone set in His sights, it's impossible for them to escape His attention. Just as Prince Charming was determined to find Cinderella, *Jesus is relentlessly seeking out His chosen ones.*

The idea of being chosen is wonderful. The word *chosen* evokes thoughts of all sorts of gleeful situations; such as being chosen for a date, or auditioning for a theater production and snagging the lead role. It's a spectacular feeling when someone picks you out as someone special or declares that you're the right person for that dream role. Have you ever been chosen for something before? Perhaps a better question is, have you ever been *not* chosen for something?

I grew up as a homeschooler who dreaded this activity we did once a month, called *Gym Day*. In public school you poor, tortured souls had to withstand this kind of agony every day! But we blessed homeschoolers would only meet once a month to stretch, practice good sportsmanship skills, and play something to get our heart rate up, such as Kickball or Basketball. Most enjoyed this jolly activity, gaily gallivanting around the gym with rosy red cheeks. But you see, I've been practically uncoordinated since birth. Give me a story to write, a song to sing, or a card game to play and I can succeed, but place a ball in my possession and I start praying and quoting Philippians 4:13 until the final whistle is blown!

Okay, maybe I'm not *that* horrible, but I'm just not naturally competitive when it comes to sports. I enjoy the social aspects of sports, such as chatting with your best friends while the other team is making a free throw. But when you're playing with a bunch of hardcore homeschoolers who treat every gym day like it's the Super Bowl, the girl who just wants to have fun is not exactly everyone's first choice. Actually, I was everyone's last choice.

When everyone lined up against the wall, there I stood, waiting, waiting, and waiting some more, as the two team captains chose the best players for their teams. After the superstars were chosen, they would settle for those of average skill. And soon, all that remained was the leftovers. One by one, the long line disappeared, and I was still there. They would pick *preschoolers* to be on their teams before they picked me. Yeah, it was that bad.

It might be a silly example, but being the last one picked isn't the best feeling in the world. Knowing that both team captains couldn't care less about the contribution you bring to the team, can make a girl feel kind of lousy. Being the leftover isn't fun. Perhaps you know the feeling. Maybe you've been the last one picked in theater group, for a sleepover party, or you feel like you're the bottom name on your crushes list of interest. Do you feel ignored, taken for granted, or invisible? Do people treat you like the disposable Cinderella or the purposely passed over shepherd boy?

We live in a cruel world. People constantly say and do things to tear us down and make us feel insignificant. Rejection is a feeling that stings the heart like none other. Nobody wants to feel cast out, useless, or unsatisfactory. But every true Cinderella has been there.

One of my favorite love stories in the Bible is the story of Rebekah and Isaac. It's the story of a humble young woman who lived an average life and dreary existence, then was suddenly, all at once *chosen* to be a Cinderella, of sorts.

John 15:16 says, "You did not choose me, but I chose you..." I think we can all relate with Cinderella, David, and Rebekah on one level or another. We've all felt the pain of rejection. But my dear sister, I don't want you to get too used to that feeling because there is another experience that God wants you to have. He wants you to relish in the part of the story where Cinderella's glass slipper fits, where David is anointed as King, and where Rebekah is chosen by Isaac! It's the part of the story where the amazing joy of being hand-chosen by God crashes over your spirit!

Rebekah grew up in a culture very different than our own. Abraham wished to find a lovely bride for his son. So he sent out one of his servants to work as a *Shadkhan*. The Hebrew word literately means "matchmaker." In Hebrew culture, parents chose and prearranged who their daughters would marry. Can you imagine the craziness of your parents choosing your future spouse? Most of us cringe at the thought of it. Some girls were lucky enough for a *Shadkhan* to slip into the village and work his romantic magic while most were assigned to the choosing of their parents.

Rebekah was *chosen* and then she was *cherished*. The Bible says that Isaac loved her the moment he laid eyes on his beautiful bride. Abraham wanted to choose the ideal bride for his beloved son so he sent out his *Shadkhan* to find her. Abraham was like a Biblical king. He had so much wealth and such a highly esteemed stature among the surrounding communities that when Isaac, Abraham's only son, came along, He wanted to choose the *absolute best* for his dear son.

Does this remind you of anything? Perhaps of our Father in Heaven and His only, beloved son, Jesus? 2 Chronicles 16:19 says, "For the eyes of the LORD run to and fro throughout the whole earth, to show himself strong in the behalf of them whose heart is perfect toward him." Jesus' heavenly Father has sent out his *Shadkhan*, the Holy Spirit, to find a bride for His beloved Son. Just like Prince Charming, He is searching for the one whom the shoe will fit. He is scanning the earth for His chosen ones. Where will He find a Royal Princess Bride? *Where is she*?

Ephesians 1:4-5 says, "For He *chose* us in Him before the creation of the world to be holy and blameless in His sight. In love He *predestined* us for adoption to sonship through Jesus Christ, in accordance with his pleasure and will." Before the foundations of the earth were laid, God knew that He wanted you to be the

Princess Bride of Jesus Christ and would do anything He needed to in order to capture your heart. Isn't that beyond amazing?

Just like Rebekah, you have been *chosen* and you have been *cherished*.

I encourage you to read all of Ephesians 1, and let the words sink deep into your heart! Memorizing Ephesians 1:4-5 would be a great way to let this truth renew your mind.

Embrace it. Believe it. Let your heart grow excited by the truth of it. You are God's chosen Cinderella!

Day 4
Destined for Greatness

Yesterday we talked about what it means to be God's chosen Cinderella. Now, I'm not sure how you feel about this, but I'm the type of girl that when I start to get attention from someone, all my inner sirens go off. My head shoots up like a deer frozen in headlights, and I feel the sudden urge to bolt. (See why I relate so much to Mia?) I'm just not used to that kind of attention. When Jesus came along and started singing His songs of love, affirmation, reassurance, and endless attention, I didn't know what to do! Should I run? Should I stay? How is a girl supposed to process this kind of attention from the King of the Universe?!

When Cinderella went to the Ball, all eyes were on her. Everyone wanted to know who she was, where she was from, and why the Prince was so obsessed with her. We can be sure Cinderella wasn't used to that kind of attention either. Her closest friends were barn mice!

But something supernatural happens when Jesus chooses us as His Princess. People begin to notice. We are suddenly illuminated with the Spirit and very nature of Jesus Christ. We shine like stars in the heavens and sparkle with splendor. When we light up and glow, the darkness takes note.

Cinderella's evil step mom knew this girl was marked for greatness. There was something radically different about her, and this fearful Mother was un-nerved. She trembled at the possibility of her stepdaughter doing something greater or being more powerful than she. So this fearful woman grappled for control and took immediate action.

In the same way that Prince Charming chose Cinderella as the target of his affections, evil made Cinderella the target of merciless attacks. Cinderella was ambushed with every possible obstacle her enemy could think of. She was loaded down with chores and her dress was ripped to shreds, all done to keep her from going to the Ball and uncovering her true identity. Though Evil Step Mom never physically hurt her daughter, she attacked the one place that was sure to be detrimental...her mind.

"If only I can abuse and abase her," the evil woman must have stroked her chin while scheming her profoundly wicked plot, "if I can twist her mind into thinking she is an ugly, worthless, cinder-scooping loser; then she will stay in my prison forever. She will never go outside of these walls and be the light that she is. Cinderella will never shine if she is too afraid to believe."

We see this evil tactic of trickery repeated throughout fairytales (remember Rapunzel's Mom?!) and throughout human history. Just like the frightened ruler in Exodus (check out Exodus 1), we must come to the realization that our enemy is drop-dead afraid of us. Just like Cinderella, your enemy *dreads* you. The more he attempts to oppress us in fear and dread, the more we rise up and turn to Christ! The enemy cannot win, but he is desperately giving his best fight. And he is a good fighter. He knows that your Prince is determined to crown you as a victor, and that you are predestined to be a Princess. The enemy trembles in fear because he can't do ANYTHING to stop that glass slipper from fitting your foot.

Don't you see the beauty of this thing? It's *impossible* for the devil to win. Jesus has already promised your victory! In the same way that Cinderella's slipper was tailor-made for her foot, you have a royal destiny that is all yours. No one else can fit their foot into the shoe that He has made for you.

Read Exodus 1:6-25. I've added the verses below so you can read along (emphasis added), but be sure to take the time to read it in your own Bible.

"Now Joseph and all his brothers and all that generation died, but the Israelites were exceedingly fruitful; they *multiplied greatly*, *increased* in numbers and became so *numerous* that the land was *filled* with them. Then a new king, to whom Joseph meant nothing, came to power in Egypt. "Look," he said to his people, "the Israelites have become far too numerous for us. Come, we must deal *shrewdly* with them or they will become even more numerous and, if war breaks out, will join our enemies, fight against us and leave the country." So they put *slave masters* over them to *oppress* them with forced labor, and they built Pithom and Rameses as store cities for Pharaoh. But *the more they were oppressed, the more they multiplied* and spread; so the Egyptians came to *dread* the Israelites and worked them ruthlessly. They made their lives *bitter* with harsh labor in brick and mortar and with all kinds of work in the fields; in all their harsh labor the Egyptians worked them *ruthlessly*. The king of Egypt said to the Hebrew midwives, whose names were Shiphrah and Puah, "When you are helping the Hebrew women during childbirth on the delivery stool, if you see that the baby is a boy, kill him; but if it is a girl, let her live." The midwives, however, feared God and did not do what the king of Egypt had told them to do; they let the boys live. Then the king of Egypt summoned the midwives and asked them, "Why have you done this? Why have you let the boys live?" The midwives answered Pharaoh, "Hebrew women are not like Egyptian women; they are vigorous and give birth before the midwives arrive." So God was kind to the midwives and the people increased and became even more numerous. And because the midwives feared God, he gave them families of their own. Then Pharaoh gave this order to all his people: "Every Hebrew boy that is born you must throw into the Nile, but let every girl live."

Why did the Egyptian leaders try to destroy all the Israelite people? Verse 12 reveals the root: "But the more they were oppressed, the more they multiplied and spread; so the Egyptians came to dread the Israelites." The enemy was afraid of the ones he was trying to attack, so the fearful leaders attempted to destroy new life. They wanted to eliminate any chances of hope arising and snuff out all joy and success. They were dreading the possibility of a new leader rising up, someone from this fruitful nation to overthrow the oppression and slave mindset of being a captive. We have seen this pattern repeat itself throughout history over and over again. We've seen this with Haman in the book of Esther, Adolf Hitler in World War 2, King Herod during the birth of Jesus, leaders in Iran and Iraq who oppress women, and controlling leaders in Asian countries who discourage the birth of baby girls. We've even seen this in the United States with abortion. Any nation killing its own children has some serious, serious problems. So why is this happening? Why is the enemy so vicious about snuffing out new life?

When it's time for a leader to be born, the fearful ones in power become even more afraid. The enemy has attacked us so viciously as girls because he is afraid of us. He wants to abort our dreams, our future, and keep us bound to fear with a slave mindset.

"But you just don't understand," you reply. "The enemy cannot possibly be afraid of me. You've got the wrong girl. I've never done anything heroic or even halfway awesome. I've been told my whole life that I am worth nothing. My parents, friends, and people I trusted have all hurt me deeply and treated me like trash. I wish I could believe that God values me as much as you say, but I'm so beyond the point of being salvageable. Everything good about me has burned away."

Sweet sister, if you feel like this, draw courage from these following words. I know you've been burned and scarred by people who spoke searing words of hatred and shot burning arrows of pain into your heart. You feel like you've been through Hell. Everything about you has been consumed, and you don't feel like there could possibly be anything good left. You've been bullied, beat up, and spit back out. You feel like Cinderella, a worthless slave sitting by the ashes of her dreams with nothing left but a pile of cinders. The "Evil Step Mom" and "stepsisters" in your life have spoken so many damaging words. BUT there is a reason for the violent assault that's been on your life. Please don't take these bitter attacks personally because they have nothing to do with you, but have *everything* to do with Jesus. If you carry the name of Christ, by being a born again Christian, His name is written brightly on your forehead! Every weapon that comes against you is coming against the Spirit of Christ *in* you. Jesus said you will suffer persecution for His sake. He promised that you will have trouble in this world. "But take heart," He finished, "for I have overcome the world." (John 16:33)

Lovely one, you are *not* the ugly, worthless, cinder-scooping loser that everyone says you are. Cinderella's family despised her, yet she was so beautiful that she captured the heart of a Prince! She was predestined to be a Princess, therefore the enemy tried to beat her into the ground. Those lying voices have been trying **so** hard to discourage you because you're part of the Royal Family. The attack has been declared against your Father and His family. The enemy forces don't want you to see or understand your royal position. They don't want you to know how crazy the Prince is about you. For if you did, you would be absolutely *unstoppable* in spreading the Kingdom of Light. We must take great hope and gird ourselves in the unwavering confidence that the victory has already been won. Just like in every fairytale, we are promised a Happily Ever After. We know how this story ends. But until the scarlet curtain falls and Satan is thrown into his final prison, we have daily choices to make to defeat this violent monster in our lives.

Girl, your adrenaline-pumping, high-action story of greatness is unfolding. Just like Cinderella's evil stepmother, the enemy is jealous of our potential and royal position. He knows we are stunning and splendorous so he tries his very best to lie to us and convince us that we are not. He says we are worthless, powerless, ugly, and unloved. But he knows the truth and it frightens him. We are priceless, powerful, beautiful, and radically loved. Imagine what damage an army of girls, who understand who they are in Jesus and walk in their royal identity, could do to the enemy's plans!

If we don't know or believe the truth, we offer no threat to him. But once we grasp and understand this truth, we become unstoppable! The enemy tries to keep us from our Cinderella-style, God-given destiny that is more exciting and exhilarating than we could possibly dream. He would like us to continue gazing into the mirror, despising, comparing, and hating ourselves. But it is time for the Sleeping Beauties to awaken, for Snow White to be washed in absolute purity, and for Cinderella to move into the palace. Sisters, now is the time for action!

The potential of you partnering with the King of Kings and Lord of Lords, to be all that God created you to be, has caused the enemy to fear you greatly. Perhaps your life hasn't given him much to fear so far. Maybe you've been dabbling around in sin, chilling on the fence with one foot in God's presence and the other in the world. Perhaps your life looks a tad bit like Mia's, who is ignoring the call to be Princess, or like the girl in the Worthlessness Camp who would rather stay in her old familiar, muddy place. But the enemy isn't afraid of what you have done. He's afraid of what you *might* be.

We might still be a little disoriented, foggy, and confused by what took place in the Worthlessness Camp. Your life might be in ashes, or shredded up like Cinderella's ball gown which was ripped apart by her stepsisters. We may feel inadequate, weak, or unfit for the Ball. But we are going anyway! We are God's girls who are marching into the City of the Chosen! We will embrace our royalty identity and put on our royal robes!

Cinderella's name means *"girl by the cinders."* They gave her such a lowly name because fire seemed like such a low, humbled, and abased element. But Jesus does not see fire the same way that we do. He sees His beloved Cinderella, the girl by the cinders of her burned up life, and says, "I have come to provide for you, to bestow upon you a crown of beauty instead of ashes. I've come to give you the oil of joy, instead of mourning and depression, and a garment of praise, and the strength of my joy, instead of a spirit of despair!" (Isaiah 61:3)

You, dear one, hold a special place in the King's heart. You are His priceless Princess whom He has given everything for. Cinderella, this isn't the end of your story. This isn't where the ashes consume you. The King is waiting to bestow a crown of beauty upon you. All you have to do is close your eyes, crawl up into your Daddy's lap, and ask Him to hold you, heal you, and restore you.

Day 5
Princess Rebekah

I've painted a short story about Rebekah, in hopes that this will give us a colorful look into what life might have been like the day she was chosen. Let's visit the day that Abraham's matchmaker showed up on her doorstep, and checked to see if the glass slipper of destiny fit her foot.

As the Arabian sun inched its way up the horizon, darkened nighttime shadows were eaten away by its glorious brilliance. Calling this sleepy village to wake, the usual morning activities started to stir. A young maiden descended down a grassy hill with two large water jugs in hand. The empty jugs would soon be filled with what was needed for cooking the morning meal. Rebekah was not the only young woman sent from the community on this task. Girls from each family appeared on the grassy knoll, water jugs in tow. Rebekah had been doing this chore ever since she was strong enough to lift and haul without spilling any of the precious commodity. Though this chore was painfully mundane, she truly didn't mind the short trek from home. The walking distance gave her time to think. Dismissed from the busyness of life and chores at home, her brisk walk served as a quiet sanctuary for Rebekah. She took a deep breath of the crisp morning air, relishing in the coolness which still hung over the desert. The breeze offered a welcome reprieve from the glaring heat which was soon to come. A flock of birds descended from a myrtle tree, singing their sweet song of the dawn. A small smile slipped across Rebekah's soft, olive-toned face, her dark brown eyes looking heavenward.

"Wait!" the voice of a child came from behind, "Wait! Wait for me Rebekah!"

The trip to the well *used* to be a place of serenity, until her younger sister became old enough to come along. She paused patiently as little Nohla came running with a jug in hand. Rebekah shook her head playfully, "Little Nohla, always running behind."

"I stopped to watch the ravens feeding on an olive bush," innocent, chocolate-colored eyes pleaded with Rebekah.

Rebekah could not be harsh with her. The sweet, adventurous girl was the youngest in a family full of rowdy boys. "I understand, little one. Come." Rebekah wanted to reach the well in time to catch up with her friends and hear the latest news in the village.

"Hello Rebekah!" her friends called. Upon reaching the well, Rebekah gave her greetings to all who gathered.

A young woman named Leah was the first to fill her jug. "Have you heard the news?" she began the usual excited chatter. "About Sarah?"

All the girls replied that they had not, and listened intently. Leah fed off their eagerness, and carried on with her story. "Just last evening I saw handsome Simon wander over to Sarah's tent. While he was there, he offered a bride price and asked for her father's permission to marry her!"

Hilgah snorted, placing impatient hands on her hips, "Of course that would happen to Sarah, why Simon has been sweet on her since childhood."

Rebekah smiled to herself. Hilgah was a good friend, but sometimes she spoke without thinking. Rebekah suspected a hint of jealousy in Hilgah's voice. Sarah was three years younger than her and Rebekah. Sometimes Rebekah battled depressing doubts that said she would never find a match, and perhaps this was one of those days for Hilgah.

"They should've waited for the *Shadkhan* to come to our village," another voiced. "It's foolish to arrange a marriage without the Matchmaker."

"How can that be foolish?" little Nohla spoke up. "Aren't they in love?"

Her comment was ignored, as Hilgah spoke, "It could be years before the *Shadkhan* appears again. If one wants to get married they must make their intentions known to the young man they are smitten with. There's no time to wait for some village Matchmaker!"

"Oh really?" another teased. "If you're so sure of the way it is, why hasn't Dan asked you to marry him yet? You're always making sheep's eyes at him."

Hilgah withdrew her second jar from the well and tossed a cold look at the one who teased her. "Dan will make his intentions known very soon. Just wait and see."

Rebekah laughed at her friends' silliness as the dunked her jar into the well.

"Excuse me, miss." A male voice came from behind, startling Rebekah. She turned around to see an old man whose wrinkled face had seen many years. He was weary from a long journey, and his tired voice cracked as he spoke, "Please give me a little water from your jar."

Rebekah lowered her head respectfully and offered the jug to him, "Drink, my lord." The young women remained silent, having immediately ceased from their chatter. The distant stranger gulped his helping as though he hadn't tasted water in days. As soon as he finished, Rebekah spotted his small caravan of camels loaded with supplies. She spoke softly, "I'll draw water for your camels too."

She loved animals of all kinds and could only imagine how tired they were. She had no idea how far this man had come, nor what kind of conditions they had traveled in. The least she could do was offer this small act of kindness. Slowly, each young woman filled their remaining jars and slipped away from the well. Soon it was only Rebekah and her sister who remained, as Rebekah watered the camels.

Nohla stood in silence as she stared at the man, examining his foreign attire. He looked deep in thought and Nohla wondered what he was thinking. This man had been taken aback by her simple words. Rebekah had not known what was going on behind the scenes. For just moments earlier, this man was praying. As soon as the camels finished drinking, the man reached for a gold nose ring and two heavy bracelets made of pure gold. Rebekah's eyes were struck by these lovely ornaments.

The man proceeded to ask, "Whose daughter are you? Please tell me, is there room in your father's house for me to spend the night?"

"I am the daughter of Bethuel," she responded quickly, then smiled shyly at the hungry camels. "We have plenty of hay and fodder for your animals." She quickly added, "As well as a room for you, sir."

Without warning, the man suddenly fell to the ground face down and cried out, "Praise be to the Lord, the God of my master who has not abandoned his kindness or faithfulness to my master! As for me, the Lord has led me on the journey to the house of my master's relatives."

He stood up and proceeded to slip the heavy, gold bracelets onto Rebekah's arms. Suddenly realizing that this man was near kin, Rebekah abandoned her water jars and ran back home to tell her family.

Rebekah pushed past the curtain which draped over the entrance of their humble abode, rushing through the threshold in such a wild furry that she scarcely stopped to catch her breath. "Papa, Mama, aunts, uncles, cousins, listen! A visitor is coming!"

Rebekah's announcement sent the whole household into a buzz of preparation activities. Laban, Rebekah's eldest brother who was preparing to check on their flocks, spotted the dazzling bracelets on his sister's arms and suddenly realized what was going on. He hurried down to see the man at the spring. Delilah, one of Rebekah's many cousins, admired the jewels on her arms, for she had never beheld anything so lovely.

Meanwhile at the well, little Nohla was sent home and the water jugs were abandoned as Laban and his this traveling stranger spoke.

"Come," Laban greeted with outstretched arms, "you who are blessed by the Lord. Why are you standing out here? I have prepared the house, and a place for the camels."

The man was very grateful, and the men walked in silence back to

Laban's tent. Upon entering, this stranger was welcomed like a long-lost family member into their home. Rebekah and her two sisters immediately brought water for washing the man's feet. They knelt before him and performed the customary courtesy, slipping off his sandals and washing the travel dirt from between his toes. Laban and his brothers fed and watered the camels outside, and Rebekah's mother quickly spread out a variety of foods before him, "Eat," she insisted, "Rebekah tells us that you had a very long journey."

The man raised his hands in protest, "I will not eat until I have told you what I have to say."

Then tell us!" Laban spoke eagerly, "And do not spare a detail."

"I am Abraham's servant. The Lord has blessed my master abundantly, and he has become wealthy. He has given him sheep, cattle, silver and gold, menservants and maidservants, and camels and donkeys. My master's wife, Sarah, has borne him a son in her old age and he has given him everything he owns." The man explained that he had been sent to find a wife for his master's son.

The family stood in silence after he finished his story. Rebekah could scarcely believe what her ears were hearing. She tossed a quiet glance at her father who appeared to be deep in thought. Fingers ran through his thick beard, contemplating the words that were spoken. He looked at Laban and then answered, "This is from the Lord; we can say nothing one way or another."

Upon hearing this, Abraham's servant bowed down on the ground before the Lord and worshiped. Then he brought out gold and silver jewelry and articles of clothing from his caravan of camels and gave them all to Rebekah. Her little sisters and young cousins swarmed around the gifts which this man gave liberally to her. They were all very beautiful, and she had never seen such great wealth. The excitement of it all nearly made her dizzy, and eager voices buzzed all around her. He also gave costly gifts to her brother, Laban, and her mother. The bride price had been offered from her father, and Abraham's servant agreed. Rebekah's beautiful mother could not contain the soft tears which fell from her eyes as she spoke, "The choice is Rebekah's. Will you go with this man?"

Rebekah took a deep breath and spoke, "Yes, I will go." With those words it had become official. She was to be married. The day was filled with preparations for her long journey, and Rebekah slowly began to realize the reality of what was happening. It wasn't until she laid her head on her mat that evening that the weight of it all hit her.

I am to be married. I am to leave my family. I am to travel to a land I've never known, to marry a man I've never met.

A cold shiver traveled through her warm body, as she fought back terrified tears. *Will he love me? Will I be happy with him? O Lord, God of Abraham. The One who searched me out, and called my name, I am afraid. I do not wish to leave my family, friends, and all I've ever known. Help me to be strong. Help me to be a wife whom this man will be proud of.*

Day 6
Shifting Our Perspective

Jesus Christ came to this earth for a divine purpose. He came with a one-track mind. Do you know what the heartbeat of His mission was? *To reveal the heart of our Heavenly Father.*

Why did he have to do that? Why was it so vital that Jesus represent the true image of God? Because after the fall of mankind, Satan launched a full-blown campaign, an all-out attack on the reputation of God. He wanted to twist the way that we see the Father, to shroud His goodness and love. The enemy wants us to see God in a distorted, dark, evil, and depressing way.

In the Old Testament you can imagine why the Israelites thought that God was cold, harsh, legalistic, and angry. But Jesus came to completely shift all of our preconceived ideas about who God was (John 17:26). Jesus came to destroy the works of the devil (1 John 3:8).

One of the most beautiful illustrations of what Jesus did to shift the way we see God can be found in John 8:1-11. I encourage you to read this passage in your own Bible. Here, a fearful woman is caught red-handed in the middle of a sinful act. She committed adultery and was dragged into the center of the city by the Jewish rulers, with perhaps nothing more than a blanket covering up her nakedness. She was embarrassed and ashamed. They were ready to stone her and watch Jesus slam down the hammer of justice. They believed Jesus would be the first to cast a stone and carry out the written law (Whoever had sex outside of marriage was to be killed!) because this was all they knew about God. They knew His royal, righteous decrees, but they hadn't the slightest idea of His mercy (Matthew 9:13).

I can only imagine the horror in this young woman's eyes. Her end had come. The past had finally caught up with her. She was guilty, guilty, guilty; and there was nothing she could do to change that. But Jesus did the most beautiful, shocking, and gracious thing that humanity has ever seen. He didn't condemn her. He didn't reach down, wind up, and smash a stone onto her head, even though the Law of God said she deserved it. He *forgave* her. He extended such a beautiful mercy; a mercy that caused everyone in the crowd to gasp and walk away in astonishment. Here, Jesus revealed a side of the Father's heart that no one had ever seen before.

"And provide for those who grieve in Zion-- to bestow on them a crown of beauty instead of ashes, the oil of joy instead of mourning, and a garment of praise instead of a spirit of despair." (Isaiah 61:3) Our shadowy pasts do *not* phase the One who has chosen us. He's much too excited over who He has called us to be and what He sees in us, to throw us away over past mistakes.

Verse 7 continues to say, "Instead of your shame you will receive a *double portion*, and instead of disgrace you will rejoice in your inheritance. And so you will inherit a double portion in your land, and *everlasting joy* will be yours." Beloved, you've been chosen. Embraced, accepted, and fully adored by the King of the Universe. Humility *is* royalty. Your lowly, difficult, life circumstances have placed you in the perfect position to be exalted as a princess. God cannot work with puffed up pride and ridiculous egos. When we are crushed and broken in spirit, He is near and working on our behalf. (Psalm 34:18)

Let's return to the story of Isaac and Rebekah for a moment. Can you imagine the excitement and sheer joy Isaac felt over the thought of finally seeing his promised bride?

A handsome, dark pair of eyes brushed over the horizon. The scenery had not changed. He squinted harder, wishing he had the eyes of an eagle to spot what would be soon coming his way. He glanced at the watchman standing beside, wishing he might see with such clarity. It was the watchman's duty to keep nonstop lookout for enemies who might unexpectedly raid his master's land. Isaac rose to his feet, paced back and forth several times, and then paused to strain his eyes once again. In an instant, Isaac thought he saw dust rising in the west. Eagerly he prepared to sprint and greet the coming caravan of camels, but the watchman grabbed his arm.

"Rest," He commanded. "It's only your imagination."

Isaac let out an exasperated sigh, and kicked at some loose stones below. "When will my Father's servant arrive with her? When will I finally see her?"

The watchman did not know the answer to the young man's question, so he only continued doing his job.

"Isaac!" a voice called from below. Isaac peered over the edge of the rock he stood upon and spotted his father preparing to climb the summit. Father Abraham was considerably old, and climbing the mountain proved to be a chore. He relied heavily upon his thick staff made of sturdy oak. Finally he reached the top, and Isaac asked, "Father, are you sure we sent enough gifts? What if they refuse our generosity and don't allow their daughter to return? What if they treat our kindness with contempt and stick their noses in the air at our lofty bride price? Oh, Father, do you think we paid enough? Perhaps we should have sent more livestock, more jewels, or clothing..."

Abraham placed a gentle arm on his anxious son's shoulder, "We offered all that we could. May God be their judge if they refuse what we have given them. If she is a young woman of virtue and integrity, she will come. Let your mind be at ease, my son."

"Oh, I can only imagine what she shall be like," Isaac began pacing eagerly once more, "stunning eyes, with a face painted by heaven itself. Delicate figure, but not too delicate; she must be strong. Strong in heart and vigorous. A joyful companion, one who makes me laugh and challenges me to reach new heights, one who is gentle and kind. Oh, Father, I have not seen her, but I know I shall love her! If she's anything like I dreamed she would be..."

A sudden hint of movement in the distance brought Isaac to an abrupt stop. A cloud of dust rolled in the desert, and Isaac knew it was her. Without saying a word to anyone, his feet took off running as he rushed to greet his new bride.

I can only imagine the eagerness of this young man as he sprinted across the desert. The Bible says that after Rebekah asked, "Who is that man in the field coming to meet us?" she then took her veil and covered herself in it.

I may be reading into this more than what the Bible offers, but I see an eager Isaac who may have been overwhelmingly friendly! We don't know if he swept her into his arms and kissed her on the cheek, offered to help her down from her camel and began talking a million words a minute, or if he simply stared at her in wonderment. The Bible makes it clear that Isaac loved Rebekah from the moment he laid eyes on her. It does not state Rebekah's feelings. Perhaps she felt shy, bashful and frightened. She may have blushed silently at his handsome features, but kept her mouth locked shut. She may have carried anger and resentment in her heart toward him for forcing her to leave her family, relatives, and all she had ever known. All we know is that she *hid* inside her veil.

Sometimes, we do that with Jesus. Our overwhelmingly-, exuberantly-joyful Savior comes running up to us as he desires to wrap us in His arms. But we sometimes hide from his affection and shudder under His warmth. Whether we are frightened, mistrusting, or angry; you can't blame a girl for wishing the Man would keep his distance!

"...as a bridegroom rejoices over his bride, so will your God rejoice over you." (Isaiah 62:5)! He rejoices over us just like a man rejoices over his bride! He sings love songs, and desires to dance with us and share all the secrets of His Kingdom and His heart. It may sound a bit extreme, but Jesus actually wants to have such a dynamic, intimately close, heart-to-heart relationship with you. It's the kind of relationship that the Bible likens to one a man would have with his bride. He desires to have a passionate, authentic friendship with you! This crazy love He proclaims for us is a little bit radical. We're not used to the idea of having this kind of affection from someone we scarcely know. Imagine if your next-door neighbor pounded on your door and suddenly started proclaiming his undying love to you. Chances are, you'd slam the door in his face, call 911 and report that creeper!

Isaiah 54:5 says, "For your maker is your husband, the Lord Almighty is His name." If the idea of Jesus desiring to cherish you like a bride makes you want to toss this book out the window, hang in here with me for a moment. Although it's true that Jesus is crazy in love with us, He is also a complete gentleman. He will *never* force us into a relationship we do not desire to have. His gentleness and respect for each human heart means that He will never, ever, *ever* force us into a place of closeness we desire not to have.

Just because Rebekah was chosen did not mean she was totally comfortable with the idea at first. The man was an absolute stranger! For some of us, Jesus is this intimidating God-Man, whom we picture seated on the clouds with a terrible frown, a long scraggly beard, and lightning bolts shooting out of His fingers. Or maybe your image of Christ is like the picture from your coloring book in Sunday school with little sheep and children gathered around him. Maybe Jesus is nothing more to you than someone you sing about on Sundays.

Our first impression of people can be powerful. Sometimes we create such a strong opinion of a person, that we don't give that person any room for change in our hearts. But there is something even stronger than a first impression, and it's called a second impression.

One of my closest friends in grade school once thought I was a stuck-up, little brat who hated her guts. She held this prejudice about me in her heart for months until one afternoon my mother invited her over to play. In our carefree timelessness together she discovered that I was very different than what her original image of me was. After the lie had been trumped by the truth of my identity, we became great friends.

Jesus desires to do the same with you. He wants to smash apart any shadowy, tainted, distorted or preconceived ideas that you may have about who He is. He wants to invite you over for an afternoon of time spent together so that He can prove His true identity to you. He wants to debunk the lies and profess the truth about Himself. Ask the Lord to remove those false images in your mind of Him, which you have in the past subscribed so faithfully to, and ask Him to reveal His true self. Because once you catch a glimpse of the pure heart of Christ, you'll feel compelled to let down your guard, take off your veil, and *truly* get to know your Prince.

It's my prayer that this book be just that; an opportunity for you to spend time with the Prince of Peace and King of Kings. Use these words, Bible verses, and stories as conversation starters. I encourage you to begin journaling through your journey. You are just like the young girl who was rescued from the Worthlessness Camp and called into the City of the Chosen. I invite you to start writing about your life experiences as if *you* were the Princess on this amazing journey of getting to know her Lord and King.

There is no greater adventure than the one you are on right now! You've been whisked into an amazing plot, the sweetest Cinderella story ever told. Just think of it!

Abraham sent out his matchmaker to find a bride for Isaac. Prince Charming searched the whole kingdom for that one heart he knew was completely his. And in the same way, in the Old Testament, God sent out His Holy Spirit to search the entire earth...for what? A heart that was completely His. A princess bride for His Son, Jesus Christ. But what did He find?

"I looked for someone among them who would build up the wall and stand before me in the gap on behalf of the land so I would not have to destroy it, but I found no one." Ezekiel 22:30 He found *no one*. Can you imagine the devastation in this Father's heart? What if Abraham's matchmaker came home having found no one? What if Prince Charming never found his chosen Cinderella? That would make a really sad fairytale, wouldn't it? Of course it would! Because every beautiful story has to end with the guy getting the girl! But there was a time in God's grand fairytale that things looked pretty bleak. God longed to restore relationship with humanity, but he found NO ONE to stand in the gap and restore righteousness.

Romans 3:10, "There is none righteous, no, not one: there is none that understandeth, there is none that seeketh after God." (KJV) So right then, in the earth's darkest hour, Jesus stood up and said, "I'll go. I'll be the last Adam. I'll restore humanity's relationship with my Father, by living a perfect life, doing ONLY what He says and does, to represent Him...then I will become sin, and bear the wrath of God, and completely pour myself out."

What LOVE Jesus had for His Father! To step out and sacrifice everything. I mean, hello, He was the royal one of heaven! He did not have to do that. But Jesus loved His Father so much...and the Father loved the Son, that He promised Jesus he would have an inheritance. He *would* have a Princess Bride. And the most mind-blowing part of this story is that the Princess Bride is *you*. If I was God, I would have just created some kind of a goddess to be Jesus' beautiful Bride. I mean, He is the Creator, after all! But no, *we* were what He wanted. A royal Prince is never one to marry below Himself, so why would He choose us? Girl, God PICKED YOU OUT and CHOSE you for Jesus. Holy Spirit, the Royal Matchmaker, was like...."Yep, this girl, right here, she's the one."

The love of Christ reminds me of Prince Philip and his amazing attitude with every trial he faced. In the original version of the tale, Philip faced dazzling temptations from Maleficent, just like Jesus did in Matthew 4; including the temptations of wealth, honor, glory, and women. But he said, "No, no, no!" and slashed through the thick weeds, slaying the dragon to rescue his Chosen Cinderella, his beloved princess bride!

Day 7
The Queen of Persia Beauty Contest

"But what will I wear!?" Panicky shrieks overflowing from hearts of pure happiness, and excited screams escaped from the lungs of every eligible young maiden in the land. Closet doors flew open and clothes that "just wouldn't do" were flung across the bedroom. Daughters begged their fathers for more cash before racing down to the mall in great pursuit of "the perfect outfit." Every shelf in the cosmetics department was empty. Every tube of lipstick and every wand of mascara were completely sold out.

A mad mob of teens argued so fiercely over the remaining items at the jewelry store that a shop owner had to close early that afternoon. The way that every girl between the ages of twelve and seventeen rushed through the stores, it caused some to think that the end of the world was near! The screams were heard from miles away, and some folks speculated that One Direction had come to town. But no, the world had not reached its end, and neither had a boy-band of British heartthrobs arrived. So what was the madness all about?

We will find our answer in the book of Esther because that is where this crazy story is found.

In the land of Persia, a king named Xerxes reigned from his royal throne. (How about we just call him King X? That's so much easier to pronounce!) King X, this abundantly wealthy dude, was hosting the party of the century. He invited the most popular and highly influential men in the area, and all his party buddies infiltrated the palace.

In Esther 1:4-6 it reads, "For a full 180 days he displayed the vast wealth of his kingdom and the splendor and glory of his majesty. When these days were over, the king gave a banquet lasting seven days, in the enclosed garden of the king's palace, for all the people from the least to the greatest who were in the citadel of Susa. The garden had hangings of white and blue linen, fastened with chords of white linen and purple material to silver rings on marble pillars. There were couches of gold and silver on a mosaic pavement of porphyry, marble, mother-of-pearl, and other costly stones."

What a place! Can you imagine a one-hundred-and-eighty-day banquet hosted by the king himself? Sounds like my kind of party! Everything was decorated beautifully, and each element set in place. Each stone on the pavement had been scrubbed and polished by the servants, and the flowers in the garden were pruned just the way the king had asked. Everything about this party was flowing smoothly, and all the guests were comfortable as they sat around the garden fully relaxed and totally at ease, sipping from their golden goblets of wine.

As the King sat there looking at how blissful things were, he thought of the one thing that could make this party the absolute bomb. He would bring out the showstopper; His gorgeous (and little did he know, gutsy) wife, Queen Vashti.

Verses 10-12 says, "On the seventh day, when King Xerxes was in high spirits from wine, he commanded the seven eunuchs who served him – Mehumam, Biztha, Harbona, Bigtha, Abagtha, Zethar, and Carcas – to bring before him Queen Vashti wearing her royal crown, in order to display her beauty to the people and nobles for she was lovely to look at. But when the attendants delivered the king's command, Queen Vashti refused to come. Then the king became furious and burned with anger."

Uh-oh. So much for keeping this party clean from anything the paparazzi would just love to dig their claws into. Talk about a royal conspiracy! Did this Vashti lady ask for it or what? The hungry tabloid hounds sent to hide in the bushes quickly scribbled down a story that would shock the nation on the cover of *Star Magazine*. They quickly snapped photographs of the Queen, imagining a killer caption like, "Queen Vashti Has a Hissy!"

I've heard many opinions and commentary on why Vashti refused to come when the king called. Some say she was stubborn and non-submissive, acting like a snooty Sharpay Evans from *High School Musical*; and others say she was asked to perform for the king's friends in a seductive way and was tired of being treated like a devalued object of pleasure. The Bible doesn't tell us what her reasoning was. So whether Vashti was acting out as a complete snob or as a woman standing up for righteousness, King X was not going to let this fly.

Thankfully King X was a bit more merciful than other kings of the past. He didn't pull a King Henry and chop off her head, but he talked it over with the guys (AKA the "experts in matters of law and justice" vs. 13) and executed his decision.

Esther 2:1-4 continues, "Later, when the anger of King Xerxes had subsided, he remembered Vashti and what she had done and what he had decreed about her. Then the king's personal attendants proposed, 'Let a search be made for beautiful young virgins for the king. Let the king appoint commissioners in every providence of his realm to bring these beautiful girls into the harem at the citadel of Susa. Let them be placed under the care of Hegai, the king's eunuch, who is in charge of the women, and let beauty treatments be given to them. Then the girl who pleases the king may be queen instead of Vashti.' This advice appealed to the king, and he followed it."

And so it was official. Every eligible, young maiden in the land was given the chance to become queen. Can you imagine? This was the chance of a lifetime for these local girls of Persia. Forget American Idol and a fleeting five minutes of fame. This was the chance to rule by the King's side! Not only was it a chance to be somebody, but it was the chance to be *the* somebody. *Her Royal Majesty.*

I can just hear the wired-up announcer telling every T.V.

watcher in Persia, "If a simple, small town girl can capture the heart of the king, in turn he will give her everything she's ever dreamed! The world will be hers on a silver platter, decked out with flowers, frosting, sprinkles, and sparkles on the side! Jewels, riches, gold necklaces and diamond rings. This one lucky girl is going to get the works! Who will rise above the other maidens, seduce the King, and claim the crown? Find out next time on, "Queen of Persia Beauty Contest!"

Think about how crazy girls can get when there are shoes, dresses, a cute guy, and a tiara involved. Now add a heaping scoop of "Royal Power" for dessert, and tell me who wouldn't want a slice of that?

So what exactly were the *rules* of this wild competition that King X was hosting in his grand palace? Esther 2:12 says, "Before a girl's turn came to go in to King Xerxes, she had to complete twelve months of beauty treatments prescribed for women, six months with oil of myrrh and six with perfumes and cosmetics."

If you're anything like me, the first thing you thought when you read that verse was, "Oh. My. Was looking gorgeous and smelling like roses actually such a big deal to King X? What about inner beauty? Was he really that shallow?" If you haven't figured this out by now, it might be about time someone told you. Guys like pretty girls. Always have, always will. And when you're the King of Persia, you wouldn't want a semi-pretty wife would you? I mean you're the king! You would only want the best of the best! Why would you settle for average? Can we really blame the king for wanting a woman near perfection?

Now before you write a letter to the king of Persia telling him how unbelievably shallow and prejudice he is for choosing a wife simply by the way she looks, let's practice being graceful and give this guy the benefit of the doubt. We know that looks aren't everything. And maybe King X didn't choose his girl on that one depending factor. Hopefully he looked past fading superficial beauty and took a glimpse into the unfading beauty of his queen's heart, Esther.

So what about our King Jesus? He is much more royal than King X ever was; and although King X's reign was only for a season, Jesus is going to be King forever. So, is looking beautiful and smelling lovely really that important to God? If King X only wanted the best of the best, wouldn't God want the same?

"But the Lord said to Samuel, "Do not consider his appearance or his height, for I have rejected him. The Lord does not look at the things man looks at. Man looks at the outward appearance, but the Lord looks at the heart." (1 Samuel 16:7).

"Phew!" I can hear you say as you wipe your brow. "What a relief! I thought I was going to have to undergo twelve months of beauty treatments, lose ten pounds, and get plastic surgery!" Okay, so maybe you already knew that God is much more concerned with our hearts than He is with our clothes, but sometimes we just need to be reminded.

Our King loves beautiful hearts *so much more* than King X ever loved beautiful faces. So are we concerned with the fact of whether or not our hearts are beautiful before Him? Or would we rather fix our make-up before we fix our hearts? Does our way of living as His daughters honor Him? He desires that our hearts be beautiful, clean and purified. Just like the orphan turned princess in our story there comes a time in each of our lives where we need a major heart wardrobe change.

After wallowing around in things like envy, jealousy, unforgiveness, self-pity, and pride, our hearts can end up looking pretty ugly. We come in contact with these germs every day, things that try to contaminate our hearts and separate us from God. The good news is that just like the girls of Persia, we can go through daily *inner* beauty treatments that will prepare us for our heavenly Prince. Any contact with darkness taints who we are and leaves a smudge of dirt on our hearts. Jesus desires that we be without spot or blemish (Ephesians 5:26).

Jesus has a spa that every girl can slip into, to set her heart at ease and get her looking like a Princess. That spa is called the Bible. In Ephesians, it says that we are washed by the water of the word. Soaking in the Bible is just like slipping into a bubbly, steam-filled hot tub after a long day of stress and craziness. Every care of this world melts away beneath the heat of God's love being poured into our souls. God's word comes and surrounds us with servants who shampoo and condition our hair, clean under our nails, give us manis and pedis, and leave a bright bubblegum pink robe for us to wear. Getting pampered is something that most every girl loves, and God wants you to do it every single day!

It's so important to spend time getting beautified! Why? Because as a Princess I cannot afford to think like a pauper. Sometimes I get caught up in all the superficial stuff of this earth, all the lies and everything temporal about this life. But I am receiving a Kingdom that I cannot see. A Kingdom that will not be shaken. (Hebrews 12:28.) Something unseen. Something eternal. Something more beautiful than I could dream. I need to remind myself of this every day or else I end up conforming to the world around me instead of transforming it. Without washing in the water of God's word, I let the mud from the Worthlessness Camp seep into my thinking and mess up my clean heart.

We have to renew our minds in God's word *daily*. We have to soak ourselves in God's presence because the more time we spend with the Prince, the more we will start to look like a Princess. 1 Peter 2:9 says, "But you are a chosen people, a royal priesthood, a holy nation, God's special possession, that you may declare the praises of him who called you out of darkness into his wonderful light."

I love the story of Esther. It paints a beautiful picture of a royal scene, where a young woman chosen by God was used to save her entire nation. If you haven't read the full story of Esther, I encourage you to read the whole book. Esther never got caught up in the deceitfulness of riches, nor did her head inflame ten sizes larger as she indulged in the perks of being "Queen". She remembered who she was, and she understood her true identity.

What about us? Can we say the same? We too are living in a similar land as Esther, in a world that places a high price on external beauty and tries to make us think that what we see is eternal. Are we caught up in the things of this world or have we kept our hearts set on the Kingdom of God?

Maybe it's been awhile since you've just soaked in the spa of God's word. Do you feel anxious, worried, afraid, or not at peace? Now would be the perfect time to slip into that spa and ask God to wash all the dirt away. He specializes in making insecure, selfish, ugly hearts into radiant, confident, humble Princesses. With his sweet love and never-ending patience He can place you on an inner beauty treatment program that will change your heart forever. So go ahead sister, set down this book and step into the beauty parlor of the King. Ask him to wash the dirt away and transform your mind.

Listed below is a treasure trove of some of my favorite verses about being royalty. These golden words are laced with pearls of truth. Read them. Embrace them. Memorize them. Post them on your Facebook page. Text them to your friends. Use sticky notes to plaster these words all over your bathroom mirror. Write them on the tablet of your heart. (Deut. 11:18.) Allow the words of a Prince to daily transform your mind and heart.

From the outside, we may appear to be Converse-, cowgirl boot-, flip-flop-wearing girls. But on the inside, we're adorned with a supernatural splendor and glow. Something that shines from the inside out. It's the light that can only come from being a Princess of Heaven.

Beauty Treatment Bible Verses

(For best results, use daily. Wash, rinse, and repeat.)

"I adorned you with jewelry: I put bracelets on your arms and a necklace around your neck, and I put a ring on your nose, earrings on your ears and a beautiful crown on your head. So you were adorned with gold and silver; your clothes were of fine linen and costly fabric and embroidered cloth. Your food was honey, olive oil and the finest flour. **You became very beautiful and rose to be a queen.** And your fame spread among the nations on account of your beauty, because the **splendor** I had given you made your beauty perfect, declares the Sovereign LORD. " ~Ezekiel 16:11-14 "You came to greet him with rich blessings and placed a **crown of pure gold** on his head." ~Psalm 21:3

"All glorious is the princess within her chamber; her gown is interwoven with gold." ~Psalm 45:13

"God redeems your life from the pit **and crowns you with love and compassion.**" ~Psalm 103:3

"Awake, awake, Zion, clothe yourself with strength! **Put on your garments of splendor**, Jerusalem, the holy city. The uncircumcised and defiled will not enter you again. Shake off your dust; rise up, sit enthroned, Jerusalem. Free yourself from the chains on your neck, O captive Daughter of Zion." ~Isaiah 52:1-2

"Arise, shine, for your light has come, **and the glory of the LORD rises upon you.** See, darkness covers the earth and thick darkness is over the peoples, but the LORD rises upon you and his glory appears over you. **Nations will come to your light, and kings to the brightness of your dawn.**" ~Isaiah 60:1-3

"Surely you will summon nations you know not, and nations you do not know will come running to you, because of the LORD your God, the Holy One of Israel, for He has **endowed** you with **splendor.**" ~Isaiah 55:5

"O afflicted city, lashed by storms and not comforted, I will build you with **stones of turquoise,** your foundations with **sapphires.** I will make your battlements of **rubies,** your gates of **sparkling jewels,** and all your walls of **precious stones.**" ~Isaiah 54:11-12

"For this is what the LORD Almighty says: "After the Glorious One has sent me against the nations that have plundered you—**for whoever touches you touches the apple of his eye-** " ~Zechariah 2:8

"The LORD their God will save his people on that day as a shepherd saves his flock. **They will sparkle in his land like jewels in a crown.** How **attractive** and **beautiful** they will be! Grain will make the young men thrive, and new wine the young women." ~Zechariah 9:16-17

"You are the **light of the world.** A city on a hill cannot be hidden." ~Matthew 5:14

"Blind Pharisee! First clean **the inside** of the cup and dish, and then the outside also will be clean. Woe to you, teachers of the law and Pharisees, you hypocrites! You are like whitewashed tombs, which look beautiful on the outside but on the inside are full of the bones of the dead and everything unclean." ~Matthew 23:26-27

"Charm is deceptive, **and beauty is fleeting**; but a woman who fears the LORD is to be praised." ~Proverbs 31:30

"And we all, who with unveiled faces **reflect the Lord's glory**, are being transformed into his image with ever-increasing glory, which comes from the Lord, who is the Spirit." ~2 Corinthians 3:18

"So we fix our eyes not on what is seen, but on what is **unseen**, since what is seen is temporary, but what is unseen is eternal." ~2 Corinthians 4:18

"For he **chose** us in Him before the creation of the world to be **holy** and **blameless** in his sight. In love He **predestined** us for **adoption** as His sons through Jesus Christ, in accordance with his pleasure and will." ~Ephesians 1:4-5

"So that you may become blameless and pure, children of God without fault in a warped and crooked generation in which **you shine like stars in the universe**." ~Philippians 2:15

"But you are a **chosen** people, a **royal** priesthood, a holy nation, a people **belonging** to God, that you may declare the praises of him who called you out of darkness into his wonderful light." ~1 Peter 2:9

"**Your beauty** should not come from outward adornment, such as elaborate hairstyles and the wearing of gold jewelry or fine clothes. Rather, it should be that of **your inner self**, the unfading beauty of a gentle and quiet spirit, which is of great worth in God's sight." ~1 Peter 3:3-4

Going Deeper (Bonus Study)

Inner Beauty Treatments aren't the only way that the Lord causes us to shine from the inside out. Another way that He makes his daughters sparkle like jewels is through the more *painful* beauty treatments called "The Trials of Everyday Life." Oh yeah.

Ouch.

1 Peter 1:6-7 says, "In all this you greatly rejoice, though now for a little while you may have had to suffer grief in all kinds of trials. These have come so that the proven genuineness of your faith—**of greater worth than gold,** which perishes even though refined by fire—may result in praise, glory and honor when Jesus Christ is revealed."

Sometimes I think God's value system is really messed up. He values beautiful hearts higher than lovely faces, and He places more importance on our faith then He does our own comfort! Ugh, how rude! But He says our faith is of greater worth than gold.

What if we *really* understood what that means? I believe if we valued our faith as God does, maybe we wouldn't complain and cry "woe is me!" so often during those times when everything in our world seems to be falling apart. When trials come, maybe we would actually have the courage to do what the Bible says and rejoice in our suffering! If Jesus thinks my faith is of greater worth than gold, and He is eagerly awaiting the day when He will bestow on me praise, glory, and honor when I first see Him face to face, maybe I should try thinking more like Him. Maybe the trials of this temporary life aren't as huge as I make them out to be. **Maybe these trials and hard times on earth are like inner beauty treatments.** Heart makeovers and long spa days before we meet our King face to face. I know, it's a stretch. But maybe, just maybe, He has a reason for all this pain. Perhaps it is intended to make us beautiful as well.

Does Jesus really turn ashes into beauty? Does He take the ugly things we go through, and make something beautiful out of it? Does He turn tears into diamonds and ashes into roses? I know in my heart this is true because I have been thrust into seasons of ugliness of death and pain, and have come out with a crazy abundance of treasures. But what about you my sister? Has God turned any of your toughest times into jewels? If He hasn't yet, continue to hang in there, and He will! That is the beautiful thing about a story...it's not over until it's over. Things can get pretty ugly halfway through, but if we cling to Him and endure the fire, we are promised the beautiful ending of a *happily ever after*.

"Everything is good in the end. If it's not good, it's not the end." -Lisa Bevere

Day 8
The Banquet Table

"He has bought me to his banqueting hall, and his banner over me is love." (Song of Solomon 2:4) One of my favorite parts in the story that I shared with you earlier is when the orphan is rescued from the Worthlessness Camp and ushered into the courts of the King. She arrives at the palace feeling totally dirty, unworthy, and completely wide-eyed at all the grandeur of the palace. After undergoing her inner beauty treatments, she sits down in the Banquet Hall with Jesus. But it's just too much for her. She can't handle it, and so she runs away. From the outside looking in, this makes absolutely no sense. Why would someone who was starving, run away from a table of delicious food laid out before them?

In this story, the Banquet Table represents the living Word of God. His Word is the extravagant meal of love, peace, and wisdom that God has provided us to feast upon with our hearts. That's right sister, your Bible *is* the Banquet Table. How often do we place God's Word on the shelf as we run to our friends, magazines, or our Netflix account; desperately seeking advice, comfort, or encouragement? Only just about *every day* of our human lives.

"There was no way that every dream she never knew she had could be coming true, all at once, all in one place. Absolutely free. What was the catch? What did this Prince want from her in exchange for everything He was giving? Was she to be a servant destined to scrub palace floors and clean out golden bathrooms the rest of her life? Wouldn't freedom be better than having to report to someone daily? It seemed so simple, yet so extremely difficult. How could she just sit down and receive it? How could she possibly say 'yes' to his offer? She had not earned any of it, and she knew in her heart-of-hearts that she didn't deserve it. How could she simply sit and eat?"

Why do we run outside the umbrella of God's protection and

wisdom as we make a mad dash through the pouring rain with companions like Self and Envy, only to make a miserable mess of our hearts? This world provides us all with a Teenage Survival Manual, and words from this popular publication are printed all around us. Every day we get bombarded with messages that are candy coated in the deceptive shade of "We are just trying to help."

But don't you see? That's the problem! It's a *Survival* Manual. Why settle for surviving along with the rest of this world when in God's word we could be *thriving*?

"But," I hear you sigh, "could an old book written thousands of years ago actually solve all my modern-life problems? No offense to God or anything, but I really don't think He was too concerned with things like friendship issues, dating, and the high school popularity totem pole. All I'm saying is that it seems like God just doesn't understand this stuff we go through these days."

If that's the way you've been thinking about God's Word, I think it's time to take another look. Hebrews 4:12 says, "For the Word of God is living and active. Sharper than any double- edged sword, it penetrates even to dividing soul and spirit, joints and marrow, it judges the thoughts and attitudes of the heart." This Book is living and active meaning that God breathes His breath of life onto those pages every day. His advice is totally up to date! Believe it or not, Jesus does understand the times. He understands everything about your life, and He cares more than you could ever imagine.

His words are sharper than any double-edged sword. Unlike this world's advice, He doesn't just give you the scoop on what meets the eye. No, He goes much beyond the obvious. He divides the soul and spirit and discerns the thoughts and attitudes of the heart. Not just the attitudes of your heart, but the heart condition of others as well! He knows us all better than we know ourselves! His wisdom goes so deep. His banquet table is so full. And it's all right at your fingertips.

Isaiah 55:1-3 says, "Ho! Everyone who thirsts, Come to the waters; and you who have no money, Come, buy and eat. Yes, come, buy wine and milk without money and without price. Why do you spend money for *what is* not bread, and your wages for *what* does not satisfy? Listen carefully to Me, and eat *what is* good, And let your soul delight itself in abundance. Incline your ear, and come to Me. Hear, and your soul shall live; and I will make an everlasting covenant with you—The sure mercies of David."

What girl in her right mind would turn down a banquet? Eh, nobody. So why do we spend our days chasing things that can never truly feed and satisfy our souls? I think it's time for a reality check. We each have 24 hours in the day. How much time do we spend reading the Word of God, flipping through the pages of our Bibles, asking the Lord to speak to our hearts and guide us in His truth? Be honest with yourself. It is an embarrassingly small amount of time.

Now, may I ask, how much time do you spend talking with your friends, texting them, or surfing the internet? How much time do you spend on Facebook, Pinterest, Tumblr, or Twitter? How much time do you spend watching Netflix or movies on the weekend? How much time do you spend reading novels or studying for school?

When we take a step back and look accurately at how much time we spend feeding our brains with temporal, fading, earthly things, instead of eternal, princess, kingdom things, it's no wonder we don't live like princesses.

Princess Mia may have been born royalty, but she was raised in an Americanized culture that taught her to set her attention and focus on temporal things. Princess thinking didn't come naturally for her, and she had to be taught. The same is true of us! Now, don't get me wrong, there's nothing wrong with having some girl time on your favorite social media sites, having sleepover parties, and watching chick-flicks with your besties, but we cannot expect ourselves to live and think like fearless world-changers if we fail to take the time to attend our "Princess Lessons."

Mia found this struggle to be a challenging one. She really enjoyed her old life as an average girl, and it was more comfortable for her to live like everybody else, rather than spend hours studying her Princess manual. She needed to learn the history, language, customs, laws, rules, and traditions of the Genovian people. But it took up so much of her time! It was like learning a whole new way of life.

She sighed and asked Joe, her Security Guard, "Can't I simply quit?"

He replied, "You can quit the job, but you can never stop being who you truly are. A princess."

Queen Clarisse (Mia's Grandma) sensed how much Mia was struggling and offered an appealing compromise, "You don't have to do this Mia." She said, "You don't have to do the job."

Mia didn't know it at the time, but if she chose not to continue her Princess lessons, if she quit studying the Princess manual and decided to continue on with her average teenage life, someone else was lurking in the shadows, ready to pounce on her throne of power. There was a usurper who was more than eager to take her job. Who was this usurper? Baron and Baroness Von Troken! (Don't you remember, the man who said to his wife, "Your nose would look lovely on a postage stamp!"?) These long-lost, distant cousins were quietly waiting in the wings, ready to take Mia's authority as soon as she set down her royal scepter.

We too have a usurper lurking in the shadows of our lives. Satan is waiting for us to sigh and say, "This is just too hard. I don't like the responsibility of being a daughter of the King. I'd rather just do my own thing." He wants us to hang up our crowns and continue life as royal daughters who refuse the job.

The Lord is saying to us, the same thing that Grandma told

Mia. "You don't *have* to do this. You can quit and forfeit your royal authority to another; but if you do, things are going to get messy. Someone is going to take control of your life, and it won't be you."

Mordecai told Queen Esther, "If you remain silent at this time, help will arise from another, God will surely raise up a deliverer, but you yourself will be destroyed."(Esther 4:14). The whole Kingdom is *not* resting on your shoulders. If you decide that Princess living is "too hard," and that you'd rather spend hours with the world rather than in the Word, deliverance will arise from somewhere else. *But* your own personal life will be consumed by the sickness of selfishness, and you won't be fulfilling the purpose for which God made you! The people around you will also suffer if you don't be who God has called you to be in their lives. Sounds really depressing, doesn't it!?

There is nothing the enemy enjoys more than watching a Princess who is rightfully royal never take action. If the crown of royal authority is hanging on a hook in your closet, the enemy can slip in and wear it. Nothing is stopping him from doing so! *You* are the one who has been entrusted with the responsibility to manage your life, your environment, and your mind. You are to be the reining governess of your thought life! You must choose and control your own thoughts. Don't allow your thoughts to control you.

So often, we walk around like helpless captives, struggling to make it from Sunday to Wednesday night youth group, crying because the enemy is beating us up so badly. Instead of rising up in our God-given authority and using our Princess rights which are to walk in personal victory and triumph, we give the devil WAY too much credit declaring that every crappy day we have is an "attack!" Maybe it's not an "attack," maybe your own mind has simply been thinking about the wrong things. Perhaps you've been focused on the wrong thoughts, and you are simply walking in the fruit of what your own mind *thinks* about your life!

Dale Carnegie wrote, "Two men looked out from prison bars; one saw mud, the other saw stars." I know there are days when it feels like everything is crashing down around us, but the truth of the matter is that the posture of our hearts and minds will affect the way we experience both negative and positive things that happen to us. If our hearts are rolling around in the mud, everything is going to seem negative and depressing and dirty. But if our minds are fixed on the reality of heaven and what it means to be a Princess Daughter of the Most-High, we will experience the pain and trails of life with a measure of great joy, because we are seated in heavenly places with Christ! (Ephesians 1)

There is a reason that Paul told us to fix our minds on everything that is "true, noble, beautiful, praise worthy, pure, excellent, and lovely." Jesus desires that we reign in this life, and soar on wings like eagles, allowing the burdens and struggles to lift us high and closer to Him, rather than push us down into the mud.

Do you know how to reign in your own life as a Queen? Do you know how to take authority over your own thoughts and lead them captive into the obedience of the Lordship of Christ? Do you know how take authority over the enemy when he really *does* attack and attempt to wear your crown?

"For if, by the trespass of the one man, death reined through that one man, how much more will those who receive God's abundant provision of grace and the gift of righteousness, *reign* in life through the one man, Jesus Christ!" (Romans 5:17, emphasis added.) In other words, if Adam changed the whole course of history through a simple choice and allowed such evil to rush in, how much MORE can we, who have the gift of grace and righteousness, radically change this world through the power of God's Word and His love?! Just imagine how much we can flood this earth with God's goodness! We can totally reign with Him! Authority belongs to Him who authors or creates something, and

God the Owner and Author of this life has given us the pen to be a co-author with Him. He has given us the creative ability to write on the tablets of our own hearts and etch a tale through our daily choices, affecting the story of those around us.

If we choose to submit to what Jesus is doing in our lives, ask Him what to write, and start writing alongside Him, we will have such a beautiful story! But if we ignore the radical responsibility we have been given to be a steward of each moment, thought, word, and deed, we give the enemy opportunity to pick up the pen and begin scribbling. Don't let him steal your pen or your crown!

The job isn't easy, but it is what we have been called to. Sisters, we must daily realize the value of each moment we've been given. We must see the value of Jesus, His Word, and spend significant amounts of time with Him each day.

Everything we could possibly need, want, or dream of is found in Jesus Christ. It's all there! But just like anything else in life, it's up to you to make the first move. You have to reach your arms across the room and pick it up off the shelf. You have to wipe the dust off the cover and open it up. You have to use your fingers to flip the pages. And you have to use your heart to seek God for His answers.

Think about it like this: Exploring God's word is like digging for gold. You have to dig a little here and dig in a little bit deeper there, and you may not find what you're looking for right away. You have to keep coming back. You've got a whole 66 books to explore, but most Christians have never read their Bible cover to cover once.

When we run away from God's Word and choose not to worship and honor Him by spending time with Him and sitting quietly at His feet, it seems almost as foolish as a Princess running away from a royal ball held in her honor.

Day 9
Royal Secrets to Success

"Moses my servant is dead. Now then you and all these people, get ready to cross to the Jordan River into the land I am about to give them-to the Israelites. I will give you every place where you set your foot, as I promised Moses. Your territory will be from the desert of Lebanon, and from the great river, the Euphrates-all the Hittite country-to the Great Sea of the west. No will be able to stand up against you all the days of your life. As I was with Moses, so I will be with you, I will never leave you or forsake you. Be strong and courageous, because you will lead these people to inherit the land I swore to their forefathers to give them. Be strong and very courageous. Be careful to obey all the law my servant Moses gave you; do not turn to it from the right or to the left, that you may be successful wherever you go. Do not let this Book of the Law depart from your mouth; meditate on it day and night, so that you may be careful to do everything written in it. Then you will be prosperous and successful. Have I not commanded you? Be strong and courageous. Do not be terrified; do not be discouraged, for the Lord your God will be with you wherever you go." (Joshua 1:2-9)

God was telling Joshua to get ready because they were headed into the Promise Land. The Israelites had been wandering around in the desert for forty years. This generation of people had grown up with sand between their toes, sand in their teeth, and sand in their tents! When God delivered the nation of Israel from slavery in Egypt, He told them they were headed to their new home. It was the land that had been promised to them, but God had to take them on a little detour first.

Because of the condition of their hearts and the way their minds were programmed, God had to remove the slavery mindset before He could bring them into the land He promised. He wanted them to enter it like kings, not paupers. They were called to reign, and to drive out the enemies in their land! (Remember Romans 12:2? God had to teach them not to conform to the ways of their old word, Egypt, but instead to be transformed by the renewing of their minds. It took this nation forty years to throw away that old mental material fashioned after the world, before they could put on the new! Only after their mindset had changed could they enter into God's will for their lives...His good, pleasing, and perfect will.)

Can you imagine? Forty years of camping out in the desert?! One weekend is plenty long enough for me! After enjoying (more or less) the great outdoors, nothing beats that feeling when you walk through your front door and settle back into your house. Home. It's a place the Israelites dreamed about for forty years, but sadly most of them died before their nation arrived there.

So can you imagine the excitement when God told Joshua, "Now then, you and all these people, get ready to cross to the Jordan River into the land I am about to give to the Israelites. I will give you every place where you set your foot, as I promised Moses." Those folks must have packed up their suitcases right away! When reading about all the land God was going to give them, we may think,"Uhh who cares?" But to the Israelites, their mouths must have watered as God spoke of the land as far from the Euphrates River all the way to the Great Sea of the west and beyond. Their hearts must have ached with a mixture of anxiety and joy as the word "home" rang in their spirits.

So what does that have to do with us? Keep reading what God told Joshua and you'll see in just a moment. ***"Be strong and very courageous. Be careful to obey all the law my servant Moses gave you; do not turn to it from the right or to the left, that you may be successful wherever you go. Do not let this Book of the Law depart from your mouth; meditate on it day and night, so that*** *you may be careful to do everything written in it. Then you will be prosperous and successful. Have I not commanded you? Be strong and courageous. Do not be terrified; do not be discouraged, for the Lord your God will be with you wherever you go."*

To the Israelites all they wanted was the land. That was their prize; it was their fairytale dream. To be home at last! To have land to plant crops and raise livestock. To have open fields for their children to run, and a safe place to raise their families. It was all they could ask for. All they wanted was to be free. In Bible times, if you had land to call your own, you were richer than rich. You were prosperous and successful, and people respected you for it.

So what about us today? What do we want? Love? Respect? Happiness? Popularity? Success? Fame? The list goes on and on, and everyone's list looks a bit different. Some of us may have written our wishes with our favorite gel pen, and others in crayon, and some just in plain pencil. But no matter what we use to scribble our hopes and dreams onto our hearts, we are each aching for the same thing. We all want a chance to be free. We want a chance to be loved for who we are and to experience the sweet freedom of being our true selves without feeling condemned or awkward about it. We want to feel beautiful, respected, trusted, adored, and accepted. We want to live full and rich lives, bursting with joy, happiness, and the things we delight in. We want to do what we love and be amazing at it! We want to spend every moment with the people we love the most; doing what we love, with who we love. Now that, my friend, is success – prosperity of the heart. When our hearts are full, what more could we possibly ask for?

What I am about to say might rock your boat a little bit. But that's okay, let the waves of astonishment crash over because you're sailing on the waters of truth!

God wants our hearts to be full. He wants us to live the most extravagantly joyful lives we could possibly imagine. That's right, girl, He *wants* us to be happy! He wants our hearts to be successful. He does not want us to struggle along, limping beside the rest of this world, fighting to survive. He wants us to thrive. He wants us to be free as wild horses thundering toward our dreams. (That doesn't mean our lives will be pain-free, trial-free, or stress-free. On the contrary, Jesus guaranteed that hard times will come. *But* He has promised that His joy and strength will be enough for us when they do! He told us to take heart because He has already overcome the world!)

If that doesn't change your outlook on life, I don't know what will. **God does not want us to be miserable!** I don't know where we picked up that little tidbit of misinformation along the way, but it's time we disarm that lie. John 10:10 says, "I came to give life and give it to the *full.*"

We all crave heaven, our very own Eden, our place of happily ever after. So not only does God want us to enjoy ourselves, as we thrive in our sweet spot doing what He created us to do with the people He created us to do it with, but He also provided a *way* for us to do so! That's right, girl, I am about to give you the secret to success. You ready for this? "Do not let this Book of the Law depart from your mouth; meditate on it day and night, so that you may be careful to do everything written in it. Then you will be prosperous and successful."

That's right! You guessed it, sister; it's all waiting for us at the banquet table! God has a promised land for each of us. A beautiful, unique, wonderful and absolutely fulfilling purpose and will for your life! I like to call it the sweet spot.

The people of Israel were finally headed for their sweet spot, but to get there they had to spend time at the banquet table. God told Joshua not to turn to the right or to the left of what God's Word commanded. He told him not to ignore it for even a moment, but to constantly go back to that banquet table of His Word over and over again.

The problem? There's this little root of doubt, deep down in our hearts, that doesn't really and truly believe that everything we dream of could be found in Jesus and Him alone. We set Him up as the "God" of our lives, but we sometimes fail to realize all the other little lowercase 'gods' we have set up for ourselves as well. We fail to believe that the abundance of life, love, pleasure, and absolute joy of our souls should come from our relationship with Him. Sometimes we think, "If I had Jesus plus a boyfriend, then I would be happy" or "If I had Jesus plus a record deal..." But there is no plus necessary. Jesus is the Source of everything we dream about and desire. We don't need anything else! Just Jesus is enough!

We all have a vacuum in our souls that can only be filled by our relationship with Him. When we sin, it is because we are deceived to believe that it will provide a pleasure that might be superior to obeying God. We like to pray for His blessings, and ask that He not take away our little 'gods' like comfort, pleasure, popularity or unhealthy relationships, but are we truly content with just Him? **Do we love God or do we love what God might do for us? It is true that He loves to give gifts and blessings, but He only gives us those gifts so that we can see His heart expressed to us through those things and fall in love with the Giver!**

Hosea 3:1 says, "The Lord said to me, "Go, show your love to your wife again, though she is loved by another and is an adulteress. Love her as the Lord loves the Israelites, though they turn to other gods and love the sacred raisin cakes." This verse used to make me laugh. What kind of goofy people would trade a real, genuine, relationship with the King of the Universe in exchange for "sacred raisin cakes"?! But I can't laugh too hard because I often give my attention to "raisin cakes," like when I run to my friends for advice before I run to God, seek attention from boys, or spend hours on the internet rather than in the Word. The only reason we waste time chasing after our "raisin cakes" is because we haven't had a life-changing revelation of God's utter, absolute, extravagant goodness. We have not truly encountered His love in a soul-shaking way. For if we have, we would never be the same.

C.S. Lewis said, "We are half-hearted creatures fooling around with alcohol and sex and ambition when infinite joy is offered to us. We are like an ignorant child who wants to go on making mud pies in a slum because we cannot imagine what is meant by an offer of a holiday at the sea." Wow, those are some strong words. Just like the princess in our story, sometimes we would rather stay where we are comfortable, with the stench of the Worthlessness Camp leaking out of our minds, than dine at a grand ball with the King of Kings and allow His love to transform us! Sisters, we need to know what He means by this offer of a *holiday at the sea!* What does Jesus mean when He speaks of the splendors of His Kingdom, abundant life, and being a daughter of the Most High? Wouldn't you love to know? Wouldn't you like to experience this holiday at the sea, splashing around in the ocean of His love?

I sure would! I want to daily fall more in love with Him! God has commanded that I love Him with all my heart, soul, mind and strength (Matt 22:37), but how can I love someone I hardly know? You cannot force yourself to fall in love with someone. You must get to know them and take the time to do so. After that, love just tumbles out of your heart naturally, and you can't help but get a little giddy and obsessed!

The only way we can rightly love Jesus in the way that He so lovingly deserves to be adored is to *experience the ocean of His love*. We cannot muster up any love or adoration for Him. The only way we can love is if He **first reveals** how much He loves us. We can only love Him with the love He gives us! (1 John 4:19). And if the only way we can possibly love Him is by knowing Him then shouldn't that be our first and highest priority in life?

When we set our Bibles on the shelf we are not just dismissing a dusty, old book. We are putting aside Jesus. Jesus *is* the Word! When we read the Bible, we're not just reading ancient words on a page. We're interacting and having a heart-to-heart conversation with Jesus Christ - The Living WORD who became flesh!

When we spend time with Jesus by diving into our Bible, it is no small thing. The enemy would like us to think that time is wasted when we are "lazy" and sit before the Lord like Mary did. The enemy attempts to convince our minds that reading the Bible is such a small thing, and that as long as we go to church, listen to worship music, and listen to a few anointed speakers here and there that everything will be just dandy.

But do you want to know a secret? The enemy is freaked out at the idea of you reading the Word, speaking the Word, and living the Word! Remember, he is not afraid of who you are, but who you *might* be. He has no concern if he can distract you with a thousand other thoughts and keep you from the quiet place of Jesus' presence. But if you are determined to sacrifice *time* and *energy* to sit at the banquet table...Uh oh! A royal queen is on the rise!

Moses had this same choice to make. Hebrews 11:15-16 says, "By faith Moses, when he had grown up, refused to be known as the son of Pharaoh's daughter. He chose to be mistreated along with the people of God rather than to enjoy the fleeting pleasures of sin. He regarded disgrace for the sake of Christ as of greater value than the treasures of Egypt, because he was looking ahead to his reward." So what about you? Will you dare to sacrifice the "perks" of being a blessed American girl, crucify the things from this world that steal your attention, and choose to be "mistreated" with the people of God, as you value Jesus more than the "treasures" of our sacred raisin cakes?

When I was a young teenager, I made a really tough decision. I made the decision to spend abundant amounts of time in God's presence. I'm not sharing this with you to toot my own horn, so that you can think, "Wow, she is so spiritual." Honestly, the decision to spend so much time with Jesus came out of a season of loneliness and boredom. I wasn't out partying on Friday nights and dancing with the cutest boys in town. I didn't have a huge group of friends because I wasn't going to hang around people who dragged me down into the Worthlessness Camp. I chose to hang around people who had like minds, with similar goals; to build one another up in Christ!

But quite often, all the way through my high school years, I felt like a lonely princess, locked in a tower of "Waiting." But when I surrendered in that season of barrenness, rejection, and yes, even *boredom*, He was faithful to meet me there. Did you know that feelings of boredom are actually a soul cry for more of the Lord? When we feel a dissatisfied stirring and hunger inside of us, He is calling us to seek Him, rather than scroll around on social media to pass the time until something exciting happens. He is exciting! He is what we are longing for! He wants us to respond to boredom and give it to Him!

That season of quietness is where God birthed beautiful dreams in my heart, for which I had to wait in order to see them come to pass. I embraced the strange and rather abnormal calling on my life that God had for me to be His beloved princess. At times, it was *not* fun. I would read the Word faithfully and wait for breakthrough. I waited and waited for my shining moment to arrive, for the promises He made to me to come to pass, for opportunities to do ministry and live my dreams, for new princess sisters who would actually understand me, and an earthly prince charming to come along and call me his!

It was frustrating to give up the treasures of Egypt in exchange for greater promises, because I didn't see anything happen right away. Many of these dreams I am still waiting to come to pass. But I believe that the seed of God's Word planted deep inside of me will *not* disappoint me.

Galatians 6:7 says, "Do not be deceived: God cannot be mocked. A man reaps what he sows." Time is like a seed. And I have sowed much of that seed into a field called, "Being with Jesus." The Word says that if we do that, we will reap an abundant harvest! I know that like what King David wrote about in Psalm 1, I will someday see the fruit of this field suddenly explode in my life!

"Blessed is the one who does not walk in step with the wicked or stand in the way that sinners take or sit in the company of mockers, but whose delight is in the law of the Lord, and who meditates on his law day and night. That person is like a tree planted by streams of water, which yields its fruit in season and whose leaf does not wither—whatever they do prospers." (Psalm 1:1-3)

All this time spent at the banquet table *is* going to bear fruit. One of the enemy's greatest lies spoken to our minds is that, "If I can't see it right away, nothing is happening." We pray twice, asking God to help us out with a situation, and if nothing changes, we give up. We read a Bible passage once, and if we don't understand it, we skip to the next one. We might live in a fast food, microwave culture, but God doesn't work like that. He is the One who invented the seed. He knows that everything takes time to grow, soak up the sunshine, and sprout up in the rainstorms of life. He also knows that the seed of His Word will bear abundant fruit in us! All we have to do is be faithful and stick with it! We have to be more consistent than the lies that would convince us otherwise.

Everything that is in the oak tree is in the acorn. You have Christ, living in you! Let the seed of His Word do His work in you. He will make everything beautiful in its time. (Ecclesiastics 3:11.) And one day, that little mustard seed *will* grow into a huge tree, a covering and place of rest and blessing for so many people around you! Jesus said that's how the Kingdom works!

Cinderella understood the importance of never underestimating or despising a small seed. She was a faithful steward of everything she had and made the most of each opportunity, always sowing love into the little mice, her animal friends, and even her enemies. She fully reaped what she sowed!

"Let us not become weary in doing good, for at the proper time we will reap a harvest if we do not give up." (Galatians 6:9) None of us will become the pure spotless Princess Bride that Jesus has made us to be overnight. Perfection isn't going to happen until the final curtain call when He returns for us and finishes the project! But until then, He will let us go as far as our faith will take us! Allow the supernatural power of His Word to do His "Bibbity-Bobbity-Boo" sort of miracle on you! Watch as the pumpkins in your life are transformed into carriages, the ashes turn into roses, the pain turns into gold, and your tears turn into diamonds.

Day 10
The Ocean of His Love

The love of God is *truly* unfathomable. We could be in heaven for a billion years and still not fully grasp the quality of this pure, intense, wild and wonderful love. But just because our brains don't understand it doesn't mean we should dismiss it! In fact, we should do just the opposite! We should search out this mystery of mysteries and ask God's Holy Spirit for revelation, that He would daily unfold and reveal the reality of His love to our hearts! (Check out Ephesians 3:18)

John 15:9 says, "Just as the Father has loved me, so I have loved you. So abide in my love." God's love is like the ocean. You can experience as much or as little of it as you choose. You can play on the beach, splash around and get your toes wet or you can dive into the depths and allow it to completely overtake every part of your being. If you're thirsty, you can come at Him with a thimble, a cup, or even a ginormous bucket!

Today we're going to go deeper into John 15:9. Let's dissect this verse, and really seek to understand what Jesus is saying here. He begins by saying "As the *Father* has loved..." What comes to mind when you think of a father's love? For some it invokes feelings of joy, and others it stirs up pain because of past hurts. The enemy has tried really hard to distort the image of what a good and true father is. Some of us have experienced the love of a dad who reflects the image of God the Father, and some of us have not. But no matter what earthly image we have of a dad in our minds, allow it to be shattered right now because our Heavenly Father is ten bazillion times better! He *is* love. He is the absolute ideal. He is the epitome of everything you've ever hoped for. He is proud of you, pleased with you, excited over you, never annoyed with you, not easily angered or frustrated, loves His job of protecting you, and really, really enjoys being with you!

The next word of this verse adds more, "As the Father has loved *Me*..." Remember, Jesus is speaking here. He is talking about how much His Father loves Him. How often do we stop and meditate on God's love for Jesus? It's something that tickles the brain how God the Father, Jesus Christ, and Holy Spirit can be three, and yet they are One and they each have love and affection for one another. We know that God the Father loves Jesus like crazy. He declared just how He felt about His Son while He was on earth. Multiple times in an audible voice He said to the people on earth, "This is my BELOVED Son, in whom I am WELL PLEASED. Listen to Him!"

Can you imagine the sky breaking open and the Father shouting this over His son? Can't you just hear the pride and joy in His voice? Obviously the Father gets so much pleasure from who Jesus is. Let your imagination soar as high as it will, linger on this idea, and think about how much God the Father must LOVE Jesus. Picture a proud father at a baseball game, cheering his head off in the stands. Imagine God the Father at a BBQ telling all of his friends about Jesus' latest accomplishment. Imagine the two of them walking and talking together, just enjoying each other's company! The pleasure which Father has over Jesus is radical and extravagant; it's the perfect, ideal, parent-child relationship. It's so sweet when I think about how much they must adore and respect one another.

And now, allow your mind to take this one step further..."As the Father has loved Me, so I have loved *you*." In other words, this passage is saying, "with the same intensity that Father loves Jesus that is how much Jesus loves you."

What? How can that be? How could Jesus dare to love us humans so deeply and intensely? How can He love us as much as God loves God?! Sisters, it is not anything that we have done to deserve this love. He loves us in this way because it is simply who

God is. If His character has always been (and always will be) pure, holy, exuberant, excited, joyful, amazing love then how could He possibly love us any less than with every inch and fiber of His Being?

If He were to look at you and love you any less than His normal 100-percent level of love, He would actually deny Himself and His holy character! Jesus loves you 100 percent, ALL the time, with ALL of His heart, soul, mind and strength! The reason He asks us to love Him with our all is because He loves us with HIS all. Wow!

God's love for you is never going to grow based on your behavior or performance. When you stand before Him in heaven as His pure and spotless Bride, He won't suddenly love you more. His love for you is already TOTALLY maxed out. Sister, this is the way He feels about you right now!

[Important note: just because God loves us with all His heart, doesn't mean He's not heartbroken by areas of sin in our lives. His love is *not* a free pass to live selfishly and play with sin. That is not the purpose of grace. God can love you 100 percent, but still be heartbroken about active areas of sin in your life. God disciplines us in love, makes righteous judgments in love, and commands that we live holy before Him in love. He is eager to forgive, when we turn whole- heartedly back to Him.]

Jesus finished verse 9 by saying, "Now *abide* in this love." The word "abide" means to pitch a tent, to stay, or remain. The truth of Jesus love is so overwhelming and out of this world that Jesus exhorts us to stay there and study this love for the rest of our lives. He doesn't just want us to know about God's love, He wants us to experience it in the deep places of our hearts on a daily basis!

The truth is pretty surreal, but we must embrace the supernatural reality of His love. It is the most absolute and true thing in our life...despite how we feel! Sweet sister, get this life changing truth: God doesn't just "love" you; He actually likes you.

He enjoys being with you! He loves when you chat with Him, laugh with Him, and be your goofy, old self with Him. He adores your dorkiness and little quirks! He wants you to totally enjoy being yourself because that's exactly who He wanted you to be!

Meditate on the love of Christ *right now*. Close this book if you have to. Close your eyes and ask Holy Spirit to reveal this massive love that desires to tumble over your heart and overtake you! Paul prayed that we would know the depths of this love and dive into the unsearchable riches of Christ. (Eph. 3:18)

Why would he pray that? I believe there were 3 reasons...

1. You Cannot Love Somebody Unless You Truly *Know* Them

    Where your treasure is, there your heart will be also. How can you treasure someone you don't know? You don't just see someone randomly walking by on the street and say, "I am going to make myself fall in love with you!" You adore someone because you know something ABOUT them that causes your heart's affections to be awakened. The same is true with God. We cannot even begin to love Him in the way He truly deserves to be adored unless we know who He is and allow the reality of His love to totally consume us! We have to daily experience this love; learning who Jesus, the Father and Holy Spirit are, or else why would we love them?

2. We Cannot Love God Unless We First Encounter His Love

    The only love we can offer Him is the love with which He first loved us. Genuine love cannot be mustered up or invented within ourselves. He is the author of love, which means we can only give Him recycled love...the love which He first gave us! So unless we are daily experiencing and discovering His love, we are not loving Him back the way that He so deserves to adored!

3. His Love Is Impossible To Fully Fathom With Our Human Minds

   The love of the Trinity and the affections of God are absolutely MIND-BLOWING. We can't even begin to fathom it, unless His spirit of wisdom and revelation reveals it to our human spirit. We must pray, "Reveal your love!" We need His help! We cannot love Him back unless He reveals His love to us!

I'm here to offer you a radical thought. The Father loves you just as much as He loves Jesus. He LIKES you just as much as He likes Jesus. He absolutely adores His Son, but He has always wanted a daughter. That is why God made Eve! Eve was the crowning glory of God's creation. I mean yeah, Adam was pretty cool being made in Jesus' image and all, but Eve was something special and unique. She was woman, and she was beautiful. She was a precious daughter! And so are you. It is my prayer that the reality of His love crashes over you like a thundering tidal wave!

Day 11
The Tower of Purity

Okay, so we've been hanging out together for 11 days now, and God has had us on a pretty great journey! But I believe it is time you and I get to know each other better. I'm about to lay all my cards out on the table. You ready for this? The confession I am about to make is the sort of thing a girl would say at a Truth or Dare sleepover party game. But this is total truth.

I am twenty-two years old, and I have never been on a date with a boy.

Shocked?

Well, let's look on the bright side, if I was busy dating this boy and that boy, I wouldn't have had time to write this book, so that's a big plus, right?! But seriously girls, not one single date. More than that, I've never even been *asked* out.

Now, before you start thinking, "What is wrong with this girl?! Does she have some sort of strange foot fungus? She can't be that ugly! Why no dates?" allow me to explain.

I like to think about my love life (or major lack thereof) as living like Rapunzel, in Disney's *Tangled*. I haven't been placed in this lofty tower of singleness by force of an evil step mom or religious regulations. The decision to refrain from recreational dating throughout high school was not forced on me by my parents; in fact, they weren't really sure what to think of it at first!

As a ten-year-old girl, the idea of waiting instead of dating was plopped into my head by a catchy song called "Barlow Girls" by my favorite band at that time, Superchick. Myself, and several of my friends were entranced and inspired by the idea of waiting for true love, and choosing not to date was exciting, rebellious, and gutsy. We proudly sported our *Barlow Girl* T-shirts and rallied up friends in support of our *No Dating Campaign*.

But now, ten years later, many of my friends are flashing their engagement rings and inviting me to watch them slow dance with Prince Charming at their weddings. I can't help but glance at my sisters who are still waiting with me in the tower of singleness and wonder if there's something wrong with us!

"So why on earth," you might be wondering, "have you chosen to put yourself through such misery?!"

My answer is simple. Jesus commanded me to stay in the tower of His love. Proverbs 4:23 says, "Guard your heart, for everything you do flows from it." The New American Standard Bible says, "Watch over your heart with all diligence, for from it flow the springs of life." The KJV says, "Keep thy heart with all diligence, for from it flow the springs of life."

By the power of God's Holy Spirit, Jesus has revealed just how precious I am in His sight. I was worth His blood, His time, and His attention; my heart is a rare jewel, and a priceless treasure. I'm worth more than 74 billion dollars, remember? If I had that kind of money hanging around, don't you think I would do everything in my power to protect it? I would keep it locked up tight in a vault with a high-tech security system and raging alarms! If our hearts are the most precious, priceless thing on this earth, why do we treat them as so cheap and common?

Michelle McKinney Hammond (author of *Secrets of an Irresistible Woman*) wrote: "The moment we meet a man, we snatch our heart out of God's hand, toss it at this new guy we've gotten all excited about and say, 'Here!' Small wonder the poor little thing is so banged up! I think it's time to get a clue, don't you? How about trying this approach…you meet a man, he's re-a-al cute; you like him. Your little heart is all a flutter, revving up to leap out of your chest and at the poor unsuspecting guy. Place your hand on your heart, whisper to it, "calm down," and put it back in the secret place. And say this: "God I think I really like this one. What do you know about him? What is the purpose of his being my life? Is he the one for me? Should I proceed, or should I not waste my time on him?"

I have chosen to keep myself tucked away in the tower of Jesus' love because I am not going to waste my time with someone who won't view and treat me like the jewel I am. This isn't a prideful statement...it's a smart one! As a little girl, this was kind of a no-brainer for me. I didn't have the intention of getting married at age twelve so why would I concern myself with such things? Sure, I liked boys just as much as the next girl, but viewed all the boys around me as frogs.

One of my favorite songs by Superchick goes, "All princes start as frogs, and all gentlemen as dogs, just wait 'til it's plain to see what we're growing up to be, 'cause some frogs will still be frogs, and some dogs will still be dogs, and some boys can become men, just don't kiss 'em 'til then." I decided to wait until the boys I knew grew up into men, and *then* I would take a second glance and find out who might make good husband material!

Because of the radical love that Christ has poured out into my soul, I have some pretty high standards for my future man. I believe the Lord wants to bring someone into my life who will love me in a similar way that Christ has loved me and be a reflection of that heavenly love. (Eph. 5:25) I have a lot to look forward to! No, my future man won't be perfect, but he most certainly won't be a frog! I am willing to wait because I believe in the preparation process which will make our ending so much sweeter.

Song of Solomon 8:4 says, "I charge you, O daughters of Jerusalem, that ye stir not up, nor awaken my love, until he please." (KJV)

The Shalumite woman in this passage told this to her friends three different times. In Song of Solomon 2:7 & 3:5, "Do not arouse or awaken love until it so desires..." She knew how delicate and fragile her heart was and didn't want to toss her affections on this young man before the timing was right.

In the animated film, *Princess and the Frog*, (Important note:

this is one of the scariest and darkest Disney movies I have ever seen. I am not recommending this one. It was so dark, it really disturbed me. I was able to pull out a great lesson from this tale, but I don't think I'll ever watch it again!), young Tiana has a beautiful dream. She desires to open her own restaurant. It was a dream she shared with her father, and he encouraged her to go for it. But Tiana's life is thrown a major curve ball when she finds herself conversing with a big, wet, slimy, frog. "Prince Naveen" convinces her that if she lends him a smooch, he will turn into a dashing young fella, and in return, he will give her the money she needs for her restaurant. Instead of the miraculous transformation like in *Beauty and the Beast*, Naveen doesn't change; instead, Tiana turns *into* a frog! This is so profound, because it shows what happens when a girl tosses her heart and affections on someone who is below her heavenly identity and calling…she gets dragged down and demoted to his muddy, ground-hopping level.

I have seen so many princesses sacrifice the long-term dream of what they TRULY deserve in exchange for a lame romance with a lowly frog. Sometimes we as young women can be afraid of having high standards for the guys in our lives for various reasons. We really don't want to remain in the tower of total heart purity, and we can be tempted by our very own Mr. Adorable.

Do you ever feel invisible to the guys in your life? Maybe you feel like you're the only girl without a prom date. Sometimes I can feel like a weary Rapunzel, locked in an intimidating tower of stone, which keeps my Flynn Rider far, far away.

Sneaky lies pounce on every opportunity of doubt to whisper things like, "You're unattractive. You're a major dork. All your friends have someone special to hold hands with on the Fourth of July. You dream of fireworks, sparks, and romance; but you've never even been asked on a date before! You don't get special attention from guys because you're not worthy of it. Your high expectations are scaring them all away. Nobody is going to be brave enough to climb that tower and pursue you. You're going to be utterly disappointed!"

In fear, we can often lower our hair, slide out the tower window, and go explore the world of boys with an insecure heart. If we are not secure and confident in the love of our Father, Jesus Christ, and the Holy Spirit; we run the risk of settling for something *way* below what is fit for a princess.

We should never be out "looking for love." When a young man decides he wants to pursue you, the right one will not ask you to lower your standards; instead he will get super creative, scratch his head, start praying, and figure out a way to climb UP that tower!

Think about Rebekah. She was not out searching or "looking for love." She was in the middle of her mundane, everyday life, serving humbly and washing in the water of the Word (Eph. 5:26). Her pursuer was *seeking after her* and found her by the well! The best place to be hanging out while we are awaiting our earthly prince charming is in the Word and presence of the True King! How else will we recognize His sons and know who is fit to rightly love us?

In Job 24, Job talks about a deep, dark place. He speaks of hidden treasure buried underground. A mine of glorious, priceless jewels are hidden, but the sparkly diamonds resting there are not for the eyes of man. Only God sees the "place where gold is refined." (Job 24:1) Verse 10 says, "He tunnels through the rock, His eyes see all its treasures, He searches sources of the rivers, and brings hidden things to light."

My favorite verse in this passage is verse 6, "Sapphires come from its rocks, and its dust contains nuggets of gold." One might look at these verses and say, "What kind of injustice is this? Why are those lovely pieces of gold, silver, and sapphires forced to live in the dirt where no one can see them? They should be honored and adored, noticed and cherished! Why would God hide them away like that?"

These treasures would only be found by those who would seek them out. God didn't make these treasures obvious and place them on a display table. He knew that lazy men would never dive into the depths of the earth. He knew that only those men who truly desired and valued the treasure would take the effort to seek it. The men who would humble themselves and be willing to get their hands a little dirty; those are the guys who are forever rewarded with the prize.

The same is true with you. You are beautiful. You're a dazzling diamond. The Bible says that you were woven together in the depths of the earth. Because you are so valuable and lovely, the Lord desires to hide you in the shade of His right hand. If you choose to abide under His covering, you may feel as though you're locked in a tower. You're tucked away, but not to rot. You've been hidden so that your beautification process can continue without being tainted by the fingerprints of man. If you choose to stay hidden in God's presence, a young man will one day set out on the greatest adventure of his life as he humbles himself and trails through the deepest places of life just to find you, his eternal treasure.

Cinderella was hidden for a purpose. A parade of guys didn't pound on her front door. We all know that Cinderella wasn't ugly, socially awkward, or unattractive in anyway, yet she was never asked out on a date before it was time for love to awaken!

Do you remember the magical scene when Cinderella entered the Ball Room for the first time? Every jaw dropped and Prince Charming stared at this mysterious girl. Who was she? Where had she come from? Prince Charming was suddenly hit with an astonishing realization...he didn't know anything about this girl, but he wanted to know everything. She was like nothing he had ever seen. Some say Charming fell for Cinderella because of her sparkly blue dress or luxurious blonde hair, but I believe he saw something beyond sparkles and glitter...He saw the defining element, the one thing that set her apart from every other pretty face in the room. He saw a beautiful heart. Patience and kindness were glowing from her eyes. She didn't flaunt and strut into the room; instead she gracefully walked in thankfulness. Her humble heart posture enabled her to be exalted to the high place of Princess.

In order to walk in the heavenly splendor of a Princess like Cinderella, we must first allow ourselves to be humbled and changed in the hidden, secret place. Dirt is the place where diamonds are discovered.

The beauty of a woman, which can only be cultivated in the secret place of Christ's love, is what I believe Peter talked about in 1 Peter 3:3-4: "Your beauty should not come from outward appearance, such as braided hair or fine jewelry, but instead it should be that of your inner self, the beauty that comes from a quiet and gentle spirit, which is of great worth in the sight of God." This verse really encouraged me because I used to believe that if I wanted to snag a boy's attention, I was going to have to get a little bit loud, dress in a way that would capture his attention, and learn a few jokes! I thought my personality was a bit boring and rather drab compared to the colorful girls I saw dancing around on Disney channel. This verse reminded me that I didn't have to follow the Teenage Survival Manual to finding true love. I didn't need to have hair like Taylor Swift, or run up to my dream boy singing, "Hey, I just met you, and this is crazy, but here's my number, so call me maybe!"

The world has taught us that we must take an abrasive, hard core approach to chasing down our dream dudes; as if simply and sweetly being our own unique self isn't enough. It can be hard to wait in the tower, for something you've only imagined would happen once upon a dream. In this life we have been taught that if we want something, we have to go out and get it. While that is true for many things, it isn't the way God set up relationships. We don't have to chase down our dream man. No, when the right guy comes along…he will be the one chasing *you*.

Day 12
Trusting the Author

Yesterday we talked about everyone's favorite topic: boys! I shared my story of epic singleness (Ha, ha, I suppose we could call it that, right?). So how can a girl be brave enough to remain in the tower throughout middle school, high school, and perhaps even early college years and beyond? How can we trust the One who has asked us to remain and not go seeking for the approval of frogs?

We know that His perfect love casts out all fear. If we are in love with Jesus, we can be totally fearless. We can be secure and confident in our royal identity when we know who the King is and how He feels about us. But we must learn how to *abide* in God's love.

The Lord has challenged my heart with a radical purpose. I am nowhere near the finish line on this thing, but really, it will be a labor of love throughout my whole life. What is the challenge? Learning to abide, remain in His love, and stay safely hidden in the Tower of His Presence. How do we do that? By choosing to be in a 24/7 conversation and relationship with the person of Jesus Christ. Truth is, He wants to speak to our hearts ALL the time, and He wants our 100% attention every day of our lives.

Jesus is calling us to return to the Garden of Eden. To live the life that Eve once had! What must life have been like? The Father loved hanging out with Eve and walked with her in the cool of the garden. Can you imagine their conversations?! What would your conversations look like if you had unlimited talk time with the Creator of the Universe? What would you ask Him? I'm pretty sure my first question would be, "Lord, what were you thinking when you made *One Direction*?! Where did you get such divine inspiration for those cuties?!" Ha-ha! Kidding! But really, what topics of discussion would you bring up with the Creator of the Universe? Would you ask Him about your future? Ask for help with your math homework?

You might be thinking, "Those topics don't sound holy enough! God doesn't really care about those things!" 1 Peter 5:7 says, "Cast all your anxiousness on Him, for He cares for you." Trust me, sister; if it matters to you, it matters to God. I talk to Jesus about all sorts of unconventional things. We talk about boys, cute clothes, and anything else that happens to pop up during my day! Nothing is too small, or unimportant to God. He wants to talk about everything!

Because of the sacrifice of Jesus Christ, we have the same, exact, 24/7, unlimited access to chat with the King of kings! Just like Eve did! Everything was like a dream world for Eve. She was loved perfectly by the Father, Jesus, Holy Spirit, and even dashing, young Adam. But we all know that the enemy came along and messed everything up.

This is a very familiar story, but let's return to the beginning of human time, for just a moment, as we revisit what really happened in that garden.

"Now the serpent was more crafty than any of the wild animals the Lord had made. He said to the woman, 'Did God really say you must not eat from any tree in the garden?" The first thing Eve did was set this serpent straight. She explained the rules, "We may eat from the trees in the garden, but God did say you must not eat from the tree in the middle of the garden, and you must not touch it, or you will die." (Gen 3:1) Now it sounds to me like Eve was totally okay with these rules. She was rejoicing in all the goodness around her and was focused on all the good stuff her Father had provided. She was in love with the King and everything was good!

But then came the sly stinger. "You will not certainly die. For God knows when you eat of it, your eyes will be opened, and you will be like God, knowing good and evil." Wow, talk about cunning. He begins with a flat out lie, but finishes it with a candy coating of truth.

What happened here? The enemy took Eve's focus that was so zeroed in on God's abundant goodness and turned her eyes to look at the one thing she *couldn't* have. This caused her to question, "Wait a minute? Is God holding something back from me?"

Her whole perspective of who God was suddenly shifted. The words the serpent said caused her to see God in a different way, as if there was some darkness or hidden evil about Him that he would hold something GOOD back from her.

James 1:16-17 says, "My dear brothers and sisters, do not be deceived. Every good and perfect gift comes from above, the Father of heavenly lights, who does not change like shifting shadows." Do we really truly believe that God desires to give us good and perfect gifts? Do our hearts rejoice in the fact that He wants to shower us with His attention and blessings with each new sunrise? Do we *really* believe that He will take everything evil that has worked against us in our lives and ultimately turn it all around for our good? If we believed these things to be true, we would be lit up with a deliriously crazy joy as we abide in the tower of His love. We would believe that God *desires* to give us "every good and perfect gift," including true love with a God-loving hunk someday! Oh how silly we are to think that we can write a better love story than the Author of Love! Why do we try to yank the pen out of His hands in fear and distrust?

To be deceived is to believe that God is holding something back from us. The enemy desires for us to turn our eyes away from focusing on all the abundant trees of blessing in our lives and zero in on the one thing we *don't* have. He attempts to convince our minds that waiting for God's timing is utter foolishness; and that if God had something good for us, He would give it to us RIGHT this second.

So dear sister, tell me, how do you see God? When you

envision Him in your heart, what do you know about Him to be true? I often hear people describe our Heavenly Father as if He's a terribly angry man, ready to shoot lightning bolts at us the moment we mess up. If we see God with His arms crossed, judging us because of sin, telling us we cannot do this or that, and that He is holding back good gifts from us, then we don't see His commandments as boundaries of love because He has something **better**. We are deceived about who He really is and who we are.

Mr. Adorable attempted to make this Princess think the King had lied to her. *"I just don't understand," Adorable kicked around a few pebbles before resting his arm on the tower wall, "Why would someone you said cares about you so much do this to you? Why would he forbid you from living your life?"*

I once saw an adorable image on Pinterest of a sweet, little girl clinging to her raggedy, old teddy bear. Jesus kneeled down beside her, and asked her to surrender the bear. She held it tightly to her chest and cried out, "But God, I love it!" What she couldn't see was the big fat, ginormous bear, hidden behind Jesus, held in His right hand. He wanted to give her something far better than she could dream, but first she had to surrender the old!

We must let go of any preconceived ideas we have about our Heavenly Father, and the way He feels about us. The enemy's goal for our lives is to distort the way we see God. He does not want us to see our good and perfect Father for who He really is because that would change the way we see ourselves, and we would be absolutely unstoppable.

"If you who are evil know how to give good gifts, will not your Heavenly Father give good gifts to those who ask Him?" (Matthew 7:11) Girls, we can absolutely trust Him with our hearts. He's got this whole romance thing *totally* under control. He is the Author of every good and perfect fairytale...can't we trust Him to write each of ours?

Eve was deceived into believing that her Daddy didn't really love her as much as she'd hoped. And this is what the enemy challenges each of us with: "Does your Daddy REALLY love you?"

Daughters, our Daddy loves us just as much as He loves Jesus. Not only that, Jesus said, "As much as the Father loves Me, that's how much I love you!" Jesus loves you even more than He loves Himself. How do we know this to be true?

The Bible says, "Let nothing be done through strife or vainglory, but in lowliness of mind, let each esteem one another better than themselves." (Philippians 2:3) God never gives us a command that He himself doesn't first follow. Jesus actually esteems us higher than Himself. He loves us so much that He was willing to step out of the limelight, come to this earth, live a life of humility, suffer and die while bearing the wrath of God, BECOMING sin to be a sin offering in our place. Jesus lifted you high in his heart, you were His treasure, and He esteemed you even higher than himself!

When Jesus looks at you, He doesn't see a weak, pathetic, little girl that He just has to tolerate. No, He sees the potential of a glorious Princess Bride inside of you! He sees someone He could spend all of eternity with walking in the cool of the garden of your heart, talking about anything and EVERYTHING, sharing the secrets of His heart with you. He sees the strong, valiant, humble makings of a queen inside of you. And He is absolutely committed to transforming you with His radical love.

Psalm 18:35 says, "You have stooped down to make me great." In other words, "You have humbled yourself to make me look amazing." That is what we are called to do with one another because Christ first did it for us.

Honestly, sometimes I'm not so sure why we girls are in such a hurry to throw ourselves into romantic relationships. Christ-centered relationships are all about dying to yourself, esteeming the other higher than yourself, and stooping down in humility to make your boyfriend or husband look ridiculously amazing.

Maybe we should slow down a lil' bit and enjoy life in the tower, and first learn how to love those around us; our best friends, family, and even strangers. Married life will be here before we know it! We will have to chase around our kiddos, clean up messes in the kitchen, and sacrifice sweet hours of sleep. Let's enjoy the freedom while we have it and focus on all the trees from which we can enjoy the fruit right now!

One of my favorite verses is Ephesians 5:19 which says, "Encourage one another with psalms, hymns, and spiritual psalms." Again, God wouldn't tell us to do this without it being something that He Himself does. His heart is *always* to encourage us. His mouth is ALWAYS full of affirming, encouraging words and songs for you! He doesn't want you to be discouraged and think badly about yourself, He wants you to see what He sees in you! Romans 8:29 says you're predestined to be conformed to the image of Christ Jesus!

We don't have to feel inadequate or afraid that we will disappoint Jesus; it's been established in heaven that the Father, Son, and Holy Spirit are going to transform us into EXACTLY who we are called to be – a strong, pure, spotless Princess Bride. We can rest in that. The seed is already inside of you!

Words of encouragement are ALWAYS on His tongue. Even if they are convicting words of correction, He is a good Father who limits correction to the point of what we need, and always offers chastisement with the reward of a greater, closer relationship. He's not going to condemn us, make us feel bad about ourselves, and constantly be harsh and critical.

Did you know that God wants good things to happen to you, in you, and through you? He wants to give you good gifts, and cause you to be a GOOD, sparkling gift of encouragement to those around you! If you trust Him with your love story, it will be one of the most beautiful things your heart has ever experience. My dear sister, know that it is well worth the wait. Be patient. God makes everything beautiful in *His* time. You can trust the Author.

Day 13
Princess Hadassah

Let's look at the story of Esther. I find so much strength in her tale. We glanced over it briefly, but that was in a much more light and comical way. The story of Esther is actually a very intense and emotionally riveting story. I've often imagined what life must have been like for her.

She was orphaned at a young age. The Bible does not explain what happened to her parents, but says she was adopted by her sweet cousin, Mordecai. During this particular time in Biblical history, the Jewish people were in captivity. They had been conquered by the Persian Empire and were forced to live in exile in a land that was not their own. They were severely hated and ridiculed by the people around them. The Jewish people were like Cinderella. They had a promise that land would one day be their own, but they were in the midst of stinky, depressing, persecuting trial.

Esther's real name was actually Hadassah. She was given the name Esther, a pagan name, to hide her true identity, when she was forced to live at the King's palace. We all know that Hadassah was chosen as queen, and used by God to save her entire nation, but we often forget her humble, painful beginnings. Let's explore what life was like for our dear sister...

A thick cloud of smoke rose from the fireplace where a young woman coughed. The strong scent stung her nose. She quickly removed a smoky black kettle from the hearth.

"Hadassah?" the cautious voice of an older woman spoke from the other room. "Is something burning?"

"No, Hannah," she responded quickly, fanning the wispy smoke spirals out the front window, "supper is ready."

The old woman poked her silver-haired head into the small room, "Very well. Mordecai should be home any moment. Empty the ashes please, Hadassah."

"Yes, Ma'am." Hadassah swiftly swept up a pile of cinders which had clung to the foot of the fireplace, scooped them into a bowl, and made her way to the back door. Stepping outside, humming a soft tune, Hadassah took a deep breath, relishing in the fresh air. An array of colors meshed across the eastern sky; a glorious mix of pink, orange, and purple, as the sun held its breath and prepared to dunk under the horizon. As soon as Hadassah completed her chore, she returned indoors to set their small table with the humble set of cracked clay bowls and utensils. The old pottery was worn and chipped, but it was more than many others had and for that they were grateful.

"Hadassah," the old widow clicked her tongue, "You mustn't let our food stick to the bottom of the pot like this! I fear you'll never find a husband if your cooking is less than satisfactory." Hannah added extra water to the sticky pot, vigorously stirring it with her strong right arm.

Hadassah sighed as she placed a third bowl on the table, "Forgive me, Hannah. My mind was elsewhere."

"As it usually is my child," Hannah chuckled, adding her own secret remedy to Hadassah's failed meal. She taste-tested the ingredients a second time. Her furrowed brow relaxed, and she nodded confidently to herself. The meal finally reached her approval.

"Just like your mother," Hannah spoke gently as she whisked a black strand of hair from Hadassah's face, "always a day dreamer."

Hadassah squeezed the old woman's hand and spoke softly, "I wish I remembered her better. Sometimes I think I can still hear the old lullaby she used to sing to me, but other times I think I must be making it up. "

Hannah's dark eyes grew moist as these old memories were relived, "She would be so very proud of you, Hadassah. You have grown up to be a beautiful, young woman, who one day will make a lucky, young man a very proud husband. Your Father would be proud too, just as Mordecai is."

Just then, the sound of an opening door was heard. "Cousin Mordecai!" Hadassah greeted, "You're just in time for supper. Come sit. May I take your shoes, wash your feet?"

Mordecai's weary eyes from a long day's work stared gently at his cousin. Hadassah had been orphaned as a young girl, both parents killed in a tragic accident, leaving the sweet, little child fatherless. Mordecai immediately brought the frightened child into his home, providing for her a place to eat, sleep, and feel protected. But as Hadassah grew older, Mordecai realized that he could not provide her with the proper education and asked Widow Hannah to come live with them. Twelve years had passed now, and Hadassah would soon be approaching her sixteenth birthday. Together, the three had forged a strong bond, a three stranded chord which was not easily broken. But now, something was attempting to rip this little family apart. Mordecai had just learned of the new law which was posted on nearly every building in town. Still drifting away to sea in the wake of this tsunami tidal wave of news, a strange look of grief fell upon Mordecai's face. Hadassah immediately knew something was wrong. Terribly wrong.

"Mordecai, what is troubling you?"

The man tried to wipe the look of fear and distress off his face and attempted a shaky smile. "Nothing, my child; other than the fact that I have built up quite the appetite." He ducked into the other room where a wash bin was awaiting his hands.

Hadassah quickly buzzed over to the hearth where she scooped a generous helping into each bowl. She could hear Mordecai reciting the familiar Hebraic blessing, "Blessed are You, *HaShem*, our God, King of the Universe..."

Hadassah felt a troubling stir deep in her heart. The look on Mordecai's face caused a terribly uneasy feeling to arise. She bit her lip, worry engulfing her mind. *Lord*, she prayed silently, *please help Mordecai.*

After Mordecai returned, the three were seated, each grabbed hands, closed their eyes, and offered this simple prayer up to heaven:

"Blessed are You, *HaShem*, our God, King of the Universe, who brings forth bread from the earth."

~*~

She could hear the subtle hush of whispers coming from the other room. Hadassah's head lay on the hard, cool ground, enveloped by darkness in the security of her small bedroom. Hannah and Mordecai were still awake, kindling the fire, and speaking about the events of the day. Hadassah rolled over, unable to allow her body to be still. Her mind raced with worry. *What was it that Mordecai was so worried about? Why did he look at me like that?*

Hadassah felt a shiver of fear tremble down her spine, as she began to entertain all the possibilities. Had he lost his job? Had the crop failed? Was a famine approaching, desiring to strip the land of all their food? Were their rumors of a war stirring with the Persian Empire? Hadassah had always preferred prayer over worry, so she lifted each concern up to the One who made her.

Oh Lord, I do not know what Your mighty hand has in store for us. Every night I pray for peace in our land, enough food to be on the table, and for Mordecai and Hannah to be blessed and happy in their hearts. But what was that look of fear in his eyes? I have never seen my dear cousin appear so threatened by trouble and so vulnerable to pain. Have mercy on us, dear God. Oh Lord of Abraham, Isaac and Jacob, the One who led your children the Israelites into the promise land, and through the desert; deliver us from the great oppression of this Persian rule, just as You delivered our forefathers from the Egyptians. I pray that one day we might return to Israel, and be released from this land of exile out from under the mighty hand of King Xerxes. Give us strength to face whatever storm might be coming our way. Hold my hand, and make me strong for I am afraid. Make me like Sarah, Rebecca, or Deborah, a Godly woman who is strong in faith. Remember Your faithfulness, and Your promise to Your children. Don't leave us now, Holy One, because our small and humble family needs You now more than ever before.

~*~

The small yellow and brown kernels were crushed beneath the sharp rock as Hadassah tirelessly worked at grinding the corn. Hannah also worked diligently at her task, working just as vibrantly and full of life as the young woman decades younger than herself.

"Have you heard that Elisha proposed to a Persian girl?"

Hadassah chatted easily, enjoying the special time with Hannah. The old woman's company was greatly desirable, and Hadassah treasured each day with her more than the first. When she was younger, her heart used to ache for more companions and she daily begged Hannah to let her play outside, run to the market, and meet new friends. But that was not a proper place in society for young girls, and most were confined to the safety and shelter of their own homes. But unlike most Hebrew girls, Hadassah did not live with a passel of cousins, siblings, and other girls and boys her age to play with. She went through a short phase in which she wished to run away and never return, seeking grand adventure; but soon the desire to live elsewhere dwindled away as she realized that Hannah was growing old and needed her assistance. Someone would have to take care of Mordecai as well, when Hannah passed. Even so, in all her contentment and joy with her current role in life, Hadassah still harbored secret hopes of grand adventure, finding true love, and doing something radical with her life. Quite often she dreamed of venturing out into the market place and meeting a handsome young fellow who struck her fancy and desired to know her better. She would invite the brave and charming young man over for dinner, and he would fit into their family like the perfect missing puzzle piece. Mordecai would eagerly say yes when he offered a bride price for Hadassah, and then...

"A Persian girl?!" Hannah's brown eyes flickered with shock. "Elisha's parents must be heartbroken. God has forbidden intermarriage with other nations, warning us that our hearts may grow loyal to foreign gods and forget the one true God. We must pray for Elisha that his heart will remain faithful."

Hadassah nodded, feeling somewhat guilty for the excitement she felt for Elisha and his soon-to-be bride. Elisha was one of the few Jewish boys her age who she conversed with from time to time, before and after synagogue on the Sabbath. She was very happy for her friend when he first shared the news, but felt an unwelcome twinge of disappointment. Elisha was a handsome, hardworking, young man with a heart eager to study the Torah. From the family line of Levi, Elisha desired to be a priest, but Hadassah knew that now he would be forbidden the privilege.

"I wouldn't have minded marrying a man like Elisha," Hadassah spoke softly, "He was so gentle and kind."

Hannah let out a barbaric-sounding display of disgust, "Pshh! You don't really mean that Hadassah! A man who chooses a woman with a pretty face over his loyalties to the One True God is no man at all. He is a worm. Elisha is not capable of loving and treasuring a woman in the way she is to be treasured; for if he abandoned his love for God, he will just as easily abandon his love for his wife!"

Hadassah sat in the silence that followed, contemplating Hannah's wise words. She had never thought of it that way before.

"Nevertheless," Hadassah smiled, still wishing her friend well, "I pray Elisha and his new bride will be happy and be blessed with many children."

Just then a violent knock came on the front door. The pounding shook the threshold of their home and was accompanied by a harsh voice which barked,

"Open up! By order of King Xerxes, Prince of Persia, ruler of one-hundred-twenty-seven provinces! Open this door!"

The shade of white on Hannah's face suddenly matched her hair. "Go! *Hide!*" she whispered desperately, shooing away Hadassah.

"No!" Hadassah refused, "I won't leave you!"

"Go!" she demanded. Hadassah had never heard Hannah use such a frightful tone.

She quickly obeyed, slipping into the back room, frantically looking every which way for a hiding place. Hadassah could hear the sound of Persian officers storming into the front room. She waved her hands up and down frantically, nervous feet pacing from one side of the small room to the other. A few bedrolls leaning up against the wall were not large enough to duck behind. She examined a small crevice in the wall which she used to crawl into as a little girl, but now she could not fit. Finally, she spotted the large ceremonial hand washing basin which stood in the corner. It was large enough to squeeze her entire body into, and she pulled a blanket overtop her head, desperately trying to tuck the stray edges in. She was breathing so loudly that she was sure they could hear her in the other room. She placed a frightened hand over her mouth and prayed she could keep silent.

She heard voices seeping through the thin walls, "By Order of King Xerxes, King of the Persian Empire, His Royal Majesty has issued a decree: *Queen Vashti has been expelled from the presence of His Royal Majesty. Therefore, I command commissioners in every province of my realm to bring every eligible young virgin, stretching from the land of India to Cush, to be brought into my Royal Harem. They are to be placed under the command of Hegai, my eunuch, who is in charge of the women. Beauty treatments will be given to them, and the girl who pleases me will be made Queen instead of Vashti. Let this decree be carried out swiftly across the entire land, and may no man stand in the way of my law.* Signed with the royal signet ring of King Xerxes."

Hadassah felt her ears burn with a fire of fear. Her mind flashed back to the terrible look in Mordecai's eyes the night before. Had he known about the law?! Had he known this was to come?! Hadassah could hear a cry rise from Hannah like that of a woman who had just gotten news that her child had been killed.

"Are there any young women in your home?" one of the gruff soldiers asked. Hadassah could hear the heavy metal on their shoes stomping through their home, performing a search. She cringed, fighting back frightened tears which stung her eyes. *Please God, please, don't let them find me! Don't let them take me away...*

"No, sir, no!" Hannah tried her best to protect her beloved treasure. "There is no one here but me. I am only a widow who lives

195

alone, and tries her very best to-" But the men were blocking out her frightened, stuttering, mouse-like words.

CRASH! The sound of the table being pushed over, and clay pots crashing to the ground made Hadassah jump.

"We were ordered to search for *every* virgin!" The man spat out those sharp and cruel words which shot an arrow of pain through Hannah's heart.

"But there is no one here!" Hannah begged, "no one at all! You have no right to destroy my home searching for someone who does not-"

Hadassah closed her eyes. She could hear the footsteps enter the room. She could hear the man breathing. Suddenly, a terrible flash of light flooded in. The solider had removed the blanket. She was exposed. He grabbed her wrist so tightly that Hadassah felt as though he fastened her with a chain, pulling her to a standing position. A dark pair of beady eyes in a face scrunched up with anger, studied her. "Get outta there!" He yelled at her, even though she was within whispering distance. She tumbled out of the wash bin and struggled to regain her footing as the man dragged her into the main room.

"Please!" Hannah shouted, tears welling up at the sight of the man dragging Hadassah, "Sir, please I beg you! She is a Jew! Surely the King would not wish for an outcast from Israel in his Harem; he would be appalled at such a find! Let her stay; the King will not want her!"

Those cruel eyes flashed at her, as if he was contemplating the crazy, old woman's words. Would the King refuse a Jewish woman? He turned to look at Hadassah whose tear- stained face was choking back sobs, trying to be brave. This servant girl had a dark complexion, soft brown eyes with a natural array of captivating eye lashes, bold crimson lips, and a gently built chin. She was thin and had a good figure, but didn't look weak or sickly either. She looked vigorous, and for one strange moment this soldier thought perhaps he could even see the beauty of a queen in her. He yanked at the girls arm and headed for the door.

Hannah let out another terrifying cry, and clasped Hadassah's left arm, "No, please no!" She clung to the beloved girl who was slipping away. The muscular men ripped them apart without much effort at all.

"Hannah!" Hadassah cried, as the strong man led her out the door, "I love you!"

"Hadassah!" Hannah called back, refusing to allow herself to crumble into a pile of tears on the floor, "The Lord is with you! Never forget, He is with you!"

And with that, the door was slammed in Hannah's face.

~*~

Hadassah couldn't recall any of the events in her trip to the palace. It all felt like a blur, and she wanted nothing less than to curl up in a ball and cry. She wanted to hug her knees, rock back and forth and plead for them to take her home. She desired to scream, and shout a slew of choice words at that terrible man who snatched her away from Hannah's arms. In her mind's eye she imagined herself hurling stones at the man who did this to her. She thought of Mordecai. Why didn't he warn her?! If he knew what was to come, couldn't he have sent her to hide somewhere in the countryside?! She tried her very hardest not to be angry with him, but she felt as though anger was controlling her. The grief was too much to bear. What would become of her now? And what would happen to Hannah and Mordecai without her at home?

Upon arriving at the palace, she was whisked into a room with hundreds of other girls, some of them much younger than her. Some young women were sniffling; others wore a stiff mask of determination and bravery. Some eyes were glazed over with disbelief; others were wide- eyed with horror and fear.

The room which they entered was magnificently designed with regal marble pillars, beautiful and strong, sprouting up like a majestic oak tree from a foundation of mosaic pavement made of porphyry, marble, and mother-of-pearl. The stunning floor sparkled beneath the sunlight pouring forth from the Eastern windows. The room was pampered and cared for with fresh flowers every day, including roses, hanging of ivy on the walls, and posies from the Royal Garden. As Hadassah entered, she was greeted by the sight of enslaved women on their hands and knees scrubbing the floor vigorously, style coordinators placing flowers, and servant men cleaning an indoor fountain. Surrounding the fountain was a generous array of flowers. Though this room was the most glorious man-made structure Hadassah had ever laid eyes on, she didn't admire it. She doubted if any of the others did as well.

Persian soldiers kept a sharp eye on the girls as they stood around waiting. But what were they waiting for? Hadassah didn't know. They had all been collected and herded into a line, just to stand in this room like a bunch of cattle at the market. Just then, a man entered. He had a large pot belly, long black beard, and friendly eyes.

"My name is Hegai," the man's voice boomed through the room, an unwelcome echo bouncing off the walls. "I am in charge of the harem. I will be directing every activity in which you young ladies are to be involved in during your stay. Many of you have been forced to come here against your will, and while you may see this as a great disadvantage to leave your families, you must know that the King only commanded that we search for the most beautiful virgins. Consider it an honor to be here. For from now on, you will be treated like royalty and pampered with the finest of foods. The King's wealth and the wealth of Persia will be bestowed upon you, as you dine, wine, and lodge in this glorious palace! Each young lady is in a unique and honored position. For one standing among us, here in our midst today, may be the next Queen of Persia." Hegai paused, letting the weight of his words settle in like a fog. Several girls glanced at one another, as if to ask themselves, 'Could it be me?'

"King Xerxes has required each of you to complete twelve months of prescribed beauty treatments; six with oil and myrrh, and six more with perfumes and cosmetics. Until your opportunity to attempt to win the King's heart, you are not to speak to him or even so much as see him until then. Any interaction with the King is gravely forbidden. You shall not enter the King's quarters, nor leave the place assigned for you. Each young woman must remain in her assigned spot in the quarters of the harem. While there is much freedom for the young ladies in our harem, there are also rules. Strict ones. And you must remember that this is a palace, not a royal *zoo*. We all know why Queen Vashti was banned, and I suggest you make it your highest priority to guarantee that does not happen to you. Now, follow me out into the corridor as I lead the way into the harem quarters, where you will be spending the night. Try and sleep well, for first thing in the morning we will begin our treatments."

Hegai paraded out the doors, and each girl followed in single file. Hadassah was close to the front. As soon as she reached the long hall, Hegai ordered the girls to stop. "Silence! Heads down! King Xerxes has entered the hall!"

Every girl obeyed his command. Hadassah peered at her mud-stained feet and could hear the King's footsteps coming closer.

"Forgive me, Your Majesty, we did not know your way of travel," Hegai spoke quickly. "They will vanish from your sight as quickly as possible; we've just received the other shipment of women."

"Very well," a voice replied. It was the King. Hadassah realized that his pace had slowed, and she wondered if he were examining them. Everything within Hadassah fought the urge to glance up. She seared an imaginary hole through her toes with her eyes and bit her bottom lip. She clamped her eyes shut and listened. His footsteps slowly inched closer and closer. Without warning, her eyes shot open and stole a forbidden glance at His Royal Majesty. From the corner of her eye, she saw the tall man who was surprisingly lacking a crown. Hadassah had never seen a real King before and thought it strange that he wore no sign to declare himself so. He was tall and strong like the pillars which held this very palace upright. She was surprised by his handsome features. His dark brown eyes gazed into the distance then shifted and met hers. She fought back a gasp. He had seen her!

She averted her eyes, ashamed and fearing for her very life. She felt her breathing quicken, and her heartbeat pounded in her head. Would he call her out? Would he put her to death for stepping out of her place of submission? What was she thinking? Why had she glanced upward? His feet continued on down the hall and when she could hear his footsteps no more, Hegai called for the women to move forward. Hadassah breathed a heavy sigh of relief.

~*~

That night she scarcely slept at all. Just like every other girl spending her first night at the palace, she experienced a wild mix of emotions. She shed tears, found herself angry with Mordecai, angry at the palace guard, and angry at the stout Hegai who would be directing and micro-managing the rest of her life. *Why,* she asked the Lord silently through exhausted tears, *why did You let this happen?!* But after her short prayer, Hadassah realized that "Why?" wasn't a question she wanted to battle with. Not tonight anyway. It was a word with too many unknown answers. It wasn't right for her to demand answers from her Creator. It was like marching into the presence of King Xerxes and shouting at him to let her return home. Foolish. She clamped her eyes shut and tried to remember the lullaby that her mother used to sing to her. But all her ears could hear was the muffled whimpers and cries of the girls around her.

~*~

Morning dawned much sooner than she had hoped, and every young woman was served a ginormous breakfast. She had never seen so much food all in one place before! The elaborate table was bursting with colorful fruits, playful vegetables, robust meats, savory breads, and dainty deserts. Hadassah silently thanked God for the meal, but refrained from all unclean meats. Hegai, who was making rounds, noticed the little which Hadassah had on her plate.

"Why is your plate so empty, Miss? You must eat! The King will not choose a weak woman to be his Queen!"

"Thank you for your concern, Sir," Hadassah replied graciously, "And I mean no offence to the King nor his hospitality. But if I am to look my very best when presented to him, I do not wish to allow fatty meats nor oils to ruin my skin."

Hegai was genuinely impressed with the girl's statement. Her thoughtfulness to what she ate was obvious, and it was more than he could say for many of the young women stuffing their faces.

After breakfast, each of the ladies was to soak in a bath of myrrh. Hadassah gratefully melted into the steaming, hot water which settled in the tub made of pure gold. Her entire body tingled with warmth as the herbs and minerals in the water hugged her skin, causing her to feel as though she were washing away the dirt and grime from her very core. Several maidens brought a light purple garment made of silk and matching slippers. After drying off, she wrapped the soft silk around her and took a deep sniff of the lavender scent which was rolling off her clothes. She couldn't believe the luxury and comfort of her new attire, compared to the old and rough woolen dress she used to wear.

Her slipper-covered toes walked over to an outdoor fountain in the courtyard where a few girls flocked around the water. "Isn't this palace just dreamy?" one girl dressed in a beautiful ocean blue silk sighed. "I could get used to living here."

"Scrumptious foods, spa treatments, and one glorious night with the king," another spoke quietly. "What more could a girl ask for?"

Hadassah couldn't resist the urge to speak, "But don't you desire your freedom? Your home? Your family? Isn't that better than all of this?"

The girls were taken aback by her passionate words and met them with opposition. "Freedom?" one snorted, shaking her head. "I was pledged to be married to a man whom I don't love. My parents were forcing the arrangement. There is nothing at home I wish to return to."

"Our family has never had enough to eat," the girl in blue spoke. "I didn't have a dowry, and my Papa could never afford a bride price. They would be happy for me to be here. They couldn't imagine the riches here even if I were to describe them. It's better for me here."

Hadassah shook her head, not believing their words, "Don't any of you miss them though? Your families?"

"I do," a small girl dressed in pink sniffled, "very much so."

The woman dressed in blue offered Hadassah an icy look. "Thanks a lot. You made my little sister cry." She shot her pointy nose into the air, "Come along, Anna."

All the young women left the scene, leaving Hadassah standing alone by the water. She sat down on the ledge, peering into the fountain. Silence enveloped her, and she treasured the moment spent alone. Something inside told her that it would be a rarity. A delicate blue- and white-winged bird entered the scene, perching several feet away, singing a sweet tune. Hadassah stared affectionately at it, the words which Hannah called out to her still ringing in her head, "The Lord is with you! Never forget, He is with you!"

All at once, Hadassah heard the sound of a rock smacking the ledge of the fountain beside her, causing the bird to fly away in fear. She jumped, peering around to see who had thrown it. Her eyes studied the scenery and saw nothing. Her heart settled again and she brushed a gentle hand across the water. Without warning another rock flew towards her, this time landing in the water. She gasped, as a voice called her name, "Hadassah! Over here, Hadassah!"

She twirled around, eyes wide, slowly walking toward the courtyard gate. *Who is calling me? I have told no one my name…* She inched closer, until she heard him again. "Hadassah. The Lord is with you."

This time she recognized the voice. "Mordecai?"

"Shhh," the man placed a weathered hand over top the gate, and Hadassah eagerly grabbed it.

"Mordecai! It's you! Oh, you found me!" She felt her heart flutter with joy as she pressed his wrinkly hand against her cheek, and a whole new wave of tears crashed over her.

"Quiet, my daughter! Let no one hear you." He squeezed her hand then removed it. "How are you my dear one?"

She pressed her ear against the iron courtyard gate, wishing she could see through it. "Oh, Mordecai, I am well. Only my heart aches with a terrible sickness to be home. How is Hannah?"

"She misses you dreadfully, as do I. But Hadassah, my daughter, listen to me carefully. I don't have much time. No one can see you speak to me. I will come by the palace gate every morning at sunrise. Meet me here, and make sure that no one follows you. Hadassah, I have prayed the entire duration of this long night for you and am confident that all of heaven has heard my cries for my beloved daughter. I prayed for strength, bravery, and much favor. My dear one, do not reveal your true Jewish identity and heritage. You must keep the fact that you are a Jew a secret and rid your Hebrew name! You are to go by the name of Esther. It is a pagan name which means star. And that you are, my darling."

"Yes, Mordecai," she replied eagerly, clenching her eyes tight, hoping to stop the flow of tears, "I will do whatever you tell me. No one shall know my true identity. But Mordecai," she paused, feeling a sting of bitterness at the words she spoke, "Why didn't you tell me?"

"I did not think the soldiers would come so quickly. Believe me, I would have done anything and everything to protect you. But perhaps God has a plan in all this. Don't stop trusting Him Hadassah. Know that you are loved. I must leave. Remember all I have told you."

"Yes, yes I will! I love you!" she called out. No voice replied, and she knew he was gone. She sighed, clutching her hand tightly to her heart, wishing there was a way to stop the throbbing pain which exploded inside.

~*~

The dinner feast made breakfast appear as though it was only an appetizer. Hadassah's stomach knotted anxiously and even the intoxicating smells of roast beef, bacon, and ham could not tempt her. As Hegai watched each of the girls, he spotted the odd girl who refused meat for the second time that day.

"Are you sure the King would approve of this? Are you certain that you will not wither away to nothing?"

Hadassah replied honestly, "Test me in this, Sir. I will eat only fruit and vegetables, and drink water. I will refrain from wine and choice meats. In time, compare my complexion to that of another who ate the King's finest meats. If my skin is not healthier than hers and my face glowing brighter than all the rest, then I will set aside my ways and prescribe to yours."

Again, Hegai was amazed by these wise words. "Very well," he nodded. "And what is your name, Miss?"

"Esther." The name sounded foreign on her lips, but she hoped it wouldn't sound as strange to Hegai as it did to her.

"Esther," the man repeated, very much liking the name. "Your wisdom has spoken well of you. You will be one in the first group to undergo their beauty treatments. I will ascribe to your diet, give word to the cooks, and provide you with special foods. If your diet proves to be successful, I will order every other girl in your group to eat in such a way."

A woman who sat beside Hadassah licked her fingers of bacon grease and tossed her a dirty look. Hegai didn't seem to notice, "I'm going to assign seven maids from the palace to do your bidding, and tonight you will move to the best place of the harem."

Hadassah was taken aback by this man's generous words. She bowed her head graciously, "Thank you, Sir."

~*~

"Upon entering the King's presence, each young lady is to conduct herself like that of a Queen...," Hegai's dry and scratchy voice continued droning on, until a maid offered him a glass of water. He paused from his lecture to drink with welcome reprieve. The cool water refreshed his throat, and Hegai continued with his many words.

Hadassah tried to focus her thoughts on Hegai's words, as she had learned that his advice was of great value in this competition. Many girls dismissed his words, tossing disgusted eye rolls behind the back of this stout little man. But Hadassah knew that disrespect was not going to help any of them. A little girl fanned Hadassah with a large palm branch, not helping much in the scorching heat where the royalty-in-training spread across the West Courtyard lawn. Hadassah offered a smile to the servant girl who had been assigned to her. Milcah, the eight-year-old sweetheart, took a strong liking to her master, Esther. Esther told her they could be friends and Milcah let out an excited squeal, telling Esther that she had never had a real friend before.

Six months had passed since Hadassah first arrived at these royal gates, and she had felt much change since then. Sure her skin was softer and her body healthier, but she felt as though something had shifted on the inside of her as well. Hegai treated her with abundant favor, and she had his word that she would be one of the first fifty ladies to meet the King. It was a great advantage, for as soon as His Royal Majesty chose the woman he desired for his wife, the rest would never get a shot at it. Though her night with the King was still months away, Hadassah found herself growing quite anxious at the thought of it.

Nervous energy flowed through the sweltering summer heat, and the patience of every young woman was being severely tested. Even Hadassah found that she wasn't as quick to tame her tongue the past few weeks. Vicious catfights and petty arguments over extravagant pieces of jewelry and gaudy jewels reigned predominantly in the atmosphere. Strife, jealousy, bitterness and backbiting were nearly impossible to be avoided. Hadassah prayed every day for strength and patience, but the reality of this competition set in like an oppressive heat wave.

Many young ladies deeply hated Hadassah without cause, in bitter envy of the favor Hegai was constantly bestowing upon her. He had promised to be her personal consultant and help her choose wisely what to wear and how to accessorize for her night with the King. Many of the other young ladies were all too aware of the special attention and favor she was getting from Hegai, and some plotted against her. Several evenings before, one of Hadassah's maids found a deadly snake hidden in her bed when she turned over the covers. Hegai was furious and believed it to be some sort of plot. Hadassah was shocked that someone would aim at her so viciously, but at the same time it wasn't a complete surprise. Several of the more beautiful girls had died from poison hidden in their food. The assassinations were frightening, and Hegai assured that whoever was behind it would *not* go unpunished. But how could he know who it was? There were eight hundred women at the palace now.

Hadassah's enemies whispered nasty words behind her back, words that stung her ears every time she caught the whisper of them. But she tired always to trump their lies with truth. "But perhaps God has a plan in all this," the words of Mordecai refreshed her soul daily. "Don't stop trusting him, Hadassah." And Hadassah couldn't help but wonder...did God *really* place her in the midst of all this for a reason?

She thought of her forbidden eye contact with the King, something she should have never been so brazen to do. What would it be like when she stepped through his chamber doors, finally seeing him face-to-face? In Hadassah's mind his title was so regal, and his fame spread across every providence. He was brave, unconquered, and as unapproachable as a terrifying lion. Who was she to tiptoe into his presence? Wasn't she merely a simple Jewish girl? She had no ounce of royal blood in her veins. An orphan. A child of an exiled and seemingly forgotten nation of Israel. A byword of many, and to others not even worth mention. An unwelcome shiver of fear clung to her body, despite the extreme heated temperature. Her palms grew cold as the petrifying and vivid image of his eyes flashed into her mind. They were handsome yet fierce, beckoning yet paralyzing all at once. She had sensed a gentleness tactfully hidden under his staunch bravado, but then she second guessed it. Had those eyes deceived her? What was really written there? Could a three-second glance into a pair of eyes serve as a window to one's soul? In the terrible fury of a ravenous king, would he devour her like a lion taking down an antelope or gentle deer? Or would he have mercy on her fears? Hadassah had so many questions, but no answers. She shook her head, forcing her mind to center on what Hegai was saying.

"...and so you must allow these beauty treatments to not only transform your outward appearance, but also your mind. You must believe in your heart and mind that you truly are a queen if His Royal Majesty is to treat you as if you were. There can be no room for doubt or insecurity. The King will without a doubt choose for himself both a stunning and confident bride. Now, mediate on those words, and we will continue this session tomorrow at high noon." Hegai finished his speech and left their presence, allowing the ladies to be dismissed for the day.

"The old coot is right," a voice came from behind Hadassah, "there's no way the King is choosing some weakling. Lucky for me I've always been strong-headed and confident. I'm sure His Majesty will find my spunk entirely impossible to resist."

Hadassah recognized that voice. It came from Francesca, an outspoken Persian native. She lived in the same cubical as Hadassah in the harem, so Hadassah had gotten used to her prideful comments.

"Or perhaps he shall run out of the room screaming, "No!?" a whisper greeted Hadassah's ear. It was Milcah. Hadassah's eyes smiled brightly at the sweet little face which was beaming at her.

"Shhh..." Hadassah corrected gently. "We mustn't meet rude words with others of their kind. We must contradict them with kindness."

"Yes, Esther," Milcah nodded in eager obedience. Hadassah's heart ached for the little girl who was so eager to please her. Milcah was estranged from her parents at birth and sold to the palace as a slave because a debt needed to be paid. Milcah had worked every day of her little life and miraculously had not grown bitter. Hegai assigned Milcah, along with six other ladies, to serve Hadassah by waiting on her hand and foot. It took everything inside Hadassah to refrain from joining her maids in their tasks. For not too long ago, *she* was the maid. Hadassah wished she could offer Milcah her freedom and send her away with Mordecai and Hannah, to be lovingly cared for just like she was. But for now, all Hadassah could offer the girl was herself. Little did she know that was more than Milcah could ever ask for.

"Perhaps I'll serenade the King with a love song," Francesca continued, talking to whoever might catch wind of her words. "I've been told that I have the voice of a queen or that of a mystical sea goddess."

"I think I'll flutter my eyelashes," another spurted out, showing all how she planned to do it, "like this."

"I'm planning on laughing flirtatiously at all his jokes," another displayed her not-so-rare skill, letting out a roll of completely unflattering, human laughter, "Hahahahaha!"

Francesca rolled her eyes, unamused, "*You're* a joke. What will *you* do Esther, in attempt to capture the King's heart?"

Hadassah turned to face her question, quietly contemplating a few seconds before answering, "I'll do whatever Hegai recommends."

Day 14
The Battle for Beauty

I hope you enjoyed reading Hadassah's story yesterday! It's really powerful when we place ourselves in her shoes and think about everything that she walked through. Her life wasn't nearly as glamorous as we imagine it to be. She faced some pretty terrible trials. The colorful painting of Hadassah's story isn't over yet though, so keep journeying with me! Before we get back to Hadassah's story, let's talk about what we just read.

When I was sixteen, I auditioned for a Disney Channel Open Casting Call in Nashville, Tennessee. The website announcement encouraged singers, actors, and dancers to come and take a shot at impressing the casting directors at Disney. I thought it would be a really fun experience. Besides, the worst thing that could happen is nothing, right?

I hadn't a clue how to prepare for something like this other than with prayer, vocal exercises, and emulating my favorite, perky Disney Channel stars in my bathroom mirror. When I arrived, the room was filled with hundreds of kids who all desired to be the star of their very own television show. Hyper-active radio waves of pure excitement radiated off the walls, as every contestant dreamed of becoming the next *"Hannah Montana."* With attractive young men strumming guitars, stunningly-gorgeous girls reapplying their makeup, break dancers getting funky in the hallways, and adorable little kids who look like Shirley Temple drilling lines with their parents, I felt strangely out of place. I was surrounded by intense soccer moms who looked like they would kill anybody in order for their kids to have a chance at stardom, driven daddies who encouraged their children to pursue "one more audition," and seasoned actors and actresses who have been doing this since diapers. Then there was me and the other hundred or so handful of people who decided the week before to show up for this thing.

I am a total "people watcher. Send me to the mall and you can go shopping for the perfect pair of stilettos, but I'd rather sit on the bench and watch everybody pass by. So for me, this experience was totally fascinating. As I was observing (cause that sounds so much better than eavesdropping, right?) my "competition," I couldn't help but feel that every girl was prettier, more stylishly dressed, more experienced at acting, and basically much more qualified for this than I.

Have you ever felt that way? Maybe you've auditioned for the school musical, a local theater production, or your high school volleyball team. Tryouts can be nerve wracking, butterfly enticing, and fear creating. When eyeing your fellow competitors you can begin to feel really small. It's easy to live your dreams when you're alone in your bedroom lip-syncing and dancing around with your hairbrush. But place your dancing shoes on that same stage where others are competing for your dream, and intimidation begins breathing down your back.

Maybe Esther's life at the palace felt something like one massive Disney Channel audition, basketball tryout, or job interview. It's like *reality TV* to the highest degree! It appeared as though orphaned Hadassah had a great disadvantage in this competition. Perhaps she glanced around at the breath-taking beauty of the girls surrounding her and thought, *I haven't got a chance. Vanessa's got a perfect body, Sophie looks like she could be on the cover of Popstar!, Ellie sings like an angel, Trisha can answer Algebra questions like nobody's business, Natalie's Dad has more money than...*

Do you think it was easy for Esther to get discouraged in that situation? She was thrust into a world that was so self-saturated, where nearly every girl cherished her image, fussed over food, and worshiped her mirror. I imagine it must've been the ideal breeding ground for low self-esteem, terrible self-image, anorexia, and bulimia. It would be much too easy for a girl to doubt herself.

In this Pagan culture, Hadassah may have felt like she didn't quite fit in. If anyone knew her true identity, she would be persecuted for it. Gossips would have nothing better to do than whisper behind her back, "Did you hear about that Jewish girl? Does she seriously think the King would give her a second glance?"

To be a Hebrew was a great disadvantage in this competition, and as you can imagine, the competition was stiff. In Persian society, Hebrews were looked down upon. Hebrews were those exiled servants who were conquered and brought in from a tiny country. The ones who went on fasts and diets, didn't eat meat, didn't sin, didn't work on their Sabbath, and sacrificed to only one god. The girls may have whispered behind Hadassah's back, "Psh, she hasn't got a chance."

Maybe you can relate. At school we hear these things from our toughest critics, our jealous steps sisters, from teachers, and sometimes even from our own parents. Because of the light of Christ that is burning brightly in us, the favor of God that is on our lives, and the Cinderella-like destiny awaiting, the enemy hopes to ambush our dreams. He hopes to discourage us. He hopes that we will just take a tiny look around at everyone who's got it better than we do. From the girl with shinier hair, bigger breasts, and the hottest boyfriend, to the girl who's gracing magazine covers and living the life we thought *we* were supposed to get.

When I was thirteen years old I thought God had made a huge mistake. He was supposed to deliver a vitally important package to a certain address thirteen years prior. But his carrier pigeon (also known as a Stork) got it *so* wrong. Didn't he know I was supposed to be delivered on the certain doorstep of a certain house in Nashville? How in the world did I end up being shipped to a tiny town in Michigan? God's GPS must have really glitched! Let me explain.

As a preteen, I was totally star struck with Hollywood glitz and glamour. I have to say that what I saw happening on Disney Channel was majorly attractive to me. *Hannah Montana* was just coming out, and if *High School Musical* was a fever I must've been out with it for weeks. I watched that movie so many times it's almost shameful.

I absolutely adored a young starlet on my favorite TV show. She appeared to be perky, fun-loving, kind, and an outspoken Christian. She wore the cutest outfits, spoke the funniest lines, and dated my dream boy! Soon I had bought the lie that her life was better than mine. It started out with a simple thought, 'I wish I was like her.' But the desire for my life to be hers grew like an uncontrollable weed in the garden of my heart, choking off the life source of my creativity and individuality. I wished I would've been born thirteen years ago into this celebrity's family. Mine was boring and average and thousands of miles away from Hollywood. It was so unfair! Why would God give this girl all of my crazy dreams on a silver platter and leave me with the tasteless leftovers of an average existence?

Have you ever wished you were someone else? Or had someone else's hair, friends, or popularity? When we start comparing and contrasting ourselves with others, somehow we always seem to end up on the short end of the deal. Can you imagine what would've happened if Hadassah started doing that?

Just like Hadassah, we are living in a culture that is constantly calling out to us, letting us know that God screwed up with our lives. He messed up our bodies, families, (and in my case the geographical location where I was supposed to be born)! What on earth is the Man Upstairs thinking!?

This world has given us impossible images of perfection that we are expected to conform to. But a message which God spoke to my heart at thirteen caused me to stop dead in my tracks. I turned and started swimming like a salmon upstream, fighting against the all too easy flow of this world. My Maker let me in on a little secret. Wanna know what it is? *He didn't mess up.*

Okay, maybe you already knew that. Great! You're already a step ahead of where I was at thirteen. But there's more to His secret. He whispered to my soul, "It breaks my heart when people are not themselves." I love Jesus so much and would never want to break his heart over anything. So it was a crazy thought to think that the Creator of the Universe is actually *heartbroken* when I'm not myself. When I'm wishing that I were someone else or not embracing every inch of who He made me to be, I am actually dissing my Creator.

Questioning your unique, God-given existence (the entire package; your body, brains, heart, location, sphere of influence, destiny, etc.) is just like telling God, "HEY! I don't like what you're doing, and I think I could do it better." Ouch.

Isaiah 45:9 says, "Woe to those who quarrel with their Maker, those who are nothing but potsherds among the potsherds on the ground. Does the clay say to the potter, 'What are you making?' Does your work say, 'The potter has no hands?' " Imagine creating a beautiful piece of artwork. You've just finished pouring your heart into it and have placed the finishing touches on your masterpiece. A smile eats up your entire face. A certain kind of pride that only comes from when you've imagined something in your mind, designed it with your hands, and breathed it into existence, floods your entire being. You're thrilled to share your project with your best friend, so you call her over and eagerly wait for the moment she steps through your front door.

"Ta da!" You motion to your masterpiece. You know she'll love it just as much as you do, "It's for you! I spent what felt like eternity pouring my very self into every part of this, and I want you to have it. I was thinking of you the entire time I worked on it, and I hope you think of me every time you sit back and enjoy it."

There is silence. Your best friend wrinkles her nose, placing hands on her hips. "Well…" she starts slowly, "it's not perfect. You really messed up in quite a few places. I could point them all out to you. Actually, Abbi designed something like this just last week, but hers is so fantastic! You should really go look at hers and get some pointers. Yeah, nice try, but this just doesn't measure up to what I want."

You choke. Did she seriously just say that?! No, actually you just said that. You say that to God every time you slam his marvelous creation, *you*.

This is the Artist who was so madly in love with his piece of perfection that He was willing to die for it. Why are we so hard on ourselves when Christ says we are fearfully and wonderfully made? Who are we trying to impress? Why is it so hard to cherish the priceless masterpiece that we are?

The battle has *always* been about beauty.

There has never been a time in human history when the temptation to compare our lives with the lot of those living on the "other side of the fence" has been so strong. We've all been there. We strive to enhance our natural beauty and chase things that will help us feel better about ourselves because we don't realize who we *already* are. We are shown nonstop images of cute boys, pretty hair, dazzling bags, flawless faces, flashy cars, glamorous lifestyles, and skinny models. The temptation is real. Everything is screaming at us, "You really should have this. You really need to be this. You really should chase this. Why didn't God give you this? Look how ugly you are compared to her. He doesn't really love you as much as you think He does because He has denied you the pleasure of a good gift."

Why does the enemy work so tirelessly to discourage us as young women? I believe the enemy hates us so intensely because he is jealous of our beauty. This sounds like a wild thought, but it's a Biblical one. Ezekiel 28:12 describes the enemy in this way: "You were the signet of perfection, full of wisdom and perfect in beauty."

Lucifer (also known as Satan or the devil) was a handsome, attractive angel. 2 Corinthians 11:14 says he disguises himself as an angel of light. God said he was perfect in beauty! But apparently Lucifer enjoyed looking at himself in the mirror. He became obsessed with himself. But God couldn't stand to be around pride. "Your heart was proud because of your beauty; you corrupted your wisdom for the sake of your splendor." (Ezekiel 28:17) Jesus said that Lucifer's bad attitude got him kicked out of heaven. (Luke 10:18).

Only Satan himself knows just how much his puffed up arrogance and selfishness cost him. And now aware of how short his time is on earth before he is cast away into eternal torment in the Lake of Fire (Revelation 20:10), his evil goal is to drag everyone he possibly can down with him. Although he cannot shake our eternal security of being heaven bound (as long as we are following Christ), Satan attempts to discourage us in every way possible, with such a great wrath, hatred, and jealousy. He knows what a slippery slope it is for God's beautiful ones to become obsessed with ourselves and worship our own images.

Many of us can scarcely believe that Eve threw away her entire life in the Garden for a silly apple or orange. If it was Dove's chocolate or a mocha from Starbucks that might be a little more realistic, right? But just like today, the enemy whispered lies into Eve's ears about herself and her existence. He fixed her eyes on everything she didn't have, everything she couldn't have, but everything she thought she was supposed to have. She started to question God. Is He really so good and pure and lovely and kind? Was I really meant to look like this? Was I really born in the right location? If only I... *If only* is a lie.

1 Thessalonians 1:16-18 says, "Be joyful always, pray continually, give thanks in all circumstances, for this is God's will for you in Christ Jesus..." Jesus desires that your life be full of joy,

laughter, and sweet communion with Him; bursting with the people you love, and things you enjoy doing. In John 10:10, Jesus declares that He came to give life and give it to the full. He wants us to live full, love-filled lives! He wants us to run to Him and those open arms as our source for everything.

1 Thessalonians displays a beautiful pattern I like to call the Joy Cycle. I used to get frustrated when people said, 'Be joyful always,' because this is life! There is no way I can make myself be happy all the time. But we're not talking about happiness here. We're talking about *joy*. Paul told the Christians to rejoice always, and he wrote those words with hands shackled by chains, in a dark and musty prison cell. Surely Paul wasn't happy all the time, was he? Of course not! He was human!

In Philippians 4:12-13 He wrote, "I know what it is to be in need, and I know what it is to have plenty. I have learned the secret of being content in every situation, whether well fed or hungry, whether living in plenty or want. I can do everything through Him who gives me strength."

Earlier in this chapter he writes, "Do not be anxious about anything, but in everything by prayer and petition, with *thanksgiving* present your requests to God. And the peace of God which transcends all understanding will guard your heart and mind in Christ Jesus." (Phil.4:6-7)

Paul faced some tough times, but he had learned how to give thanks in all circumstances. "Wow," you may think, scratching the hairs on your chinny-chin-chin, "that's so deep. Giving thanks in all circumstances. How would one do that?"

It's quite simple actually. Just start giving *thanks*! Look around at all the marvelous ways God has blessed you and thank Him individually for each one. And then *never* stop. Can't think of where to start? Start with your birth. Begin with thanking Him for lovingly choosing your hair color, designing your facial features, and for your eye color. He spent so much time working on every intricate detail, perfecting every cell, tenderizing every delicate nerve ending in your fingertips, counting every hair on your head, and placing part of His crazy, diverse personality that nobody else has, in your heart. Perhaps your blue eyes were inspired by the crystal sea which flows before the throne. Maybe the brown tones which he etched into your skin were something He spent a hundred years perfecting. Maybe your laugh was one which He knew would be contagious. Sister, He put so much thought and care into creating you! Why do you think He was so quick to offer Himself as a ransom to rescue you? Because He is in love with you. Thank Him for knitting you together in your mother's womb. Thank Him for the unique plan and purpose he has for your life. Thank Him for choosing you before the foundations of the world!

If the enemy can get us focused on everything we don't have, we lose our joy. But if you keep your eyes locked in His, seeing yourself through His eyes, thanking Him over and over and over again, you cannot help but truly feel like you're the most blessed girl *ever*. You get caught up in this crazy joy cycle as He transforms your mind daily with His love. Next thing you know you're smack dab in the middle of God's will for your life. Because you being with Him *is* His will. The enemy so wants to steal our joy. But we can choose every single day to live with thankful, grateful, exuberant hearts!

When we begin COMPARING our lives to those around us and say, "I wish I had a boyfriend. I wish I looked like her. I wish I could just be a few pounds lighter. I wish I had curly hair. I wish I had straight hair. I wish I lived in Hollywood. I wish I was pretty enough to-" we begin to look around at the ONE tree we cannot have, and therefore doubt God's absolute goodness in our lives.

I used to do this as a little girl. It was almost a habit for me to spot that one girl that I wished I could look like, be like, talk like, have her parents, her life experience, etc. I could tell story after story of all the girls I wanted to be over the years, like my red-headed friend whose parents owned McDonalds, which was pretty much the coolest place in town. (Hey don't judge, I was three!) Then there was my black-haired friend in second grade who was so cool and wore the cutest clothes. As a teenager, I wanted to look like Selena Gomez and have her killer hair. I also wanted to live the life of my friend who lived on a ranch of horses and never even rode them. Ugh! I wanted to be the girl on Disney who had the recording contract. Then I wanted to be Louis Tomlinson's girlfriend. Do you see how maddening this is?! We do this to ourselves every single day.

We entertain thoughts that leave us thinking, "Why is God holding back so much goodness from me?" And in that, we are deceived.

There was a time in my life when things looked very bleak. I was in a crazy tough situation, and all I could see was the negative. It seemed unjust and unfair, and I was tempted to doubt the goodness of God. So I read James 1:16-17 over and over and over again. I said, "Only good things come from God, who is only good. Only good things come from God, who is only good. Only good things come from God, who is only good!"

And I'm telling you, this verse completely shifted my perspective. Memorize this verse. Plaster it everywhere. Get this unshakable truth down deeply into your heart so that when the enemy attempts to deceive you and steal your joy, you can say with total confidence, "Only good things come from God, who is only good!"

Day 15
For Such a Time as This

The following morning, after Hadassah had entered the King's chamber, she was told to return to her place in the harem. Mixed thoughts of doubt, relief, and anticipation swirled about in her mind as she slowly inched her way up the marble staircase leading to her shared bedroom. He had not completely devoured her, as she believed that the lion would. He was kind and patient with her. He was intrigued and interested in what she had to say. His gentle touch melted away every fear. But now, it was all over. Would she ever see him again? Had she been enough for him? Was she worthy of his love?

At the sound of Hadassah turning the door handle, every girl from their cubical jumped up and swirled about, eager to see if Esther had been crowned. "Oh no," Milcah spoke quietly, "We thought for sure he'd pick you."

Francesca grinned mischievously as soon as she saw Esther enter. She stood up from her window seat and strutted forward. "Sorry," Francesca offered sympathy with the rest, but her eyes betrayed her words. "My turn!"

"I'm sorry he didn't make you Queen, Esther," Milcah spoke with innocent eyes, "but I'm glad you're back."

Hadassah drew Milcah's head close in a soft hug. Hadassah drew away to her favorite spot by the window, and Milcah went on to do her chores. Hadassah's hand slowly chose a white rose from one of the many bouquets gracing the window and reflected on the night passed. The spell of their love had been broken, and all fairytale dreams vanished with the dawn. It had felt so real to her. She was ready to give everything to him, to stand by his side as a wife, and pledge the rest of her days to him in marriage. But it appeared as though to the King she was just another average girl amidst the long line of women whom he had merely enjoyed. She would probably never enter his mind again. But he would come to mind. Oh, Hadassah knew she would dream of him every night. It was far too great a burden to bear. How could she live in the same palace as the only man she ever loved and never see him again as long as she lives? Hadassah felt the tears sting as her hands clutched tightly to the rose, crushing the petals in her palm.

Then Hadassah heard a voice. "Which do you think the King will like better?" Francesca asked the ladies in their quarters, "the gold or silver?"

You foolish girl! Hadassah harshly chastened herself, tucking away the tears before Francesca was given the opportunity to tease her over them. *How could you possibly think the King would ever choose you? Tonight is Francesca's turn, tomorrow's Anna's, and the next Tia. Then Dolores, and Magnolia, and on, and on, and on...what possibly makes you different than any of the rest of them?*

She sniffed, determined to cry no more. The King was not worth crying over. She stood up straight, with stiff muscles and tired eyes. *Enough. Milcah needs me. I will pour out my life at the palace for her, no matter what happens. God, I don't know why you brought me here. But even if it's just for Milcah's sake...I will trust You.*

She tossed the white rose out the window and with it her heart for the King. She was determined never again to revisit that night in her mind. She would forget all about it and pretend as if it had never happened.

In that very moment, as the pure white rose touched the ground three floors below, the King watched the flower drop from above. He crouched over to pick it up and examined the soft petals with his fingertips. The purity of the flower had been defiled by the touch of another. He wished to revive it, but knew that just like the fragile wings of a butterfly, once they are marred by human fingerprints, they are never the same.

In the front of his mind, he saw his Esther. Her soft eyes of innocence beckoned him. She had eyes like doves; eyes that would be faithful to him and him alone. He could sense her love for him.

Something about her was different. There was something so fiercefully entrancing and captivating about her beauty and her heart. In that very instant, the King knew what He had to do.

"Hegai!" He called. "Hegai! Fetch the royal robe and prepare her crown! I have chosen my queen!"

Hegai rushed onto the terrace, "Yes Your Majesty, straightaway. I will summon the trumpet players, violins, and cellos. I will prepare the feast and make ready her royal attire." He bowed upon leaving, yet paused to ask with a smile on his face, "Its Esther...isn't it?"

~*~

The moment had arrived. Hadassah had done everything possible to prepare herself. The past year of her life had been the longest, most trying, most heartbreaking, yet most rewarding time of her life. And now, the joy which bubbled up in her heart made every moment worth it. Her servant girl to royalty transformation was nearly complete. The maidens whom Hadassah had grown closest with fluttered and danced about her like playfully butterflies, placing the final elements of splendor on their soon-to-be queen.

Her long slender arms were adorned with bangle bracelets of gold and silver, diamond earrings dangled from her ears, and a regal sapphire necklace hung from her neck. Milcah thought she was looking at a fairy dream.

"I've never seen anyone so beautiful," she spoke in a hushed tone, "Mistress Esther, you will make a glorious queen."

Hadassah's cheeks blushed a soft shade of red, the rosy color in as her eyes danced with inexpressible joy. Her long, black hair had been carefully braided and wrapped around her crown. A small white lily adorned her hair.

Hadassah had never felt so lovely. The gown which was chosen by the King himself was interwoven with gold. It sparkled and danced in the sunshine, reflecting Hadassah's soul.

She had been chosen by the king! The pure-white bouquet of roses, with one red in the center, shook slightly as she held them in nervous hands. A full week had passed since Hadassah's night with the king. As the wedding ceremony, celebration, and feasting plans were made, Hadassah felt as though the days flew by in an excited blur. More beauty treatments, hairstyling, and gown fitting consumed her days in which she had not seen the king. Her heart soared with anticipation. It was finally happening!

With her virgin companions, Hadassah was led to the king. Violins sang, and trumpets shouted jubilantly to declare the coming presence of the queen. Every honored citizen among the throngs of people who had been invited to this royal celebration eagerly rose to their feet, craning their necks; hoping to catch even the tiniest glimpse of their new queen.

Hadassah stepped foot into the elaborately decorated courtyard, and faint whispers began to rise from the crowd. But they were no longer shadowy whispers of doubt, nor vile words of destruction. No, these were wonderstruck words. Words of praise and adoration to the King for choosing such a lovely girl.

"Who is she?" one woman asked another. "Where did she come from?"

But Hadassah's humble beginnings mattered to no one. They wouldn't believe her now, even if they were told. The King had chosen her, and that was all they needed to know.

~*~

"Parties, parties, parties!" Esther sighed, exhausted as she flopped backwards onto her queen-sized bed. The mattress below was made of finest silk, the white comforter poofing out on either side as she lowered onto the bed. "If I must dine at another feast, dance for the King's guests once more, or smile and laugh over a candlelit glass of wine, I think I'm going to die!"

Milcah's sweet laugh lit up the darkened room as she tossed several logs into the fireplace. The room was suddenly revived with a soft glow.

"Queen Esther, you know that you're the most privileged girl in all of Persia. If you're complaining about this life of pleasure, I don't know how you'd make it through the life of someone else."

Esther's head shot up as she watched Milcah float across the room, humming a tune as she gathered the items for Esther's evening bath. The little girl was so joyful. Well, she wasn't quite so little anymore. Several years had passed and Milcah was maturing. Her wise words cut Esther to the heart as she watched the servant girl be so content to serve. Milcah was right. Since when did she have a right to complain about her high society life?

Yet, in all honesty, she was fed up with the King's ridiculous parties. She had been Queen now for three years, and he was *still* celebrating their marriage. Some marriage. She felt more like a toy or a prize, rather than a wife. She barely ever saw him, unless of course he wished for a night of pleasure or for her to be the "honored guest" at one of his wild parties. Wine flowed freely and everyone guffawed with harsh joking. Esther felt like a lioness locked in a cage. Living here was madness! If she had to listen to those fools ramble on so mindlessly without being able to share her mind on any matters…she stopped herself. Milcah was right. She had to count her blessings.

"Your wisdom speaks well for your age," Esther replied.

"You forget, your majesty, that I am not as young as I once was." It was true. Milcah was blossoming into a beautiful, young woman. No longer a little girl. In fact, Esther began to worry about her safety. Many of the young ladies at the palace had been abused by the palace guards; rough men who cared more about their own cravings than the dignity of a young girl.

Esther wished to keep her safe, but she couldn't be with Milcah at all times. The idea of her being abused terrified her. Esther could see that Milcah's beauty and innocence radiated from her like a sweet-smelling flower. She was as attractive as ever. She deserved to be protected and cared for by a young man who would have her best interests in mind. Not the ravenous, foul, disgusting men who saw Milcah as a helpless piece of prey. Esther knew this much: if a man ever touched Milcah, the King would have his head. She would see to it! At least she liked to imagine that the King would listen to her appeal if such a situation arose. But Esther was not cherished for her mind. None of these women in the palace were. Esther burned with such a great frustration and hatred. Something *had* to be done. For they were all captives, from the lowest servant girl who swept out the cinders, to the highest...her Royal Majesty. They were captives enclosed by beautiful surroundings. But despite the suffocating palace walls, Esther *still* believed that she was here for a reason. She prayed every day that the Lord would show her why. But the silence from heaven was as uncomfortable and unsettling as the silence she was getting from her King. Had she been forgotten by them both?

"Your Majesty," a young maiden entered, keeping her head bowed low, "there is someone here to see you."

Esther nodded, "Very well. You may escort our guest in."

An officer, dressed from head to toe in the typical palace armor, stepped inside. He bowed respectfully before rising to say, "Good evening, Your Majesty." He spotted Milcah out the corner of his eye and Esther wanted to banish the man from her room. But she had to hear what he was going to say.

"There is a Jewish man at the Northern Gate. He requests to see you. He says that it is urgent. He is quite unsightly, with sackcloth on his head, clothes ripped apart, crying like a mad man. We've asked him to leave, but he will not. Would you like us to remove him from the premises?"

Esther felt her heart skip a beat. Mordecai! He was dressed in sackcloth? Something must be terribly wrong! Her mind raced as she thought of sweet, old Hannah. Oh no! She hadn't...

"No, I shall go visit him." She rose and slipped a turban of purple silk around her head. "No one must know of this. I forbid you to speak of this encounter." She stared with the harshness of bullets into the man's brown eyes, "Do I have your word?"

"Yes, Your Majesty." He bowed once more and after Esther's head was fully covered, she slipped out of her bedroom and down the marble staircase. The cover of dusk helped keep her hidden as she trotted down several flights of stairs, then through the Northern courtyard. She quickly tiptoed until she reached the King's Gate. She could hear loud moaning and crying coming from the other side. It startled her and she stopped dead in her tracks. *Something must be wrong*, she thought, hugging herself to keep her warm from the sudden chill of fear. *Terribly wrong.* For it was not just one voice crying. But it sounded more like a chorus of voices, droning a heartbreaking melody.

As she prepared to exit the gate, a hand grabbed her from behind. She let out a scream, but a large, calloused hand clasped over her mouth.

"Shhhh…" he hushed, "Your Majesty, it is only I, Hathach."

He removed his hand and Esther whipped around, "I demand you never to touch me again!" she whispered loudly.

"Forgive me, madam" he spoke quietly, eyeing the other guards around her, hoping to keep her identity under wraps. Esther couldn't be associated with what was happening to the Jews outside the King's Gate. That would be disgraceful for her and would portray a bad image on King Xerxes.

He motioned for her to follow him into a corner of the wall where they could speak in private, without suspicious ears lingering. She quickly asked, "I must know what is happening to that man, Mordecai. Why is he in sackcloth?"

"Please, Your Majesty, use wisdom and sound judgment at this moment. The King would be furious if he knew you were reaching out in concern to another man. He could have both this man's head and yours."

Esther didn't know what to say. She couldn't tell him that they were family. "Thank you, Hathach for your advice, but I am quite capable of making up my own mind in matters such as this. I command you to go and offer the man some clothes to wear instead of his sackcloth. The finest this palace has to offer. Also, find out what is troubling him and report back to me."

"Very well, my Queen. Your wishes will be carried out this hour."

Satisfied that the mission would be fulfilled, Esther snuck back upstairs. Once safe in her room, Milcah questioned her about the events that took place. They waited anxiously for a man to bring word.

Hathach returned fifteen minutes later saying, "I spoke to the man, Mordecai. He would not accept your garments. He had a message for you, saying, "Tell Her Majesty, The Queen, that there is a betrayer in the palace. A man who shares the King's bread and his ear, has offered a petition to the King in order to annihilate the Jews. The man named Haman has promised to pay into the royal treasury ten thousand talents of silver in order for this task to be accomplished. The King was pleased with the petition and signed it with his signet ring. A royal decree has been sent out through all of Persia saying that every Jew must be put to death; young, old, women and children, on a single day which is to be the thirteenth day of the twelfth month of Adar. Here is a copy of this edict, Your Majesty. He wanted you to see it for yourself."

Esther's hands shook as Hathach handed her the paper which promised the murder of her people. She felt faint, and her knees nearly gave out.

"This man urges you to go into the King's presence and beg for mercy. He desires that you plead with the King on behalf of this nation."

Esther's maids noticed that her face had turned a ghostly shade of white, so they buzzed around her, offering calming smelling scents and fluffing her pillows that she might be comfortable as Milcah brewed her a cup of calming tea. Esther's mind raced. How could Mordecai possibly ask her to do such a thing?! Everyone in the Kingdom knows that to enter the King's presence without invitation is like signing a contract for your own death. He was asking her to do the impossible.

"Give Mordecai this message," she said once she composed herself enough to speak. "All the King's officials and the people of the royal providences know that for any man or woman who approaches the King in the inner court without being summoned, the king has but one law: that he or she be put to death. I have seen those terrifying men who stand by the doorway, prepared to swing their axes down on the head of any intruder. The only exception to this is for the king to extend his gold scepter toward him or her, to spare the life. But this has never been done! Mordecai cannot ask me to do such a thing, for it has been thirty days since the King has asked to see me. I fear I must've upset him in some way or he has grown bored with me. I do not have his favor."

The man hurried off to deliver the Queen's message. Even though the hour was late, the thought of sleep was ludicrous. The Queen's maids tried their best to console her, but as comfortable as her fluffy pillows or her cup of tea were, they could not detract from the great discomfort and anxiousness which tore inside her soul.

Soon, he returned with another message. "Mordecai says, 'Do not think that because you are in the King's house you alone of all the Jews will escape. For if you remain silent at this time, relief and deliverance will arise from another place but you and your father's family will perish. And who knows whether you have come into the kingdom for such a time as this?'"

Mordecai's words rang inside her spirit. Suddenly she remembered everything. The day the solders came, the anger, the fear and the lingering question, does God have a plan in all this? She was reminded of those long days, doubting that the King could possibly choose her, yet he had. Were Mordecai's words true? Had she really been sent here *for such a time as this*? Was it her duty to speak up for her people and risk her life on behalf of her nation?

But she was no heroine! She was only a woman, a victim locked up in a terrible time in history, where women were regarded without value or respect. If she approached the King, would he have her exiled just like Queen Vashti? Or could she possibly soften his ice-glazed heart?

She only knew one thing was true; she could *not* do it. If there was going to be any rescue, any deliverance, or any grand moment in history, it wouldn't be because of her. It would be because of her God. She bit her lip and thought carefully before sending her reply.

"Tell Mordecai, go gather together all the Jews who are in Susa and fast for me. Do not eat or drink for three days. I and my maids will fast as you do. When this is done, I will go to the King. And if I perish, I perish."

Day 16
Uncovering the Evil Plot

Princess Warrior, for this purpose you have been called: To set captives free, break the chains of the enemy, and liberate those who are bound. You were not rescued from the Worthlessness Camp simply to sit in the palace and sip tea. You are called to liberate others! You are called to fight the good fight!

The inspiration to begin writing about the Worthlessness Camp actually came from a dream I had when I was fourteen years old. In this dream, a long line of beautiful girls stood in front of a wall. They were all so unique and diverse. Some were pale, others had dark skin, some were from India, others from Africa and Europe, some were bright blondes, and others were red-headed girls with freckles! They ranged from all ages, colors and sizes. They were short, skinny, tall, and stout. They reminded me of a colorful package of skittles. They were all so unique and special! My heart smiled at the rainbow of individuality stretched out before me. But then, a dark group of evil men entered the scene and started poking the girls. They bugged them with nagging pokes, digging into their skin, and hurting their bodies. The poking and jabbing intensified until one man pulled out a gun. He was about to murder each and every one of those beautiful girls. My heart started pounding and I knew I had to do something...anything, before it was too late.

I woke up in a panic, wondering what happened to all my sisters in that dream. Did they make it out alive? Was I able to set them free from that wretched place of torment? I KNEW that God was calling me to do something about this massacre of true beauty. Each and every poke represented the lies which Satan throws at girls on a daily basis. They are impossible to be ignored because the intensity grows until they convince the victim that they are good for nothing else than to be destroyed.

The purpose of this disgusting scheme is to convince God's chosen daughters that they are worthless. The familiar scenery of the hour we live in, the stage which has been set, and the cast of characters in this story, remind me of what unfolded in Hadassah's day. Just like the vile and evil Haman, Satan is trying to destroy our entire generation. But an ordinary, average orphan girl was called to play a magnificent role in the Kingdom, and God used her to release her entire generation from destruction. Are you beginning to see the uncanny similarities between you and Hadassah?!

This is an all-out assault on the Daughters of the Most High; and just like Queen Hadassah, we have been called into the Kingdom for *such a time as this.*

Mordecai told Hadassah, "If you remain silent, help will arise from another place, but you yourself will be destroyed." God would be faithful to raise up a deliver no matter what she chose, but if Hadassah decided *not* to be proactive, she herself would fall prey to the evil plot. In other words, if we don't choose to be part of the answer, we will unknowingly become part of the problem.

Do you see the parallel between Haman's scheme and what the enemy is doing today? The times may have changed, but the tactics have not. We must awaken and open our eyes to the reality of what is happening in this real-life Worthlessness Camp and see that this plot is just like Haman's!

But take courage! Because all the truths woven throughout this book are weapons we can use to combat the enemy's disgusting scheme. Girls, we can absolutely change this world. That's why I'm writing this book! I believe that YOU have been called to be an answer. Once we as God's daughters choose to quit contributing to the problem and take a stand against it, we will be a powerful force to be reckoned with.

Luke 17:21 says, "The Kingdom of God is *within* you." Mark 4:11 says, "To you it has been known the mystery [the secrets] of the kingdom of God." To us, the keys have been given. We *have* the secrets of royalty. Through our royal beauty treatments in the Word, we have been given keys to defeat the enemy. Just like the princess in our tale, it is time we march into his camp, scale his intimidating walls, and use what we have been entrusted with to set the captives free!

There is an attack on true womanhood and what it means to be the Princess Bride of Jesus Christ. The assault is on our identity. This is a season when the enemy is twisting everything. He's bombarding the earth with so much confusion that even men want to become women, and women desire to become men! The role of what God originally intended each gender to be is becoming marred and confused. In the same way, the enemy has distorted our purpose as Kingdom girls and has convinced God's daughters to think *just* like our culture. The idol of being beautiful and sexy has been lifted up so high that it seems the highest goal in life is to be the best prostitute you can possibly be. I know, that sounds a bit brazen and dramatic, but think about what we see on the cover of *Cosmo*, and in all the latest, newest Hollywood blockbusters. It's ALL about being sexy and beautiful.

Just like in Hadassah's day, the majority of people around us have their minds set on the things that are seen, not the unseen things of God's kingdom. As sad and pathetic as it is, most girls are in competition with one another; obsessed with our own mirrors, attempting to win the hottest guys we possibly can. Yet, we are told that we are receiving a Kingdom that cannot be seen. What is seen is temporary, but what is unseen is eternal. So how are we going to help the lost, hurting, and dying all around us to see that this life is only a temporary vapor, a mist that is here today and gone tomorrow? How are we going to help them see that nothing else in life matters, that everything is absolute vanity other than encountering the love of Jesus?

I'll be the first to admit, it's hard to preach this truth, "Nothing matters but the love of Jesus," when I still have so many concerns and agendas on my own personal "To Do" list in life. I so admire the life and ministries of those like Mother Theresa, Heidi Baker, and Katie Davis (author of *Kisses from Kate*). All of these women are truly convinced that the love of Jesus is the only thing worth living for.

Katie surrendered her comfortable life in the hills of Tennessee, her college scholarships, a relationship with her boyfriend, and the affirmation of her other friends to move to Africa at age nineteen and take care of orphaned children! Katie's world doesn't revolve around iPhones, applying more mascara, or pushing her own personal agenda. She probably wakes up every morning with a goofy smile on her face asking Jesus, "What are we going to do today? Who are we going to serve? Who are we going to rescue from the Worthlessness Camp?" She's not a worker. She's a *lover*. She didn't surrender her life to Jesus because she *had t*o, but instead she caught a glimpse of His radical love and matchless beauty, and she could only respond by giving up everything she held dear to pursue whatever He cares about!

Can you imagine what would happen if this generation of girls lived with the same passion and abandonment to God's purposes? Just think about all the positive change we would see in our world!

I believe a lot of this obsession with temporal things started in the 90's, when marketing guru's discovered a multimillion dollar industry that had not yet been tapped into. With rising stars like Brittney Spears, Mary-Kate and Ashley, and 'N Sync, marketing experts suddenly saw the dollar signs popping up for this new "preteen" market. When pop culture partnered with marketing experts, we were taught as young girls that shopping and making our *own decisions* in our favorite clothing stores would empower us and give us individuality. The power to choose between blueberry lip gloss or strawberry flavored was exciting! We were being treated like grown-ups, and now we had entire marketing campaigns devoted to us. With the rise of this "Girl Power" feminist movement, we learned that we could wear anything we want, date anyone we want, buy anything we want, and sleep with whoever we want. This major importance on beauty and individuality has not promoted us to the strong and powerful princesses we wish to be, but rather has demoted us to the likeness of selfish prostitutes.

As a teenage girl growing up in the midst of all this, I watched so many of my favorite, perky Disney Channel stars prance onto the stage, talking about modesty and Jesus and being the best "you" that you can be. Then several years later I watched them as they tragically tumbled out of the tower and become representatives of the same lies they used to speak out against.

This whole idea of conquering men, competing with our sisters, and elevating ourselves in our own power has got this generation of females in an UGLY situation. Sadly, the "ideal beautiful woman" has become a picture of someone who sucks away life rather than one who sacrifices everything to *give* life. Jealousy, envy, and a spirit of control which attempts to divide and conquer those around us, is like a leech. You know that something is wrong when women who have the "perfect beach bodies" are being celebrated and idolized more highly than those of the likes of Mother Theresa and women who give everything for the sake of those around them.

Proverbs 30:15 says, "The leech has two daughters, they cry "Give! Give!" Girls, let's be honest. We are obsessed with wanting more. More what? More purses, more clothes, more followers on Instagram, more attention, more beauty, more perfection. But this is *not* what God has created women to be! Our royal identity is quite different. Our original, heavenly purpose is for women to *give* life. We are to bear spiritual fruit and to adorn this world and the space around us with beauty and joy!

Lisa Bevere wrote, "Men plan wars, and women plan

weddings." We bring the sparkle and the decoration, and also the loving and nurturing touch to this world of men. We bring the dazzle, the glitter, and the glam! No offense to the guys out there, but can you imagine what this world would look like if men mostly planned weddings, decorated houses, and designed scrapbook paper? Our duct tape would perhaps still only be available in one color, there would be no pink bedrooms in the world, and all the cute stocking suffers that make us squeal at Christmas time would've never been invented! No adorable Post It Notes, colorful binders, or stickers to help us organize. What kind of a world would that be?!

Let's just be totally honest here... Adam's life was really quite dull until Eve came along. He probably saw everything in black and white, then when Eve appeared...BAM! Everything was in technicolor!

We as females were created to release SO MUCH life, joy, creativity, and beauty to those around us. Yes, we are the ones who can give birth physically, but something we don't talk about a lot is giving birth in the spiritual realm, which is the hidden, unseen place. Giving birth in the Kingdom of God, to Kingdom dreams.

"You did not choose me, but I chose you and appointed you so that you might go and **bear fruit** – fruit that will last – and so that whatever you ask in my name the Father will give you." (John 15:16) Isn't it interesting that females are the biggest consumers on this earth of product and resources, when we are supposed to be the ones who are GIVING the most?

We were created to be an amazing answer to this dying and hurting world, not the ones who are self-absorbed and sucking everything up around us.

"This was the sin of Sodom: she and her daughters were arrogant, overfed and unconcerned; they did not help the poor and needy."(Ezekiel 16:49)

Are we as Americans overfed and overstimulated? We have

been brought up with a consuming mindset rather than a giving mindset. Even the very food we eat and how much we eat of it is an example of our consuming mindset. Most of us have not been trained to think about where our food comes from or make sure that we are giving back and planting new seeds. But we simply consume. It's there, and so we eat.

But Kingdom Kids don't think like that. They are always in the giving mode! They know that God's abundance is like an endless sea, and there is no such thing as lack. They don't go out hungry; they get filled up in God's presence then they leave to minster to the world from the fullness of their cup running over.

Our problem? We are running out to the world before we have been filled up by Christ. So we look for boys, attention, food, more followers on Twitter, a new iPhone, friendships, and yes even ministry opportunities, to gobble up and fill our empty souls. The problem is that we are going out with the same mindset the world has, to consume and see how we can "get the most" out of our day.

But what would happen if our attitude was radically flipped upside down, and the purpose of each day was to, "Give, give, give, give, give?!" This takes faith! Faith that God is enough for us, and that He will be faithful to take care of us even when we pour ourselves out to others.

Hadassah is an amazing example of a young woman who was surrounded and daily bombarded by this life-sucking, leech mentality, yet she had the attitude of Christ. She was so humble and had the mindset of an ocean. She was always giving life to those around her! She held nothing back! She loved courageously, in her own unique way, and God promoted her to amazing places of influence and power because she had the attitude of a true Princess Bride.

In the following days we will look at what she did and how we can *use those same keys* to remove the leeches of selfishness from our lives, selflessly love like the ocean, be givers of life, and release those around us from bondage.

Day 17
For Those Who Cannot Speak

Every maid grew tired of their Queen's restless pacing. She had not slept for days. Her anxiousness was felt inside every servant who entered her room. Everyone was on edge. Their stomachs churned with hunger as they wondered what would be the fate of their Queen, the woman they had all grown to love and serve. But no one was quite as worried as Milcah.

"Mistress Esther," she urged, "please, you must eat something."

The third day of fasting was finally through, but Esther could not find her stomach. She felt as though she was like Daniel, about to be tossed into a lion's den.

"Not today," she stood up, head feeling a little dizzy from lack of food and acting more confident than she felt, "not until I speak with the King."

The compassionate, young women hurried themselves with her preparation. She must be made stunningly beautiful before she could see His Royal Majesty. They applied face paint, jewels, skin treatments, and selected the most alluring outfit they could find. When they were finished, everyone stood back and marveled at the work of art. Esther truly did look like a Queen.

"Continue to pray to my God for me," Esther faced her maidens bravely. "Pray that I might find favor in the eyes of my King."

The ladies nodded solemnly, eyes drooping and expressions glum, as if they had just prepared Esther for her funeral and burial.

Esther lifted her chin into the air, displaying a boldness she did not feel as she paraded out of her room. She floated down the marble staircase and into the King's courtyard. Questioning stares from busy maids and royal guards would've stopped Esther dead in her tracks if she had looked at them. But she didn't. She kept her eyes fixed ahead and marched forward. The fear that clutched her heart was like nothing she'd ever experienced before.

"Please Lord," she whispered as she continued moving forward, "be with me in this moment. Calm my anxious heart."

The fear didn't go away, but miraculously she kept moving, past the inner courtyard gates and to the outskirts of the King's chamber. As she stood boldly on the sidelines, she suddenly remembered to bow and humble herself before the King. Entering with a demanding attitude wouldn't get her anywhere.

She bowed in reverent fear, tiptoeing closer to the throne. The endless row of palace guards looked at the King for direction. Someone was intruding! What were they to do? Did they have the King's order to slay this woman?

She continued walking and nobody moved. She could only guess what had happened. The King had pointed his scepter toward her.

"What is it, Queen Esther?" the King asked. "What is your request? Even up to half the kingdom, it will be given you!"

Esther reached for the tip of the scepter and brushed it with her fingertips as she looked up. She trembled with fear as her body was overcome with adrenaline, and thanksgiving to her God! "If it pleases the King," she spoke softly, words dripping with gentleness, "let the King, together with Haman, come today to a banquet I have prepared for him."

"Well!" the King laughed, "What are we waiting for? Bring Haman at once! And let us go to this feast that my Queen has prepared!"

~*~

Haman's greedy eyes feasted on Esther. His brazen stare made Esther uncomfortable. She glanced at her King, hoping that perhaps Xerxes might say something in order to distract Haman's disgusting eyes. She could tell that the man was quietly undressing her in his mind and it made her shudder with disgust and terror. But apparently the King hadn't noticed. Servants busily refilled his wine goblet and he drank freely.

"Your Majesty, I am burning with envy for your wife. She is by far the most exotic beauty in the land. How did you find such a rare and stunning jewel?" Haman's slimy words made Esther squirm. "Perhaps she will perform a dance for us?"

The King glanced at Esther, "Perhaps I am a greedy King, but I prefer to keep Esther all to myself. No, she shall not dance for us tonight, perhaps another time. I enjoy speaking with my Queen; she has very wise things to say."

Haman laughed, slamming his wine goblet down, "When could a woman possibly have anything enlightening to say? Women are good for nothing other than…"

"Forgive me for interrupting, your Majesty," Esther cut off Haman's lewd comment, "if the King regards me with favor and if it pleases the King to grant my petition and fulfill my request, let the King and Haman come tomorrow to the banquet I will give them."

Great pleasure shone in Haman's eyes, and Esther tried her best to ignore him as she looked at her King.

"How do you feel about the matter, Haman?" the King asked his right hand man who had not taken his beady eyes off of her. "Shall we feast with my Queen again tomorrow?"

Haman quickly wet his lips before replying, "Yes. Yes we shall. And perhaps she may perform that dance you were speaking of."

~*~

The moment Esther returned to her bed chamber, Milcah embraced Esther with a sudden hug. "Oh, Mistress Esther!" she cried, "You are still alive!" The rest of her handmaidens were equally as pleased. They all rejoiced as they scurried around her.

"We shall not celebrate yet," she spoke solemnly as Milcah pulled away from her spontaneous hug. "Tomorrow evening we shall know if God is truly with me and our people."

~*~

After another long night and then an as dreadfully long afternoon, the evening finally arrived. This was the moment of truth. Everyone was more anxious than they had been before, and a spirit of dread settled over Esther's quarters like a thick blanket that made it nearly impossible to breathe beneath.

Esther replayed the possibilities of what she could say or do, over and over again in her mind. She would use anything she could to save her people. She used the only three things she had. First, food (for her King loved pleasure and desired to be satisfied at all times); second, her beauty with which the King was captivated by; and third, her words. She was even willing to dance for that disgusting Haman...anything she had to do in order to set her people free.

She rehearsed the scene ahead in her mind, remembering to use quiet words, speak in a convincing tone, and most importantly...rely on God and the prayers of her people. She breathed a quick prayer before leaving the safety of her chambers. She realized in a terrible moment that she might never return to this room again. If the King grew angry with her, these would be her last few moments in the palace.

"Dear God, Father of Abraham, Isaac and Jacob, you have been so faithful to your people. You were strong on behalf of Daniel when he entered the lion's den. Be strong and give me favor in this moment, I pray. Use me if You can." Everyone in her presence echoed an "Amen" as they joined Esther in agreement. They had promised to forfeit every pagan god and worship the One True God of Israel on behalf of their Queen. Most every servant now knew the best kept secret of Persia...Esther was a Jew. All the servants in charge of orchestrating and serving the grand feast downstairs were well aware of the drama which was predicted to play out onstage tonight, and they wouldn't miss a second of it.

Esther squeezed Milcah's hand before leaving the room. "May your God be with you, Queen Esther," Milcah tried to act brave as she fought back tears, "and may His right arm work strong on your behalf."

Esther forced a smile to her lips and felt such a desperation lurch inside her stomach. She must be successful in this moment. So many lives were at stake! If the King grew sore with her, everyone associated with the Queen would be killed as well. Every maiden who served her so sweetly and diligently would be treated as worthless garbage if she failed in this moment. She must speak now. She must be strong for Milcah, her maidens, and every other Hebrew sister that she had never met. She must put on her royal robes and exercise her true identity...that of a Queen.

With Milcah's image in her mind, she now found the courage to move forward. The sweet, innocent, fear-filled eyes of a young girl are what kept her walking forward into the King's presence once more. She prayed that it would not be her last time.

The banquet scene in the garden was abundantly luxurious. Flickering candles, rose petals floating in basins of water, and many other romantic elements dazzled beneath the evening starlight. The quiet summer evening offered no noises other than playful crickets chirping in the background, and man-made fountains and babbling brooks giggling throughout the garden. The canopy which was set up in the King's Courtyard had been adorned with a hundred-thousand red roses. Everything oozed with glamor, displaying the King's vast wealth, but the King was so used to surroundings such as this that it scarcely fazed him any longer.

Haman, on the other hand, was mesmerized. His heart swelled and puffed with pride like a pastry in the oven. Earlier that afternoon, Haman had told all his friends and relatives about this upcoming banquet with the Queen. Jealous stomachs grumbled as Haman described every dainty detail of the feast the evening before. Haman bragged about being the King's right hand man, the most trusted in the entire Kingdom, and showed everyone the King's signet ring.

Though he never spoke it aloud, Haman's next conquest was to move in on the King's Queen, Esther. There was nothing that he desired more (besides the King's kingdom), but that would all come in time, and he need only be patient and let the King play into his hand.

"Queen Esther," the King asked once everyone arrived and settled in with their wine, "what is your petition? It will be given to you. Even up to half the kingdom it will be granted."

The Queen quietly spoke, lifting brave eyes to meet the King's gaze, "If I have found favor with you, O King, and if it pleases your Majesty, grant me my life; this is my petition."

"Your life?" the King appeared very puzzled. "Why would I try to take your life? My dear Queen, whatever you've heard, you must be very confused. I would never harm you." He reached out to stroke her tender cheek, "I wouldn't dream of it."

"I and my people have been sold for destruction, slaughter and annihilation." She spoke firmly, "If we had merely been sold as male and female slaves, I would have kept quiet, because no such distress would justify disturbing the King."

There. She has said it.

King Xerxes set down his wine goblet. Was he hearing her correctly? "Do my ears deceive me?" His tone was calm at first, but sudden rage kicked in and the King was acting like his old self again. "Who dared devise such a plot against my Queen!? A trusted man in my palace, betraying and attempting to kill my Queen!?" He stood up and began pacing across the courtyard, "Who is he!?" the King shouted, "Where is the man who would dare do such a thing?!"

"Your adversary and enemy is this vile Haman," Esther spoke, words feeling like acid as they departed from her lips. She had wanted for so long to say it. And now she had. "Haman came to you with a petition, in order to annihilate the Jews. A harmless, forsaken people group. A humble people who would never mean any harm against the King and his ways. Haman brewed this plot in an evil, witch's caldron and now his wrath is about to be poured out upon my people. If you desire to kill the Jews, you must first kill your Queen."

"Please, please I beg you your Majesty," Haman was terrified and feared for his life, "I-I did not know! How could I possibly know that your Queen was a Jew?"

242

The King was beyond furious. He got up in a rage, left his wine, and stormed into the palace garden.

"You miserable wretch of a woman!" Haman hissed at her as he stood up and advanced toward the couch where Esther had been lounging, "You should've kept your mouth shut! The King would've never known that you were a Jew!"

"But I would've known," the Queen replied with defiance in the face of her enemy. "I do not answer to men such as yourself, but I answer to God, my Creator. He is the one who holds me accountable for all my actions and thoughts. I had to speak. If not, his chosen people may have perished."

"You should've feared for your life!" He shouted at her, shoving a finger toward her face. "And if you are as wise and cunning as you pretend to be, you'd best take back what you said and tell the King that it was all a terrible mistake. Because believe me woman…you are making a mistake! Your life is on the line, and I wear the King's signet ring. You'd best fear for what is ahead!"

"You have no right to speak to me in such a way!" the Queen asserted herself and ditched her flowery, quiet voice; "I am your Queen!"

"You are a worthless woman!" he snarled as he lowered himself over her, his voice quieted as he spoke in a sleazy tone, "Though I must say, you are blissfully enticing; a more fierce and flawless beauty I have never beheld. Perhaps, we could strike up a bargain and I could throw myself at your feet and beg for my life."

The Queen could smell his foul breath as his face inched closer to hers.

"Will he even molest the queen while she is with me in the house!?" the King's voice was suddenly heard, protective fury rose from the depths of his being, and his voice sounded like the roar of an angry lion.

Haman leaped back from where he had inched too close to the Queen; he shivered with fear, his brave act suddenly withering away to nothing. At the King's words, the Palace Guards rushed onto the scene and covered Haman's face with a cloth bag.

"Your Majesty," one of the eunuchs attending the King spoke, "a gallows seventy-five feet high stands by Haman's house. He made it for Mordecai, the one who spoke up to help the King."

"Hang him on it!" the King demanded. And that was that. Haman was whisked from the King's presence never to be seen again. His memory would be nothing more than a foul odor which no one would want to remember.

"Oh, my dear Queen Esther," the King hastened to her side, "he did not harm you, did he?"

"Only with his words, and I have long since decided that words are weapons that I give no mind to."

"Haman is gone now," the King softly stroked her face with the back of his finger. "We have nothing more to worry about. Set that pretty mind of yours to rest, and let us enjoy this banquet you have prepared!"

"I wish that were so," Esther replied sitting up, "but no document written in the King's name and sealed with his ring can be revoked." She suddenly fell to his feet, weeping, overtaken by the great loss of the tragedy ahead. "My life may be spared, but not that of my people. Innocent lives will be taken because of the influence of one man. A disgusting enemy who plotted against the King."

"Esther," the King stooped down to where she knelt, reached for her soft hands, and spoke tenderly, "Hush, my darling. You mustn't worry about what will become of your people. The Palace Guard can rescue any family members you may have and bring them here."

"They are all my family!" Esther proclaimed as tears streamed down her face, smudging her face paint, "Can't you see? If even one life is lost...if just one, precious, God-breathed life is taken, I shall never forgive myself."

"Esther, this is not your fault," the King replied. "These circumstances are entirely out of your control. As you said, a decree can never be revoked. It was a mistake to trust Haman. My mistake. Let me bear the burden. None of this is on your shoulders."

"No," Esther replied with a courage she didn't know she had, "God has placed me here for a reason. As Queen, it is my responsibility to stand up for my people, for those who cannot speak up for themselves. I will stand in behalf of the rights of all who are destitute. There must be a way."

She stood up and began pacing. King Xerxes only watched her with compassion, wishing that he could find a way to calm his distressed queen. Suddenly, it came to her.

"If it pleases the King" she bowed down once more, "and if he regards me with favor and thinks it is the right thing to do, let an order be written overruling the dispatches; that Haman, son of Hammedatha the Agagite, devised and wrote to destroy the Jews in all the King's providences. For how can I bear to see disaster fall on my people? How can I bear to see the destruction of my family?"

The King thought for a moment, then replied, "You have suffered much. There must be a way to make this up to you. Because Haman attacked the Jews, I will give his estate to you, Esther, and they will hang him on the gallows." He stood and began pacing as well, deep in thought, "Now, I will have Mordecai, a trusted Jewish friend, help you write another decree in the King's name in behalf of the Jews, as it seems best to you, and seal it with the King's signet ring. For as you said, no document written in the King's name and sealed with his ring can ever be revoked."

Esther's head popped up. She could not believe her ears. She would see Mordecai again! Not only would she see him, she would work with him to write a decree to defend her people! Her heart cried out in joy as she praised her king, and the one True King in Heaven, "Thank you, thank you, thank you! May the memory of your name be blessed forever! You have made Esther, your servant, very glad; and surely the God of the Jews will bless you and your Kingdom for showing mercy to His people!"

"Now," the King smiled, feeling quite pleased with himself, "come and let us enjoy this banquet that you have prepared."

Day 18
Slaying Fear

Hadassah's story never ceases to inspire me. The way that she placed herself on the line and surrendered everything just to rescue her people makes me want to ride out and be a hero. I desire to see that kind of greatness and bravery be released from my heart! But if you remember from our story that took place at the beginning of this book, there was a time when fear had literally killed me. As the sword of the enemy sliced into my heart, I didn't think I would ever be whole again. Being slayed by fear wasn't just a one-time event; there was actually a season in my life where dagger after dagger of disappointment was shoved into my soul.

If we want to be free and fearless, we have to face the spirit of fear head on, discover what the root of it is in our lives, and conquer it once and for all. I was shoved down and beat up by the spirits of oppression and depression. Because of all these traumatic, negative, and disappointing circumstances, I found myself battling so many dark thoughts. "What is wrong with me? Why isn't God moving on my behalf? Why is He so silent? Why are all these terrible things happening? Why have I been abandoned by my closest friends? Why do I feel the sting of betrayal? Why is it that the things I am believing for and so desperately want to see happen haven't come to pass yet?"

During this dark season in my life, I was deadly afraid of being disappointed. Because of my mega disappointment track record from the past, I felt that it was easier to not believe or get excited about anything. I tried to keep my emotions steady, and my heart protected. Instead of expecting good things to happen, I walked around like Mia, mumbling, "Someone sat on me again today." During this time, Holy Spirit spoke to my heart and said, "Cinderella, stick your feet in the air, and your shoes are going to meet you there."

It was a cute little phrase, but I wasn't sure what He meant by that. I was reminded of a scene in the movie, *Princess Protection Program,* in which Princess Rosie (Demi Lovato) must learn how to live life as a real girl. She goes incognito, as an undercover princess, and one of her first assignments is to play a casual game of bowling at the local alley.

Carter (Selena Gomez) begs her to "Just blend in." The problem? Princess Rosie didn't think like an average girl; and so when she entered the alley, she pulled herself up onto the counter and stuck her feet in the air! Carter freaked out, saying that *normal* girls put on their own shoes. But Rosie's high expectations attracted a kind and thoughtful "prince-in-training" who desired to reach Rosie in her lofty tower. He liked her high standards, and he rose to the occasion to accommodate her. He slipped those shoes right onto her feet!

The moral of this story? God was calling me to be more like Princess Rosie, and less like Carter. I knew what the Lord was asking me. He was asking me to trust Him like never before. He was asking me to dare to hope. He was asking me to dream bigger than I was comfortable with. He was asking me to *expect* good things to happen to me.

Our expectations in life are very powerful. Girls who expect to attract lousy dudes, do. Girls who expect to attract the God-fearing, Bible-believing man dressed in the shining armor of God, do. Girls who expect to be stuck in their small town for the rest of their life, are. Those who expect doors of opportunity to open, see those doors open, and they walk through them.

Our general mindset about life is VERY powerful. And as Princesses of the Most High God, we should have very lofty expectations as to how God will use us in this earth, where He will take us, and the opportunities He will give us to be a GOOD gift to those around us.

"As the Father has loved me, so have I loved you. Now **remain** in my love." (John 15:9) That word *remain* is so vital. When Holy Spirit reveals secrets about His love, and who He is, we must pitch a tent and remain there. We have to be so firm and solid, and stand on the truth of His goodness. One way we can do that is to meditate on His word. Jesus is the Word; so when we meditate on it, think about it, read it, and repeat it in our minds over and over again, the Living Word, Jesus Christ, talks to our hearts.

Today's devo is short because I want you to spend time meditating on God's abundant love today. The Bible says that His perfect love casts out ALL fear, and those who fear have not been made perfect in love. If you're battling against fear, fear of disappointment, or fear of failure, the bottom line is this: God wants to reveal His all-consuming love for you.

When we purposefully take time to ask the Holy Spirit to reveal His love, read Bible verses about His love, and listen to songs about His love, we are filled with fresh revelation of the way that He feels about us! When that happens, the spirit of fear has to flee.

I highly encourage you, as we end today, to make it your goal to meditate on one verse for *ten* minutes. Get in a really quiet place and ask the Lord to reveal what He desires. Pick one of the verses from below and choose to stay in the tower of His love!

"If you then, though you are evil, know how to give good gifts to your children, how much more will your Father in Heaven give good gifts to those who ask Him!" (Matthew 11:7)

"You make known to me the path of life; you will fill me with joy in your presence, with eternal pleasures at your right hand." (Psalm 16:11)

"And God raised us up **with Christ** and **seated** us with him in the **heavenly realms** in **Christ** Jesus." (Ephesians 2:6) I did this verse once a few years ago and wow! It will change your entire perspective on life. Remaining in His love fills us with such joy and peace, which then equips us to release that joy and peace to the rest of the world.

"And therefore the Lord [earnestly] waits [expecting, looking, and longing] to be gracious to you; and therefore He lifts Himself up, that He may have mercy on you *and* show loving-kindness to you. For the Lord is a God of justice. Blessed (happy, fortunate, to be envied) are all those who [earnestly] wait for Him, who expect *and* look *and l*ong for Him [for His victory, His favor, His love, His peace, His joy, and His matchless, unbroken companionship]!" (Is. 30:18 AMP)

Day 19
The 1 Peter 3:3 Strategy

Disappointments are inevitable. It's just a part of life. But we cannot allow the pain of past circumstances to shift the way that we see God. We must be locked in and laser focused on His love and His goodness.

I am about to hand you a secret strategy that will enable you to powerfully penetrate the evil in this world. This strategy is so simple it can be tempting to say, "That's it? I don't get it. What's so powerful about this?" This strategy will punch the enemy's Haman-style plan right in the stomach. This secret of royalty is like Esther entering the courts of the King to invite him to a feast. It seems simple. Yet it is dynamite.

I like to call it the secret of being a 1 Peter 3:3 girl. If you've read *Beauty Boys and Ball Gowns*, you might think, "Hey! This sounds really familiar! I've already read about being a 1 Peter 3:3 girl, I can go ahead and skip over this. But wait, don't do it! The reason I've included this strategy in both of these books is because I truly believe that it's a secret of royalty we can use to set SO many captives free! So if you've already heard this, read it again. Ask the Lord to give you deeper revelation into how this works, and what it can look like in your life!

1 Peter 3:3 says, "Your beauty should not come from outward adornment, such as elaborate hairstyles and the wearing of gold jewelry or fine clothes. Rather, it should be that of your inner self; the unfading beauty of a gentle and quiet spirit, which is of great worth in God's sight." This is not the kind of beauty that is being celebrated in the earth today. Tragically, most magazine covers and TV shows do not celebrate women of virtue. In our Hollywood-saturated culture, we choose who is celebrated. We crown them as queens and dub them "celebrities." The word

"celebrity" simply means, "one who is celebrated." In our culture, trendy outfits, catchy pop-songs, and push-up bras are what is being celebrated.

But we have the power to change that. We are Princesses. God celebrates us. And He wants us to show our little sister generation what they should celebrate as well. Little girls look up to older girls. They want to wear the same clothes as them, sing their songs, and act like they do. We've all seen this kind of behavior coming from the little girls in our lives. Whether they are obsessed with the latest pop stars or Queen Elsa from Disney's *Frozen*, little girls love to copy what they see in the older women around them! This is a totally natural, God-given desire in little ones. In fact, Titus 2 instructs: "Older women, [to] teach the younger women."

Little girls are more than eager and ready to learn. They desire to become what they see displayed and celebrated around them. This can be a wonderful thing, but depending on who they are emulating, this can also be a bit of a nightmare. Who is telling these girls what is beautiful? Who decides who will be celebrated and what "cool" is?

I used to be one of those wide-eyed little girls striving to become like my "cool big sisters" in Hollywood. I can only imagine how much I freaked out my poor mother when I came running out into the living room as an 8-year-old with my t-shirt rolled up, showing off my belly button, and preppy pigtails in my hair. I wiggled my hips around and said, "Look Mama! I'm Britney Spears!"

Little girls just want to be like their babysitters, their cool big sisters, and the teen-pop icons they see on TV. Sadly, the "babysitters" on TV and in the media are teaching our little sisters what being a girl is all about, and these messages are advancing the kingdom of Satan not the Kingdom of God!

In 1 Peter 3, the Holy Spirit reveals the powerful secrets to us of His Kingdom strategy in this hour. It shows us what we can do to be proactive and how to counteract the devil's twisted scheme. God does not desire for our little sisters to be sucked into this selfish, boy-obsessed, cruel, lying, manipulating culture. Thankfully there is a flip-side to every coin! In the same way that little girls want to run around and emulate their favorite girls on TV, they also desire to emulate us.

You, as a Princess, have been entrusted with an incredible sphere of influence. You might be thinking, "Okay, so maybe there are a few girls that I influence, but I'm not as powerful as the girl on the magazine cover! Don't I have to be a celebrity to have that kind of influence?"

Not at all! You're a Princess. You're the real deal. Whenever you reflect the beauty and splendor of heaven, your little sisters take note! That is not something that can be compared with Hollywood. Your realm of influence is so important, and God has given you the power to influence others in a unique and beautiful way. Don't despise it because it seems small. Trust me. It's not small.

The strategy of 1 Peter 3:3 is just like what Jesus did when He came to this earth. He dressed Himself in the garments of humility and did things so backwards and upside down! He positioned Himself to be the exact opposite of everything this world is about.

The world says a woman's beauty comes from the outside. God says it comes from the inside.

The world says a woman's utmost concern should be looking out for herself. God says her highest concern should be living selflessly, defending and protecting, uplifting and cherishing those around her.

The world says a woman's power is in her physical features. God says it is in her humility, when she "entrusts herself to the one who judges justly." (1 Peter 2:23)

The world will consume. We will give.

The world will be jealous and tear apart their sisters. We will build one another up in love.

The world will say it's so hopeless. We will say that saving one life is totally worth it.

The world says to freak out and worry. We only have absolute peace.

The world says to take matters concerning "finding true love" into our own hands, and to push to make something happen. We only wait for God's perfect timing.

The world says one human is worth less than another. We will declare that each life was worth the blood of Jesus.

This pattern of backwards, upside down, inside out living is like swimming upstream. It is not easy. But when we submit to God, declare His Words and His ways to be true as gold, setting an example for our little sisters, it is just like what Jesus did. It is the secret weapon of humility. If we can do this, we will be like dynamite in the hand of our God! Like small stones in the sling of David, the ugly giant will come down.

Princess Sisters, we must learn the secret and walk in the unfathomable power of being faithful and obedient in small, seemingly insignificant things. These things might be some of which the world will laugh and scoff at, but these little droplets of rain will suddenly create a storm of revolution!

1 Peter 3:5 continues, "For this is the way the holy women of the past who put their hope in God used to adorn themselves. They submitted themselves to their own husbands, like Sarah, who obeyed Abraham and called him her lord. You are her daughters if you do what is right and do not give way to fear." Isn't that interesting that Peter stresses, "Do not give way to fear"? Why does he say that?

Because this kind of 1 Peter 3:3 Princess living doesn't work if our knees collapse in fear. So many young ladies conform to the world's idea of what a strong, powerful, beautiful woman is because they are afraid of entrusting themselves to God and living with such silly, carefree, childlike faith.

Sometimes we act out of fear and insecurity thinking, "If I wait, I will never find my Prince Charming. I'm getting old; I need to make it happen. I need to help him along. I need to give him a hint. I need to wear more revealing clothes so I get more attention."

Or we battle thoughts like this: "I need to ignore the smelly kid by the trash cans because I might lose some good friendships if they see me with him. I need to buy myself a new pair of jeans instead of feeding a child in Africa because I'll look so uncool if I only have three pairs when all my friends have like twenty. I need to do what my parents want me to do with my life instead of following my God-given dreams. I can't witness to my friends because they might hate me. I can't wear a modest bathing suit to the pool because my friends will laugh at me. I just can't wait for my future husband because I feel like he's never coming. I can't NOT worry about this thing because it seems so irresponsible! I can't trade my Saturday night with my girls to read the Word and be alone with God because that's the only "me" time I have all week."

What do these words sound like? F-E-A-R. The Princess mindset is total abandonment of the world's ways and believing that He, whose name is Faithful and True, is going to write out a beautiful love story for you. Don't let fear and insecurity push you out of the palace. Keep your ground!

I envision this secret, quiet, backwards, Princess living to be a lot like what happened in *The Chronicles of Narnia: The Lion, The Witch, & The Wardrobe.* Aslan, the powerful lion, gave Lucy a little dagger. She gasped and said, "I don't know if I'd ever be brave enough to use it." It was a small tool, really, maybe enough to kill a mouse, but certainly not an army of bad guys who came storming toward her on horseback. But little Lucy reached for her dagger and held it out as if it was a powerful weapon. The men came barreling forward, hoof-beats pounding. She cringed, wanting to run, thinking about what might happen if the dagger didn't work. *What if the men run me over?* She was so, so tiny. But suddenly, at the most critical moment, Aslan came bounding into action. His love saved the day. Aslan devoured the enemy in the blink of an eye. Suddenly, the danger was no more.

I think of little Lucy and how silly and nonsensical she looked, holding out her dagger even though a battle was raging around her. That's what it looks like for us being 1 Peter 3:3 girls; people will roll their eyes and say, "How are you going to change the world by following God's ways? Dressing modestly? Choosing not to date? Submitting to your God? Choosing not to worry? What's that going to do?"

Sister, do not listen to those voices. Simply hold out your dagger of faith and purity, and say, "The Lord will perfect that which concerns me." (Psalm 138:8)

Princess, hold fast and steady. You never know how many little eyes are watching you in awestruck wonderment thinking, "Wow. She is so beautiful. She loves God so much; I want to be just like her someday."

When you defeat the enemy of fear in your life, you get set free to release others. Because isn't that what it's all about? Jesus said that He came to destroy the works of the devil, and that's what we are here for too. Royal Beauties are not made to sit on thrones, wear fancy dresses, sip tea and watch television. And while beauty and splendor and elegance are part of our God-given royal identity, we must take what He has given us and use it to set others free from their dungeons.

Day 20
Use Your Voice

I don't know about you, but I am very protective over my friends. I get crazy angry when the enemy tries to mess with them. I feel like a protective mama lioness in the African Safari who will pounce on any evil hyena that tries to mess with my girls!

I feel the same way about the girls of this generation. In the retelling of Hadassah's story that I shared earlier, I decided to add a character who wasn't in the Bible, but was so symbolic of what Hadassah was fighting for. Her little servant girl Milcah wasn't related to her by blood, but Hadassah felt a compelling love and responsibility to care for her, protect her, and fight for her. Are there girls in your life that you feel the same way about? Are there people that you care about, who if you discovered an evil plot to take their lives, you would do anything in your power to fight and free them?

I know the enemy would love to devour my little sisters, but my heart is determined to use every tool that God has given me to create a better world for them to live in. I want to pave their paths with truth, remove the rocks of hardship, and tell them everything that I wish I knew at their age. Do you feel the same way about your little sisters, cousins, or friends? It is my prayer that a fiery passion rise up in you, just like it did in Esther, when you see the ugly plot, so that you will SPEAK UP for those who cannot speak for themselves, and for the rights of all who are destitute.

Sister, one of the most powerful things you have is your voice. And even though the world might not be listening to what you have to say, you have a King who sits on the throne of heaven who has inclined His ear to you! King Jesus wants to hear your voice! Esther wasn't afraid to march boldly into the presence of the King (even though her King could have chopped off her head for coming unannounced), and we cannot be hesitant to come before our King! When Esther "put on her royal robes," she wrapped herself in her royal identity and entered His courts. Do you know what the King said? "What is it, Queen Esther? What is your request? Even up to half the kingdom, it will be given you." (Esther 5:3)

Wow! Up to half his kingdom! Talk about favor! She totally had his heart and attention. The same is true for us. Jesus said, "If you abide in Me, and My words abide in you, ask whatever you wish, and it will be done for you." (John 15:7)

We have been called for such a time as this to pray and take action. Hadassah had the heart of the King, and she interceded on behalf of those who could not speak up for themselves. We must wrap ourselves in our royal robes and enter the presence of the King to intercede for our lost generation. God is simply waiting for someone to enter and petition Him. He is more than eager to act!

"But why does God need my prayers?" you might ask. "He already knows everything, and sees the mess going on down here. Can't He just take care of things Himself?"

God wants us to partner with Him, because nothing can happen on this earth without someone opening up their mouth and speaking it into existence.

John Bevere said, "Spirits are like surfers. They are always looking for a wave to ride. The waves are the words that come out of your mouth." (This is true for both good spirits – God's ministering angels; and bad spirits – the devil and his army!)

The Bible says, "The highest heavens belong to the Lord, but He has given the earth to all humanity." (Psalm 115:16) God gave authority over the earth to Adam; Adam forfeited it to the enemy then Jesus took back that authority and gave it to us. The permission to write and create whatever is on the King's heart and bring it to pass on this earth is all ours! Let's be careful that we do not hand it back to the enemy. Our prayers are powerful! And they are needed to speak into existence and bring about God's beautiful story and purposes on this planet. When we come into the Lord's presence like Hadassah and petition our King, *things change*. Even though King X didn't change the law (kings can never go back on their word, remember?) which said a day of darkness and doom was coming, He added a new law which encouraged and equipped the people of that day. This is such a prophetic story because God is doing the same thing today! So many Christians hide in their hobbit holes, shaking with fear because of the doom and gloom on CNN, and are grappling with truth that things will only get worse before Jesus returns for His bride. They shrug their shoulders and say, "It's so hopeless. If God is just going to destroy the earth someday anyway, why are we even going to try to make things better?"

Many Christians think, "There are too many people in the world to feed them all. There are too many orphans and not enough families, so why should I adopt one when there will be a million more out there that I can never touch? Why fight human trafficking and petition God in prayer to end abuse in homes, when evil will always abound and only get stronger in the coming days?"

What if Hadassah had this attitude of complacency? The law was already in place. Things were going to be utterly horrifying. Her people were going to be massacred. What could she possibly do about it? But Hadassah worked with her King, and made a dent in the evil. They made a new law. A new law called *hope*. This law equipped the Jewish people to have a backbone and reach for their weapons.

Do you know what the new decree was? Simply this: *The Jews have the right to defend themselves. If you attack them, on this day of distress, they can attack you back.*

That was it. What was so powerful about that law? Surely it wasn't going to change anything. People were still going to get killed, right? The powers of darkness would still win wouldn't they? Well, the first thing the King did was make a public display of humiliating Haman, the enemy. He hung Haman and all his sons just to show they had been stripped of their power. Jesus has done the same in our battle! He totally dismantled and humiliated the enemy. He stripped that authority away from him and handed it to the descendants of Adam. This shifted everything. The whole game was changed. Jesus said, "I've given you authority to overcome all the power of the enemy." This put the *fight* back in God's children. This caused them to reach for their swords, and say, "It ain't over 'til it's over!"

The Jews did the same thing. They were empowered with *faith*, and fear was driven away. In fact, the enemy was shaking in his boots, and people were much too terrified to even think about attacking this people group now, because the King was behind them! The Jews had so much support and reinforcement that the enemy now dreaded the idea of trying to take them down.

Do you see the parallel in this story with what God is doing today? We have been equipped and empowered. Our hearts have been strengthened with a radical hope. We have laced up our battle boots and let out a war cry. We are not going to let the enemy trample over our sisters and torment them in fear! We've been given authority over that, and God is backing us up!

When we petition the King in prayer, things most certainly change. Sometimes He changes the situation, and sometimes He changes us. He is faithful to give us heavenly strategies that will outsmart the plans of the enemy.

"For this is the way the holy women of the past who put their hope in God used to adorn themselves. They submitted themselves to their own husbands, like Sarah, who obeyed Abraham and called him her lord. You are her daughters if you do what is right and do not give way to fear." (1 Peter 3) The servants in Hadassah's palace must have said, "What is this chick thinking?! She's trying to save the world through serving fancy banquets? Muffins and meat have nothing to do with this!" Oh, but Hadassah knew. She had divine wisdom. She knew that timing, patience, and trust had *everything* to do with it.

The power lies in our faith. As we continue on in our unshakable, resolved desire to surrender our lives and please the Lord as 1 Peter 3:3 girls, holding out our little daggers, Aslan will suddenly come prancing out of the woods behind us and take down the enemy. It truly is a beautiful thing. We get to let Him be the hero. So let's not give way to fear.

We've got to remember that God's ways are *so* much higher than our ways. If you're doubting the true power of what Princess living and being a 1 Peter 3:3 Girl can actually do in this world then let's look at some examples.

Peter gives us the model of a woman who adorned herself with this kind of beauty that is precious and valued in God's sight. Her name was Sarah. Sarah was a barren woman who had a promise from God. She was promised that she would give birth to a son, but it just *wasn't* happening. She tried to take matters into her own hands (you know, just like the world advises us to do!) and that made things even worse. She urged her husband to sleep with another woman, Hagar. When Hagar finally gave him a son, Sarah hated Hagar and abused her in bitter jealousy. Then when Sarah was told that she would finally have a son, she laughed in bitter doubt. Sarah's barrenness swallowed up every area of her life. She had gotten so old and wrinkly everything seemed dead and hopeless. She made a lot of bad choices. But what did she do that was right? Why would Peter highlight her in this verse as an example?

The Word says, "She submitted herself..." Here we find that Sarah did the only thing that truly matters in her story. She *submitted* herself to Abraham and came under his covering. You see, Abraham was a man of radical faith, and his faith was credited to him as righteousness. (Romans 4:22) The blessing and favor that Abraham received from God spilled over onto his wife.

In Hebrews 11:11 it says, "By faith Sarah herself also received strength to conceive seed, and she bore a child, when she was past the age, because she *judged Him faithful* who had promised." Abraham led the family with triumphant faith which eventually rubbed off onto Sarah and spilled into her soul. She judged God faithful and submitted herself to whatever it was that He was writing in her life!

So what about us? How is this story applicable to our lives? We have all experienced the pain of spiritual or emotional barrenness. We all, at times, have lived like leeches, with a sucking self-focus that zapped the life out of ourselves and the people around us. Instead of *giving* abundant life, we took life. In the same way that it was Sarah's destiny to give birth to something beautiful, the same is true for us!

But what does it look like to bear spiritual fruit? Galatians says that this fruit is "love, joy, peace, patience, gentleness, goodness, faith, meekness, and self-control." These fruits of the spirit are living and active; they are not just character traits or things we try to produce in ourselves. They are things that flow from an intimate relationship with Jesus and then suddenly come alive in us, to touch this world in a powerful and unforgettable way.

LOVE changes the world; it reaches out to the hurting and broken. Love is the power to change everything because Love is the life source of the Kingdom of God.

JOY encourages people and totally makes their day. Joy is strength!

PEACE gives someone the freedom from anxiousness, fear, and depression.

PATIENCE shines the image of Christ and draws people to His

heart.

GENTELENESS can win the hearts of kings and influence people who need to know God's kingdom ways.

FAITH can move mountains and clear the way of "impossibility" for captives.

MEEKNESS is like Lucy standing there with the dagger. The meek inherit the earth!

SELF-CONTROL is what keeps a couple pure until they reach their marriage bed. It's what keeps people standing to believe that God's promises are better than anything the world may tell them.

All of these fruits have massive influence on the people around us.

Jesus Christ has things He wants to birth in your spirit, and the fruits of the spirit are only the beginning! He wants to use you to touch this world in such a unique way; He wants to give you ways to advance the Kingdom of Heaven, spiritual strategies in prayer, ideas to feed the hungry, new inventions to make life easier in third world countries, divine strategies to release captives from human trafficking, songs that will pierce the hearts of the lost and draw them to God, books to write that will change people's lives, or a movie to direct that will reflect and represent the Father. There is SO much He wants to birth in you!

I like to call these "spiritual births" *dreams*. Sarah's dream was to have a son. Perhaps your dream is to become a missionary, open a dance studio, write a novel, or be happily married someday with a house full of kiddos. Whatever your dream is, it was placed there for a reason. Your dream is never just for you. Joseph's dream was to become a leader, and God used him to save a whole nation of starving people. If you give yourself to Him as a living sacrifice, your dreams can be used to save a whole generation.

I used to be afraid to talk about my dreams. I was like Sarah, who was afraid to believe they could really be as big and beautiful as she hoped. The enemy wanted me to stop talking about these things that God placed deep in my heart for me to birth someday. But God wants us to talk about these things with Him! He wants us to make royal decrees and speak them out into existence in our world! He wants us to write about them, think about them, and talk about them.

Don't allow discouragement or barrenness to steal your voice because life and death is in the power of your tongue! Don't be like Ariel from the *Little Mermaid* who gave her voice to the enemy. Don't allow the enemy to speak words of fear and doubt through you. Your voice is SO powerful. Guard it at all costs. Then use it with Jesus! Speak those things that are in your heart. Shout them to the sky! Let the earth hear and respond to the sound of your voice.

Sarah struggled with doubt but she submitted herself to Abraham, and as she rested under his covering, she was blessed and her dream came true. This is what we can learn from Sarah. It's all about faith. And if you don't think you have enough faith, rest in Jesus' faith. He has enough faith for the both of you! Crawl up beneath His covering, get real close, and decide not to be moved from that place! It's okay to pray, "Jesus, I know you placed this dream inside of me, but I need You to make it happen. I cannot! In my own strength, I might do something stupid and create an Ishmael instead of an Isaac. I don't want to give way to fear, so give me fresh revelation about how faithful you are! I will, just like Sarah, judge you faithful! I want to give life and be barren no longer!"

Fear attempts to make us believe that these God-given dreams inside our hearts will never come to pass. It can be SO hard to trust our Daddy, especially after being barren for so long. When we've experienced past hurts and disappointments and even aborted dreams, it can be hard to dream again.

I encourage you to read all of Isaiah 54. It's such an amazing passage! It's about a new season of promise. Stay close to Jesus, and new life will spring forth! Sister, it is time to SING! It's time to SPEAK of those dreams He has placed inside you because they *are* for such a time as this!

Day 21
Worship No Matter What

Barrenness. Disappointment. Waiting. Believing. And then waiting some more. Hannah (1 Samuel) knew a thing or two about barrenness and disappointment. Her only dream in life was to have a child. The desire of her heart was simple, yet meant the whole world to her. So why couldn't she have it? Why were the other women around her rejoicing and dancing as their dreams came true, yet she was still waiting for the fulfillment of her dream?

Hannah's husband, Elkanah, knew how heartbroken she was and he asked, "Aren't I better to you than ten sons?" The irony of it all was that Elkanah's other wife was blessed with sons *and* daughters. The one thing that Hannah wanted more than anything, children, were abundant and flowing over in Peninnah's tent. It was beyond unfair.

Why did Peninnah have such favor? Why was she so blessed? And why was it that Hannah was forgotten?

1 Samuel 1:5 says, "But to Hannah he gave a double portion because he loved her, and the Lord had closed her womb." What? *The Lord* closed her womb? *The Lord* was the One who restricted and held back those blessings, while Peninnah danced around in abundant joy? I think we can all relate with Hannah's story. We've all walked through those moments in life, where the one thing we want more than anything, our heart's cry and our greatest dream, is shut off and closed up to us. We cannot access it, and as if that didn't hurt badly enough, one of our sisters ended up with the SAME blessing that we were asking for!

Yes, we have all felt the sting of watching a friend get married before we do, watching someone else land our dream job, standing on the sidelines while someone else gets promoted, noticed, and adored. Why is it that the Lord seems to be handing out everything we're praying for to other people?! Why are their most wild and wonderful dreams coming true while we are left on the barren shores of disappointment?

"The boundary lines have fallen for me in pleasant places." (Psalm 16:6) The Lord closed Hannah's womb. The Lord decided that your friend should be married before you. The Lord removed that relationship that you were so dependent upon. The Lord said "no" to an opportunity that you were so crazy excited about. The Lord is the one who placed those boundary lines for that season.

What? No! Sometimes we can grow so incredibly frustrated with the boundary lines of the Lord. The lot of land that we've been given in life can sometimes feel small, restrictive, and hidden. Sometimes we can ask questions like, "Why are only three girls coming to the weekly Bible Study I'm hosting? Why do I only have 35 views on YouTube? Why didn't my youth pastor ask me to share at our youth rally but asked my best friend to lead worship instead? Why am I *still* waiting for my dreams to break lose and send me soaring? Why do I still feel so barren?"

The Apostle Paul said that he learned the secret to being content in every situation (Philippians 4:12) and he admonished us to do the same. But how? It's so frustrating to be barren and heartbroken, especially when the enemy comes along and reminds us about everything that we are missing out on. "Look at all the fun you could be having if you were dating around! Look at the friendships you have lost, and the opportunities that God handed off to someone else. He doesn't really care about you. He is holding back good, wonderful blessings from your life; He doesn't want you to have them. Your dreams are never going to happen. Just look at all your friends and the people around you. The Lord is blessing and promoting them, but He has clearly forgotten about you!"

But that is when the Lord whispers to our souls, "Aren't I better to you than ten sons? Aren't I more important to you than ten blessings? Don't you want me more than ten dreams coming true? The boundary lines that I have placed in this season are for YOUR GOOD. If I opened up the Promise Land to you all at once, the beasts would overtake you. (Exodus 23:30-31) I will drive out the enemy from before you, little by little, one step at a time, and expand your territory! I will stretch out your borders, and give you the land of your dreams, but you MUST remember that an inheritance gained quickly in the beginning is not blessed in the end. (Proverbs 20:21) This is a most beautiful and glorious process! I have promised to make everything beautiful in ITS TIME. (Ecclesiastes 3:11) The boundary lines have fallen for you in PLEASANT places because you are with Me! Wouldn't you rather be in my presence in a challenging place than in the middle of the Promise Land without me? I want YOU more than I want anything else. (John17:24) What do you want? Me, My presence and My love? Or do you just want my gifts, promises and blessings? All of these blessings will come in time, but I am a jealous God! I want you to seek Me first. Before I bring your husband, before I launch your career, before I make your dreams come true, I want you to fall in love with me! Seek Me first and all these other things shall be added unto you."

King David understood this barren season of life as well. After the exciting proclamation that he would be King, young David was all pumped up and ready for his wildest dreams to come true! He was given the promise, but first he had to go through the process. And so, he returned to the stinky sheepfold where he had been his entire life. Even though he was a King, his boundary lines for that season had fallen in a pasture. It was an opportunity for David to be faithful with what was entrusted to him. David wrote Psalm 37 expressing how he was simply dwelling in the land, being content, and doing good, blooming where he was planted! He was going to trust God, sing, dance, worship and enjoy safe pasture! Even when it looked like nothing was happening, even when disappointment tried to discourage him, David set his heart upon one thing knowing and worshiping the King of kings!

When David worshiped in spite of his circumstances, he was not being passive and apathetic. He did not adopt a negative attitude thinking, "Well, if God hasn't moved yet, I guess I'm gonna be stuck here for a long time. I'd better hunker down and get used to these sheep because I don't know when God is going to move. I don't want to push anything so I'm just going to go with whatever happens."

No way! It was just the opposite! When David worshiped in the midst of his barren season, that was his warfare! He was believing for change, petitioning for change, and FULLY convinced that the Lord would come through for him! The fullness of that promise would be seen in his life because He who spoke it was faithful!

Hannah petitioned heaven for her breakthrough. She went up to the temple and poured out her soul to the Lord. "In bitterness of soul, Hannah wept and prayed to the Lord." Sisters, we must lift up our voices of intercession. Just because there are boundary lines in our life right now, does not mean that God wants us to stay here! The Lord is all about expansion and launching out to take new land! But before we expand the gardens He has given us, we must learn to be faithful with the garden we already have!

The barrenness that Hannah experienced was not a punishment from God. It was not God's will that she be barren and miserable forever. It wasn't like he had predestined her misery, and then one day she prayed so hard that it changed God's mind. The Lord had fully planned to bless her with a child all along! He wanted her dreams to come true! He loved Hannah so much and wanted to give her the desire of her heart! So why did he close up her womb in the first place?

Barrenness and disappointment is an opportunity for our character to grow and develop like never before. It is truly a blessing in disguise. Without barrenness, we will not bear the fruit of desperation. And we must be desperate for God. We must be desperate for His presence. We must fully rely on Him and Him alone. We must fully rely on His Spirit, not on our own strength! Just think, if Hannah's womb wouldn't have been closed, and if her promise wouldn't have been delayed...what glory would that be? Hannah's story would be just another tale of a lady who got married and had a child. Instead the Lord used her story to inspire thousands; teaching an amazingly important lesson about how he positions us to develop many fruits! Fruits of patience, joy, long-suffering, peace, goodness, faithfulness, thankfulness, and most importantly...total dependence on God! God got ALL the glory out of her baby's birth, and God can get ALL of the glory from your miracle too, if you let Him develop what He desires to grow inside of you!

Hannah offered her baby Samuel to the Lord. She knew that her blessings were not her own. It was simply a gift given to her to steward. But it was a gift that she had to cry out for and pay a price of patience and FAITH to receive! She had to wait and believe, then wait and believe some more. But that made the gift so much more precious when it finally came.

"The Lord is gracious and full of compassion, slow to anger and abounding in great mercy. The Lord is good to all, and His tender mercies are over all His works." (Psalm 145:8-9) Sweet sister, the Lord loves you SO much, and He truly does want to bless you. He wants those dreams and desires He has placed inside of you to come to pass. But the King is endeavoring to get us to the place where He can *safely* give us every good and every perfect gift.

Any good father knows that if he gives his daughter a check for *ten million dollars* he would be putting her at great risk! If she's never handled that kind of money before, how could she possibly be a good steward of that blessing? She would have friends (and enemies) coming out of the woodwork to ask for a chunk of change, steal from her, and convince her to spend it on all sorts of foolish things. Boys would start lining up at her front door, asking to date her; not because they're in love with her heart, but want a piece of her treasure. Ultimately, what was supposed to be such a great and glorious gift could severely hurt her.

We've seen far too many young starlets in Hollywood have their innocence stolen, purity compromised, hearts shattered, and families destroyed because a "good and perfect gift" was given to them far before they had the character, wisdom and grace to handle it! We are daughters of the Most High King, and the Lord desires to bless us far beyond all we can ask, imagine, or think. I can promise you this my sister: He is NOT going to disappoint us. The season you're in right now is simply a training ground for what is to come.

David took his "boundary lines" seriously. He took stewardship over the pasture that he was given. When a lion came to devour one little lamb, he went after it. He didn't shrug and say, "Eh, I only have three sheep coming to my Bible Study. It's not like I'm speaking in front of a crowd of hundreds of people. It's really not a big deal." He didn't think, "My following is really small. I'll wait and get serious about God when I'm actually walking in the fullness of my dreams."

He was fierce, passionate, and faithful to fight for the ONE. To be faithful in the NOW. What David did in the hidden secret place, where nobody clapped and nobody cared, God saw. The Lord saw David's tenacity, boldness, and faith to go after that lion! The Lord saw Hannah's faithfulness in the hidden place of intercession! The Lord SEES your faithfulness as you pray for the three girls who come to your Bible Study. The Lord SEES every quiet, hidden act of worship from your heart. He SEES and He is keeping a Master account of everything!

Sisters, we have to get this. It's not about the crowds. It's not about the promotion. It's not about the situation you are in, or the way you were treated unfairly by so and so...It's about the quiet movements and attitudes of our hearts in the place that nobody sees. It's about how you react when you're rejected. How you react when you're applauded. How you react when your best friend gets promoted. How you react when your enemy gets blessed. How you react when you feel like giving up.

What is the reaction the Lord is looking for? WORSHIP. He simply wants to know that our hearts are truly and fully His NO MATTER WHAT. In big crowds, no crowds, lots of friends, no friends, children, no children, blessing, no blessing, marriage, no marriage, justice, injustice, joy, pain...

Will you worship?

Day 22
Patient Princess

Let's look back and think about what we have learned so far. What does this 1 Peter 3:3 Princess Bride look like?

We have learned that she is a woman who lays down her life for her friends. She is a woman who believes in the dreams God has placed inside of her and chooses to uses those dreams to serve those around her. She is a woman who SPEAKS UP for those who cannot speak for themselves in both prayer and in practical actions, being a radiant and glowing example for her little sisters in Christ.

We have learned that true beauty is not a magazine cover. True beauty is a Princess with a big, messy bun on her head, sweat running down her face, and her eyes glowing because she's been serving all day long; laying down her life for the sake of love. We have learned that if we are fearless, just like Hadassah, we are going to change this world.

I think the Proverbs 31 Woman is really the epitome of everything a 1 Peter 3:3 girl is. Now would be a great time for you to read that whole chapter. She is surely a woman who takes action! It's quite the delicate balancing act between taking action and waiting on the Lord. There are some things that God is waiting for us to do, and other things that we must wait for Him on.

For example, we can look at Rebekah by the well. Rebekah was waiting for her future man, but she wasn't doing nothing while she was waiting. She was found by a deep well, giving drinks to the cute lil' camels! We can do the same thing by filling ourselves with the pure water of the Word and giving the Word to those around us. Let's be faithful right where we are planted with all the little things, and He will be faithful to write the stories of our lives exactly how He sees fit!

Though we've already discussed this briefly, I felt it important to bring it up one more time. I believe this speaks volumes to this world about how God's Kingdom works. And that is, choosing to wait for your future husband.

When it comes to doing things the Princess way, I'm going to be totally blunt here: chasing after guys is NOT the Princess way. You may disagree with me and think that the concept of "waiting" might seem wimpy or old-fashioned, but it's very backwards for us to be chasing guys. In fact, I believe that it violates God's divine order of how things are to be. While it's true that guys are faster than us, and we won't be able to catch them anyway, we must see how dishonoring it is to the guys in our lives to attempt and take over their God-given role.

Guys were created to SEEK out the one God has for them; to look around, go hunting for her, and attempt to win and capture their heart. They enjoy chasing and pursuing females, as well as the wild pursuit of conquering other dreams and challenges in their lives. They have a God-given desire to set out on a righteous conquest and take the land! It's not right for us to try to take that away from them.

In our world's attempt to push feminism and "girl power," we've taught our younger generation that guys are so dumb they won't even know you are interested unless you take over his role and start pursuing him. The media has been telling us for so long that males need to be "trained" and "mastered" by us girls, and we have started to believe it! Sadly, so have the guys. The enemy has launched such a cunning attack to twist the gender roles and shift the way that we see one another.

This is such a blow to the sons of Adam! When we chase them, we are quietly telling them, "I know you're not capable of knowing you need me without me showing you how much you do!" We've been taught that using the powers of manipulation and flaunting our own sexuality will be the only way to get what we want.

Seriously?! We might as well just buy ourselves the ring, tell him where to take us on our dates, tell him how to propose, and where to take us on the honeymoon. Too many ladies are wearing the pants in the relationship, which gives the guys the opportunity to shrug and say, "Huh. I guess I don't have anything to worry about. She seems to have everything under control. I'll just let her take the lead..."

When we chase and pursue guys we are unknowingly helping them shut down and turn off that God-given gift and ability to set out, conquer, pursue, take the land, and be victorious! So often we complain about not being treated like Princesses and sigh about what life must have been like to be rescued by the knights of old. "A man was so brave and fearless back then! He would win wars, just to prove his love to his ladyhood." Pretty swoon-worthy, huh? But sisters, some guys would do the same thing for us today, if we would only sit still long enough for them to do so!

One of my favorite quotes is, "When a culture of ladies arise, a culture of gentlemen will follow." Jesus said the Kingdom of Heaven is like a man who finds a costly stone in a field. The man then goes out and sells everything he owns, in order to get his hands on the jewel. The right guy will be willing to sell everything, and pay any price, in order to call you his own.

I believe that waiting for a relationship like Isaac's and Rebekah's, trusting the Holy Spirit to do His divine matchmaking, speaks *so* much to this world about the Kingdom of Heaven and the heart of God. Choosing to do this in *your* life would be such a grand testimony to your cousins, little sisters, friends, and unsaved relatives.

God designed marriages to be a beautiful reflection of the relationship between Jesus and the Bride. Even the most glorious wedding and strongest marriage relationship pales in comparison to the beauty meant for our relationship with Jesus. This was and still is intended to send a message of God's love to the world! If you allow God to write your love story, this can be a powerful weapon in a world that devalues marriage, love, gender roles, and the priceless gift of your virginity. The world tells us that this is all so cheap and common. But when we place a high value back onto these things such as love, marriage, and our own personal purity, the world will certainly take note. When we say, "This is totally worth the wait," the world will begin to wonder why we place such a high worth on true love in the first place.

Allowing a young man to search for you, sacrifice his all, and pursue you like a field with a diamond in it, allows God to paint a picture on the easel of this earth of just what He did to pursue us. This will give a young man an amazing opportunity to have the absolute honor of being "made in the image of God," by doing something just like his Heavenly Daddy would! For him to learn to love like Christ does, selflessly and fearlessly, how could we possibly rob that from him? Sisters, if we step into the role of the man, we will be responsible for stripping away his honor, tenacity, and God-given command to lead.

Don't listen to the lie that says the little things don't matter. They *absolutely* matter. Do you remember what happened when Hadassah stepped into *her* role? Mordecai was promoted into *his* role.

God desires that some special young man be given the absolute honor of pursuing you, wooing you, and capturing your heart. Step fully into the *patient princess* role, and he will be exalted into *his* own courageous role of head and leader! Then, when the two of you set out as one to change this world, you can be under the same mission as him! Do your part, and God will surely cast the role of your Prince Charming at just the perfect time.

Why are we so afraid to trust Jesus with our love life? He is the Creator! Wouldn't He know better than anyone, who we will be perfectly suited for? He knows who will complement you, make you laugh, encourage you to try harder, and sharpen you like iron.

He's got a good and perfect gift being prepared for you! So do a guy a favor, and hold tight until he arrives.

Day 23
Standing in Purity

Ready to dig into some more dynamite? This final section of our book will shed more light on why choosing purity, being a 1 Peter 3:3 Girl, and doing things God's way is such a bomb to the enemy's plans.

Let's begin by reading Revelation 17:1-6. This passage talks about an evil, demonic stronghold which will rule over the people of the earth in the last days. She is described as riding a beast, an absolute harlot, who has committed fornication with the kings of the earth. This description is clearly gross and repulsive. Her name is: "MYSTERY. BABYLON THE GREAT. THE MOTHER OF HARLOTS AND OF THE ABOMINATIONS OF THE EARTH." Yikes, what a terrible thing to be. The Mother of Harlots. The part that makes me absolutely cringe is verse 6, "I saw the woman, drunk with the blood of the saints and with the blood of the martyrs of Jesus."

So what in the world is this thing? I'm sure many scholars have argued and debated about whether this passage is supposed to represent a spirit, a real monster, a figure of speech, or a literal demon woman; but whatever it is, it makes me shudder. Why? Because the effects of this happening can already be seen on the earth. Our generation is absolutely obsessed with sex. I debated about whether to add this to the book or cut it out because it feels so controversial and perhaps a little too blunt. But if the church isn't going to speak about these issues then who is?

So last summer, I was mindlessly channel surfing, searching for something good to watch, when a talk show popped up on the screen. I don't even know what show it was or what channel it was on. I didn't have time to notice because my jaw was literally hanging on the floor. On this public television broadcast, a man joked about his favorite hobby being pornography. I flipped off the TV as fast as my fingers could scramble to the remote, and I stared at the blank screen, totally dumbfound. The audience had laughed as this man and a few of his friends joked about the pleasures of looking at naked women in their free time.

There was no PG-13 icon in the corner of the screen, and the talk show treated this topic as if it belonged in everyday casual conversation. This was a totally, socially acceptable "hobby," and a man talked about this freely in front of the whole world. People patted him on the back with their reassuring sounds of laughter and applause, telling me that the world has officially lost its marbles.

"I don't get it," you might say. "What's the big deal? Sexual stuff is on the TV all the time. TV shows and movies make jokes and comments, and we hear it in our music, see it on magazine covers, it's on the internet, it's on our iPhone's...it's everywhere. Where have you been?! Living under a rock somewhere? Oh, you sheltered homeschooler; this kind of thing is in our faces all the time. We've just gotta ignore it. What's the problem?"

The problem is this: the fact that we don't see this as a problem. The crisis of the hour is so perfectly described by one of my favorite authors, Lisa Bevere. In *Kissed the Girls and Made Them Cry* she wrote, **"When femininity and virtue are no longer honored as noble, women are tempted to turn to the lesser powers of seduction and slip on the garments of sensuality. If women never connect with the purpose for their feminine beauty, honor, and dignity, they become incredibly vulnerable to sexual exploitation. Unfortunately we have not given our young girls images of females clothed in purity, beauty, and strength."**

Where are our images of females clothed in purity, beauty and strength? The only role models out there to show our little sisters what 1 Peter 3:3 living looks like is us. That's right. *We* are the Princesses who must model what being a daughter of the King is all about. If we want to combat this beast of sexual immorality that is infiltrating our culture, we must be a powerful force of purity to be reckoned with.

"Livy" you might say, "I know you're all into changing the world, but there are some things we just won't be able to change. You cannot force your beliefs on other people, and sin will always be sin. We can be in the world but not of it. Why should we be passionate about combating sexual immorality? What people do behind closed doors isn't hurting anybody, it's not like it matters to the rest of the world."

Trust me, sister. It matters. My heart is broken over the number of young girls who are sexually abused in their own *homes*. The one place they were supposed to be safe and protected is where they were betrayed by the men who were supposed to protect and take care of them. Does this not absolutely rip your heart out of your chest? Perhaps even worse are the rising horrors of human trafficking. Human trafficking generates $9.5 billion dollars yearly within the United States, (According to thecoveringhouse.org, cited from the United Nations). An average victim of this torture and outrage may be forced to serve men anywhere from 20 to 48 times a day (according to the Polaris Project). This is modern day slavery! And this is happening *every day*, all over the world. Eastern Europe, Africa, and Asia are hot-spots for this abomination. Young girls are often sold, kidnapped, and betrayed by their very only family members. Others are often deceived into believing if they go with these convincing stranger that a new job or opportunity for education is waiting for them. Instead they are whisked away and illegally transported over borders, sometimes hundreds and even thousands of miles away from their home. They are drugged, abused, and terrorized for years. This is happening *right now* to girls and guys who are *exactly* your age.

When I first learned about the horror of trafficking, I had to ask God, "Why?! How?! How could a good Father POSSIBLY let something like this happen and run rampant on the earth? Don't you love your girls?" His reply was, "Of course I love them. That is why I have put *you* on the earth as an answer." **Sisters, we are the answers. God created *you* to be a specific, tailor-made answer to someone's most heart-wrenching and devastating problem.** We have to realize how powerful that is! We might not be able to touch the whole world or even a country throughout our whole lifetime, but one life can surely touch another. Even if you allow yourself to be an answer for just *one girl*, you are making a dent in the evil of this world! The Bible says to overcome evil with good. There are SO many ways that we can combat human trafficking and other modern evils. We just have to put our heads together, join together with our sisters, get creative, ask God for answers, and GO!

One of the ways that I believe we will resist this monster of fornication and sexual obsession in our world is to STOP supporting it. Sisters, we must refrain from listening to music that has sexual themes, watching movies, TV shows, and reading magazines that support the "THE MOTHER OF HARLOTS." Not all of us will have the opportunity to minister to prostitutes or open Safe Houses, but we can each make *daily* choices to promote purity and righteous living. We can STOP watching any music videos that suggest a woman's power lies in her sexuality. We can petition our favorite clothing stores to play cleaner music or ask them to offer more modest outfit choices.

We must rise together and take a stand to let Hollywood know that we are not okay with the way they portray women in the media. **We must cultivate within our own hearts and create a culture of honor, purity, and beauty that raises the bar for everyone around us.** Choosing to dress modestly and not be a stumbling block for the guys around you is *huge*. There are so many seemingly "small" things that we can each do to make a huge dent in what is happening. There are already examples of this. One mom told her local high school that her children would not participate in some of the inappropriate content which was 'required reading' and asked for an alternative reading instead. After she made that choice, many other moms hopped on board as well. Nicole Weber, founder of *Project Inspired*, launched *Project Cosmo*, to petition Cosmo Magazine to add an 18+ warning on their magazine and not be in view of innocent eyes at the grocery store.

At the very least, we can stop supporting these magazines, movies, and media sources that are sending out the wrong messages! We absolutely cannot participate in or support sexual immorality in any way, shape, or form if we don't want to be part of the problem and considered responsible for adding fuel to the fire of sex trafficking. Experts believe that this crime against humanity is highly driven by the porn industry, and those sexual fantasies come from what we see portrayed in movies and media. These sexually charged images stir up desires that cannot be righteously fulfilled and so many are willing to pay cash for a night of "pleasure" at the expense of a terrified, abused girl.

I have heard many teenage girls talk about inappropriate music with the excuse, "I don't listen to the words, I just like the beat! I can listen to it without it affecting me." Or the classic, "That is my favorite movie! It's so beautiful, I love it, best movie I've ever seen in my whole life...well...except for a couple bad parts, but you can just fast forward and skip over those."

We must wake up and see that until we quit buying everything the media is throwing at us they will continue selling it. We must rise up against this social injustice and say, "No! A woman is worth so much more than that! I am not going to support this twisted lie. I am choosing today that my life will be an ANSWER, an absolute shining example of purity and excellence. I will emulate what true beauty is, the kind that shines from the inside out, and I will not lend my ears or my eyes to anything that tries to tell me and my sisters otherwise. I'm willing to give up certain music, movies, social sites, and even relationships that suggest a woman's worth is in her sexuality. I will stand up and speak out whenever I have the opportunity to change something in this world for the good. I won't despise the small things, but I will make a series of God-honoring, faithful, consistent, righteous choices. I will pierce holes into this darkness with each moment of my life which is lit up by Christ."

If there is one thing we must utterly destroy in our lives, it is sexual sin and perversion. Let's not be ashamed to live holy lives. The world wants us to think that there's something creepy or wrong about waiting for true love. What a lie! Why is it that we often times go to the movies and watch a bedroom scene on the big screen and not even flinch? We must keep our standard of purity in our movies and music as well. We are the temple of the King of Kings and Lord of Lords. 1 Corinthians 6:18-20 says, "Flee immorality. Every other sin that a man commits is outside the body, but the immoral man sins against his own body. Or do you not know that your body is a temple of the Holy Spirit who is in you, whom you have from God, and that you are not your own? For you have been bought with a price: therefore glorify God in your body."

Let's be like Jael, in Judges 4. My, she was a feisty one! When the enemy commander came into her home, she didn't mess around. As soon as he fell asleep, she lifted up a tent peg and smashed it through his head. Whew! Talk about violent! We've gotta have this same kind of fire and passion for purity! Let's lift up the tent peg of purity and smash it through the devil's head.

When it comes to sex trafficking, I do not want to be part of the problem. I am called to be an answer! Dressing immodestly and supporting movies and music with major sex themes is not going to make a difference in this world. We are called to shine like stars in the universe. That means we must stand apart from the crowd. I don't want to have any part with the darkness or with the sexual immorality that is talked about in Revelation; the woman riding the beast, drunk with the blood of the saints. I want nothing to do with it, and I'm pretty sure neither do you!

Hadassah, Sarah, Rebekah, Deborah, and Jael were all 1 Peter 3:3 Girls. Do you want God to add your name to that list? You can join these women of virtue and take a stand for purity and righteousness! Can you imagine if we lived like these radical 1 Peter 3:3 women? It would totally rock this world!

Day 24
Demolishing the Enemy's Plans

My very favorite thing about fairytales is that they all have happy endings. We've talked about many different Princesses throughout this book, but today I want to talk about a Princess that you may have never heard of before. You've read about her many times, and she is scattered throughout so many places in God's Word. This Princess's name is Israel. The Lord used so many parables to talk about His chosen nation of Israel, but this one parable in particular absolutely cuts me to the heart. In this passage, the Lord describes Israel like an orphan, who is adopted to be His Royal Princess Daughter.

"On the day you were born your cord was not cut, nor were you washed with water to cleanse you, nor were you rubbed with salt, nor wrapped in swaddling cloths. No eye pitied you to do any of these things for you, to have compassion on you, but you were thrown out into the open field. For on the day you were born, you were loathed. And when I passed by you, and saw you struggling in your own blood, I said to you in your blood, 'Live!' Yes, I said to you in your blood, 'Live!' I made you thrive like a plant in the field, and you grew, matured, and became very beautiful. Your hair grew, but you were naked and bare. When I passed by you again and looked upon you, indeed your time was the time for love, so I spread My wing over you and covered your nakedness. I swore an oath to you and entered into a covenant with you, and you became Mine, says the Lord your God. Then I washed you in water. Yes, I thoroughly washed off your blood and I anointed you with oil. I clothed you in embroidered cloth and gave you sandals of badger skin, I clothed you with fine linen and covered you with silk. I adorned you with ornaments, put bracelets on your wrists, and a necklace on your neck. Thus you were adorned with gold and silver, and your clothing was of fine linen, silk and embroidered cloth. You ate pastry of fine flour, honey, and oil. You were exceedingly beautiful and rose to be a queen (succeeded to royalty.) Your fame went out among the nations because of your beauty, for it was perfect through My splendor which I had bestowed on you." (Ezekiel 16:4-14)

Isn't that beautiful?! I feel like that passage in Ezekiel 16 describes everything that we've been talking about throughout this whole book! He has adopted us, loved us, dressed us in garments of beauty, and given us His splendor. How could things possibly get any better?!

Sadly, if you continue reading through chapter sixteen, that last sentence is followed by a huge "but." Uh-oh. That can never be good. This is where Israel's story takes a heart-breaking turn for the worst.

"BUT you trusted in your own beauty, played the harlot because of your fame, and poured out your harlotry on everyone passing by who would have it. You took some of your garments and adorned multi-colored high places for yourself, and played the harlot on them. Such things should not happen, nor be. You also have taken your beautiful jewelry made from My gold and My silver which I have given you and made for yourself male images and played the harlot with them. You took your embroidered garments and covered them and you set My oil and My incense before them. Also My food which I gave you – the pastry of fine flour, oil, and honey which I fed you – you set it before them as sweet incense, and so it was, says the Lord your God. Moreover, you took your sons and your daughters, whom you bore to Me, and these you sacrificed to them to be devoured. Were your acts of harlotry a small matter, that you have slain My children and offered them up to them by causing them to pass through the fire? And in all of your abominations and acts of harlotry, you did not remember the days of your youth, when you were naked and bare, struggling in your blood." (Ezekiel 16:15-16)

This story isn't just about Israel. I believe it is also about us. We would absolutely hate to think of ourselves as harlots or adulterers who would dare to run off with other lovers and break the heart of Jesus. We would *never* do that. Right?

"She said, 'I will go after my lovers, who give me my food and my water, my wool and my linen, my oil and my drink.' " (Hosea 2:5) Idols can take many different forms and shapes. But right now, I'd like to talk about just one specifically. An idol named Baal. "She has not acknowledged that I was the One who gave her the grain, the new wine, and oil – who lavished on her the silver and gold which they used for Baal." (Hosea 2:8)

We read about Baal quite a lot throughout the Old Testament. I believe that 'Baal' was just a name given to the enemy, Satan. In ancient culture, people had many, many, many different 'gods' but the root of them all is the same...the devil! He tries to rule over people's hearts in many ways, shapes and forms, so it's important to recognize the ways that he works through deception, to make sure that we are not worshiping 'Baal.' The enemy is thirsty for worship. He wants to be loved and adored, hence the reason why he got kicked out of heaven!

So what are some ways that God's people unknowingly worship the enemy? We see an example when Moses went up to the mountain to meet with God and receive the Ten Commandments. When he left, the children of Israel totally fell into the enemy's trap. They were impatient and unwilling to wait for God's perfect timing. They didn't want to believe in something that didn't give them immediate results, so they rebelled against a leader who advised them to wait on God! The enemy always tries to plant "conspiracy theories" against God's laws. He tries to plant doubts and fears that argue with God's perfect ways of purity and righteousness, and convince us that the "quick and easy," flesh-fulfilling, "have it my way" is the best answer. The enemy tries to use our flesh to make us think that doing something "now" and making it happen in our own power will be so much better than doing it God's way and waiting until He does it in His perfect timing. But that is just another lie! We see that in Sarah and Abraham's story. Creating an Ishmael instead of waiting for God to send the promised Isaac is *never* a good idea. In the desert this is where the Israelites took all the silver and gold that God had given them, and created a golden calf to worship. They named him Baal. How often do we get impatient and fearful, and find ourselves doing the same thing?

Another way that the Baal mindset can sneak into the lives of Christians is through "religion." Jesus hates religion. The enemy wants us to come under a religious spirit and have a performance mentality that thinks we must impress God and earn grace somehow. But that is not God's heart at all! He loves us just the way we are, and we never have to "earn" anything from Him!

The enemy set up some DISGUSTING rituals for those who chose to worship him under the name of 'Baal.' They would dance around and cut themselves, hurt themselves, and kill their children in order to get the 'god's attention,' to be considered 'worthy' of their prayers to be answered. It sounds absolutely insane, but sometimes we do the same thing. We feel like we have to perform or worship in a certain way to get God's attention. It's easy to slip into a place of striving and think, "If I just work harder. If I just love more. If I just sing louder, or worship harder, or give more sacrificially, THEN God will love and bless me." This is why need to totally eradicate any performance mentality or toxic ways of thinking that say we have to earn grace. The enemy set this up as a form of self-torture for anyone who chooses to think this way.

The enemy is SO messed up. Not only does he want to be worshiped as 'king' he also wants to be worshiped as 'queen.' He is truly so psycho that he thinks he wants to be a woman also. He is jealous of Jesus' Bride, the beautiful and glorious Church!

Wanting to be more beautiful was another huge downfall for Satan. The enemy has messed up gender roles because he himself is messed up. Personally, I believe that Satan is the first 'transgender' and he has been able to transfer that deceptive spirit to others. So, he also operates under the name of "Ashtoreth," the goddess of sex. In Biblical times she was called the "queen of heaven" and was believed to be Baal's bride. People had to perform sex acts to get 'Baal and Ashtoreth' in the mood to bless them. This totally consumed the hearts of so many women as they believed this 'goddess' was the only one who could bless them with children. So these poor, oppressed women engaged in temple prostitution as much as they could, in hopes to get the 'blessing' of a happy and healthy child birth. How very sad! All they wanted was to be happy and safe and have a blessed family, but they were destroyed for their lack of knowledge. Have you ever heard the saying, "What I don't know won't hurt me"? That is not true! Throughout history, so many generations have suffered from things that they never needed to, if only they had known the truth of God's Word.

I believe the same thing is true today. We need to educate this world and teach them about God's ways so that they can experience the healing, restoration, and blessing that they so desperately long for.

From this 'goddess' we can trace back so many other things running rampant on the earth right now; such as sexual immorality, feminism, abortion, human trafficking, temple prostitution, child abuse, same sex marriage, porn, and major gender role problems. So many women in our generation don't embrace their femininity and position as the TRUE "Queen of Heaven" (God's Bride!) and have allowed the enemy to tell them all kinds of lies. Can you see how messed up Satan is? He is trying to manipulate and duplicate a FALSE COUNTERFIT of Jesus and His Bride, the Church! Jesus is King, and we are His beloved! Satan wants to be both. But he cannot. He has totally lost, but he's trying to get away with as much as he can before his time is up.

(Just a side note of something you can be praying about! I know this section has already given you a ton of food for thought, but here's something else to talk to the Lord about in prayer. The entire nation of India worships the "queen of heaven." Temple prostitution is completely legal there. Parents believe that it is a great honor to give their daughters to that role and think they will be 'blessed' and that their child will become some sort of goddess. This means that more sweet little girls, with innocent broken hearts and broken bodies, are doomed to a lifetime of sexual servitude, all because of deception. Sisters, we MUST do something about this. Petition heaven. Ask for strategies to bring unique answers to this problem. The hour is now!)

Why am I sharing all of this with you? It is not for the purposes of discouraging you, highlighting and praising what the enemy has gotten away with, or trying to magnify the kingdom of darkness. The reason I am exposing the enemy's plot in these various areas of life is because WE are here to change it. I share these things with the prayer that you will burn with compassion for those who are broken, that you will see the attack against the women of this generation and become outraged, that you will believe what God has said about you, and get excited about your royal role! You are going to change the course of history! I truly believe that!

It is time for a new generation of Josiah's to rise up. We are a new breed of royal sons and daughters and are like nothing the earth has ever seen before. Now, King Josiah was a very, very unique guy. "Josiah was eight years old when he became king, and he reigned thirty one years in Jerusalem..." (2 Chronicles 34:1) I've never heard of an eight-year-old king before! "And he did what was right in the sight of the Lord, and walked in all the ways of his father David, he did not turn aside to the right hand or to the left." In the Old Testament, we find this is a very rare thing! It says, "Now before him there was no king like him, who turned to the Lord with all of his heart, with all of his soul, and with all of his might, according to the Law of Moses, nor after him did any arise like him."

When Josiah was king, Hilkiah the priest discovered the Book of the Law, which had been hidden for a very long time. Nobody knew what God had wanted for all of these years, and the people of God were NOT familiar with His Word. So as you can imagine, they were into every shade and flavor of sinning. They were deceived and worshiping all sorts of idols because they had lost sight of the Word and God's standards of holiness. When Josiah heard the words of the Book of the Law, he tore his clothes in distress and cried out, asking how they could make things right again. Hilkiah went to ask a prophetess named Huldah what God's perspective was on the matter. Josiah decided to destroy the works of the devil. He was NOT going to mess around or tolerate any more of this Baal crap that his people had been involved with for so long.

So, the king commanded Hilkiah and all the guys to bring out of the temple of the Lord all the articles that were made for Baal, for Ashtoreth, and for all the hosts of heaven, and he BURNED them. Then he tore down the ritual booths of the perverted persons that were in the house of the Lord. He also BROKE down the high places at the gates, and he made sure that *no one would make his son or daughter pass through the fire.* He removed the horses and burned the chariots. The king broke down and PULVERIZED and threw their dust into the air. He BROKE into pieces the sacred pillars and wooden images. He BROKE DOWN and BURNED UP the high places and CRUSHED THEM TO POWDER. He took away all the shrines and he executed all the priest of the high places.

There are so many intense action words in 2 Kings 23! After this guy was through cleaning house, doing a spiritual clean sweep, there was nothing of the enemy left to be seen! Sisters, this is what we need to do. We cannot, cannot, CANNOT allow any more idols or evil mindsets to be roaming around in our hearts and our homes.

Let's talk about Huldah, another main player in this story. I have to admit, I was surprised to find this woman here when I read this story. Why? Well, I honestly thought that I knew who all the leading ladies were in the Bible! I thought that I had studied them all very closely, and I knew who my favorites were! I grew up in Sunday school, was raised in a Christian family, and I've read the Bible all the way through several times, but somehow I had never noticed Huldah! I stopped dead in my tracks as I read this fascinating phrase about her: "So Hilkiah the priest, and Ahikam, and Achbor, and Shaphan, and Asaiah, went unto the prophetess, the wife of Shallum the son of Tikvah, the son of Harhas, keeper of the wardrobe—now she dwelt in Jerusalem in the second quarter—and they spoke with her."

There are only a few women actually given the name "prophetess" in the Bible. She was also the "keeper of the wardrobe." After doing a little bit of research, I learned that the keeper of the wardrobe was in charge of the all the tailors and the laundry department in the palace. Spiritually speaking, being a "keeper of the wardrobe" is what God has called us all to do! We must each steward the wardrobe of our hearts. What garments are we wearing? God has made it very clear as to what kind of clothes we are supposed to wear in the spirit and what we need to get rid of.

Huldah brought the Word of the Lord to the situation, which is what we are called to do as keepers of the wardrobe. We must continually bring God's Words to everyone around us. We are keepers of something precious. Our hearts are our wardrobe! The Garden of our Hearts is what we are responsible for. As we continue to pour the Word of God into our own hearts, that garden begins to flourish so that we can spread, expand, and bestow the truth and beauty on so many others.

Day 25
The Garden of My Heart

"She considers a field and buys it, with the fruit of her hands she plants a vineyard." (Proverbs 31:16) Let's imagine for a moment that every heart in the universe looks like a plot of land. Every soul is a garden. Every mind has a space where plants, vineyards, and crops can grow. Everyone has been given the opportunity to design a beautiful landscape and make the most out of this priceless gift. We've all been given the same ingredients, soil, water, seed and sunshine, but not all of our gardens are going to look the same.

Some of us will take the seed, which is the Word of God, and plant a glorious garden sanctuary to testify of God's goodness. We will bud and bloom and blossom, and feed other starving souls with the abundance of our harvest. But some will allow the enemy to come in and mess with their garden. Some hearts are barren. Some gardens have been torn down, trampled upon, and cursed with bitterness. Some soil is hard. Others have soft, tender soil, and are continually pouring the Living Water of God's Holy Word into their hearts. God's Word does not return void. Faith the size of a mustard seed will produce a mighty root system for a ginormous tree. But we each have the God-given responsibility to tend to and guard our own gardens! The garden of our minds and hearts has gates. The enemy is always looking for ways to come in and steal from us. Just like in the Garden of Eden, that sneaky serpent is still looking for an open entrance into each of our gardens.

The Bible talks a lot about vineyards. I like to imagine that my own heart will produce a beautiful garden with a fruitful vineyard. Why do I want to grow a vineyard inside of my soul? Because my Heavenly Father wants me to bear fruit, fruit that will not be stolen or cut off, fruit that will remain. John 14 talks all about how God is the vinedresser, Jesus is the Vine, and we are His branches. Anything that doesn't bear fruit is cut off and thrown into the fire. I don't want my heart to be a wasted space. I want it to be a holy garden, a gift of love and sacrifice that I can give unto my King!

I believe that when God created the Garden of Eden His dream was for that garden to spread across the whole earth. He wanted Adam and Eve to carry the seeds of His goodness and love inside of their souls, plant those seeds everywhere they went, and bear spiritual fruit all across this earth! I believe His heart was to see His Kingdom multiplied and expanded, and for Eden to bear more and more fruit! The word Eden means "heaven." I believe that the Father's heart has not changed. He still wants heaven to touch this earth. That's what Jesus prayed for! "Your Kingdom come, Your will be done on earth as it is in heaven." The amazing part about this is that Jesus wants to use us to do it. He is the Vine, but He wants to extend Himself through us, His branches. He wants to reach through our own individual gardens of His goodness and glory, to spread all across the world!

Vineyards are really interesting to me. In the Bible, vineyards always had fences or walls built around them. Why? To keep the enemy out! "Catch us the foxes, the little foxes that spoil the vines for our vines have tender grapes." (Song of Songs 2:15) A vineyard without strong walls isn't going to last very long. And isn't that true of our hearts? Proverbs tells us that we must guard our hearts will all diligence, but for some reason we tend to take that command a little bit lightly. We leave our precious gates open and allow all sorts of things to come through. We allow our minds to entertain music, movies, television, toxic thoughts, toxic conversations, and toxic friendships that damage our inner vineyard. If we could peek inside and truly see what our "garden" looks like, many of us would be shocked. "Why have you broken down her hedges, so that all who pass by the way pluck her fruit?" (Psalm 80:12) In what ways do you need to amp up the security system of your heart and mind? You are the most priceless treasure EVER. So why are we filling our minds with so much junk?

Maintaining a vineyard is hard work, and we have to be diligent with it. In Mark 21, Jesus mentions some of the tasks that are required to run a successful vineyard. After purchasing the land, he fenced it in and gathered up the stones. He got rid of the stony places, prepared the soil for planting, and then built a watch-tower. "The wild boar out of the woods uproots it, and the wild beast of the field devours it..." (Psalm 80:13) Not only do we have to build a fence, we also have to build a watch-tower to keep an eye on what the enemy is doing. We have to strengthen the weak places. We have to fight for our vineyard. Why is it so important? Because our vineyard is our place of WORSHIP. Our innermost soul, the depths of who we are, was created to love and adore Jesus. We were created to have relationship with Him and worship Him in Spirit and in Truth. Fruit comes when we are intimate with Him, when we are close to Him and have relationship with Him. The enemy doesn't want that to happen so he tries to distract us with all kinds of other lovers.

"I will punish her for the days she burned incense to the Baals, she decked herself with rings and jewelry and went after her lovers, but me she forgot. Therefore I am now going to allure her, I will lead her into the dessert, and speak tenderly to her. There *I will give her back her vineyards* and I will make the Valley of Achor a door of hope. There she will sing as in the days of her youth as in the days that she came up out of Egypt..." (Hosea 2:13-15) Notice God said, *I will give back her vineyards*. This must mean that they had been stolen. So how does the enemy go about trying to steal someone's vineyard? Let's look at a story in the Bible that talks about just this! We find this story in 1 Kings 21...

"And it came to pass after these things that Naboth the Jezreelite had a vineyard which was in Jezreel, next to the palace of Ahab, King of Samaria. So Ahab spoke to Naboth saying, 'Give me your vineyard that I may have it for a vegetable garden, because it is near, next to my house, and for it I will give you a vineyard better than it. Or, if it seems good to you, I will give you its worth in money."

So Naboth has a beautiful vineyard. King Ahab wants it and makes a nice offer for it. In a normal story, it seems like Naboth would have just shrugged his shoulders and said, "Sure you have a deal!" He could have sold his lot of land to the King, gotten a huge amount of money, and bought a new lot. But that's not what happened.

"But Naboth said to Ahab, "The Lord forbid that I should give the inheritance of my fathers to you!"

Woah, harsh response? To understand this passage, we have to realize how important *inheritance* was to the Israelites. Inheritance was everything! If your Father gave you a piece of land, that was a huge treasure. You wouldn't sell it for anything! Inheritance was such a special thing, and all the Israelites understood the value of family inheritance. It was so wrong for King Ahab to ask for it in the first place! But that's what the enemy does. He never follows the rules. He does everything totally illegally. So then Ahab got totally upset.

"So Ahab went to his house sullen and displeased because of the word which Naboth the Jezreelite had spoken to him, for he had said, "I will not give you the inheritance of my fathers." And he lay down on his bed, and turned away his face, and would eat no food. But Jezebel his wife came and said to him, "Why is your spirit so sullen that you eat no food?"

Ahab goes on to explain what happened, and Jezebel decides to take matters into her own hands. This is where things start to get totally crazy. Jezebel, the queen of a demonic worship movement, (yeah, this is the same lady who was hunting down Elijah and killing every prophet of the One True God) decided to use the people of Israel to her advantage. She played the "religion" card and told the city to proclaim a fast because Naboth had blasphemed God and the king, which was a total lie. But the city fell for it, because hey a fast sounds legit right? So the city rallied behind Jezebel, stoned Naboth, and took the vineyard. Just like that. The enemy was totally unfair, played down and dirty, and broke all the rules. But the Lord saw what happened and passed judgement on the enemy. Ahab and Jezebel were destroyed.

So what's the moral of this story? It seems so random, why is it even in the Bible? There are a few things that we can extract from this story. 1) The enemy wants your vineyard, and he will use anything from his evil toolbox to do it, including lies, deception, and even "religion." 2) You must be totally aware of how precious, priceless, and irreplaceable your vineyard is or else you may be tempted to sell it to him. 3) If you've given up your vineyard in the past, God is all about restoration! Remember Hosea 2:14 says, "Therefore I am now going to allure her, I will lead her into the dessert, and speak tenderly to her. There I will give her back her vineyards and I will make the Valley of Achor a door of hope. There she will sing as in the days of her youth as in the days that she came up out of Egypt..."

My vineyard is a place of worship. I want to bear fruit so that I can bring Him wine from my vineyard and pour it at the feet of King Jesus. He so desires that fresh wine! He desires for me to pour out every ounce of my love, energy, attention, life, and breath into loving Him, because that's the way that He feels about me! He says to His bride, "'You have ravished my heart, my sister, my bride, you have ravished my heart with one glance of your eyes, with one jewel of your necklace. How fair is your love, my sister, my spouse! How much better than wine is your love....A garden enclosed is my sister, my bride, a spring shut up, a fountain sealed. A fountain of gardens, a well of living waters, and streams from Lebanon.' And my response is, 'Awake O north wind, and come O south! Blow upon my garden, that its spices may flow out. **That**

**my beloved may come into His garden and eat its pleasant
fruits.' "**

It is HIS garden. I want Him to enter in and enjoy who I am. I
want Him to find good fruits, the fruit of His Spirit, the fruit of His
labor and His love, and walk with me like in Eden! I want to break
open my worship and be like the woman who poured out her entire
inheritance at the feet of Jesus. You remember her, right? The
woman who anointed Jesus for His burial with her extravagant
worship and costly perfume, the woman who was accused and
frowned upon by the religious leaders because she had "wasted" so
much money on the King. But did you know that this woman didn't
just give Jesus a little bit of perfume that she had sitting on her
shelf at home? She broke her alabaster box which was her
complete inheritance from her family. In Jewish culture, that box
was only meant to be broken upon the feet of her husband. As a
young girl, it was given to her as a precious gift. It was her
vineyard. It was her future. It contained all of her hopes and
dreams! It was everything she was, and everything she ever hoped
to be. You don't just give that away to anyone. The only ONE who
is worthy of your everything is JESUS. Don't give it to anyone else
but Him! It is far, far too precious! The enemy tries to tempt us
with all sorts of other attractive lovers and addictions, but our
garden is for Jesus, and Jesus alone!

I encourage you to spend some time talking to Jesus about your
garden. Ask Him if your fence needs building up. Are little foxes
breaking in and eating those grapes? What have you allowed into
your heart that is separating you from God? Ask the Holy Spirit to
search your inmost being and reveal what shouldn't be there. He is
so faithful to guide us into all truth! When He asks us to clean
house, it is never for the purpose of condemnation or
discouragement. It is always for our good! He simply wants to
remove those things that are harmful for us and give us a wider,
more spacious place to walk with Him in the garden of our souls!

Jesus longs to have communion with us. Will you ask your Lover to enter your garden?

Bonus: Spend some extra time with your King today, worshiping and pouring out your heart. One of my favorite songs is "Waste It All" by Kim Walker-Smith. As you listen to the song, imagine yourself as the woman who broke her alabaster box at the feet of Jesus.

Day 26
Setting the Standard for Godly Womanhood

As we're nearing the end of this book, I realize that there's another classic Disney Princess we haven't talked about yet! Princess Leia. Okay, so she hasn't always been a Disney Princess. But ever since Disney bought LucasFilms, she has officially joined the Disney Princess list in my book! I grew up watching *Star Wars*. I darted around the backyard with my big brother, pretending to be Princess Leia fighting aliens, Jabba the Hutt, and Darth Vader himself! At bedtime we turned off the lights and full blown flashlight (ahemm, I mean lightsaber) wars broke out.

The *Star Wars* movies were a huge part of my childhood, so as you can imagine, I was one of the millions of twenty-somethings amongst excited movie goers to rush out and experience *Star Wars: The Force Awakens*. As the story unfolded, I was awestruck. I smiled, laughed, cried, and left the theater feeling totally satisfied with the film. Like many others, I left thinking, "I love all the new characters! Especially Rey. She was *so* cool."

I thought about all the little girls who found a new heroine in Rey and giggled to myself about all the Rey Barbies that would be sold. Millions of imaginations were sure to be ignited, and a whole new generation of little kids would pull out their flashlights and have epic battles in a galaxy far, far away.

The next day I decided to Google Rey's character and see what the critics were saying about her. I was also curious to see if I could dig up any information about who her parents were! Is she a Skywalker? Is she the daughter of Leia? Is she Princess Rey? Oh the great mysteries of the Star Wars Universe. Anyway, as I snooped around the world wide web a bit, it seemed like everyone was applauding her. After all, she was so spunky, fearless, and brave. She wasn't a Princess locked in a tower in desperate need of saving. Moms were so grateful and relieved that their daughters could now pretend to be Rey rather than the weak and flimsy Disney Princesses. While surfing, I landed on several Mom blogs where ladies expressed why they loved Rey. A sea of comments and a tidal wave of opinions all seemed to express the same thing, "Rey is a feminist hero!" they chanted. "She knows how to blast guns, beat the boys, and the best part is she's not sitting at home knitting, waiting for some guy to rescue and marry her!"

While I agree that Rey is a wonderful warrior role model, I was surprised at how much of an attack was being expressed toward Disney Princesses who *don't* shoot guns and save galaxies. For some reason, the kind, soft-spoken, gentle princesses are seen as "weak" and "man-dependent." While it is true that Cinderella has never been a physical warrior, she has so many noble qualities about her. It took the heart of a warrior to forgive her evil step mother. No "weak" woman could do that! The more I read what these Moms said, the more I found myself growing disturbed with the revelation that they don't *want* Princess daughters. They want to raise a generation of fiery feminists.

Feminism is a massive buzz word today. In fact, it's so *buzzy* that it makes a countryside beehive look inactive. I'm seeing this word all over social media. Celebrities are cheering for it. Thirteen-year-old girls are tweeting about it. But before we get caught up in all the excitement (and deception) of this movement, we need to stop and ask ourselves, what is feminism, exactly?

Celebrities, pop-stars, and women in the spotlight have been chanting "Girl Power!" for decades. Throughout history, "Girl Power" has meant many different things. In the 1920's, it meant women finally had the right to vote. In the 1960's, "Girl Power" meant that females were invading the workforce. In the 70's, 80's, and 90's, it meant that ladies could get away with wearing less clothes, revealing their bodies, dancing around provocatively and not being "judged" for it. "Girl Power" meant buying new clothes, trying on shoes, and loving your new lip gloss. "Girl Power" meant doing anything boys could do and doing it better. In the 2000's, "Girl Power" meant giving women the right to have an abortion. In the 2010's, "Girl Power" meant posting nearly (or fully nude) pictures on Instagram and not being "body shamed" for it.

The latest trend in this "Girl Power" movement is to hop on this steam locomotive called the "feminist" train. It's barreling ahead, rolling down the tracks of pop culture, beckoning to us girls to hop on board, call yourself a "feminist," retweet other celeb "feminists," and make sure that you're staying totally gender neutral. The sly conductor of this future train wreck is calling out to its passengers, "Say 'so long' to those God-ordained gender roles! We're girls, but we won't be put in a box! We can be anything we want to be!"

Celebrities are using their platforms to pick up a megaphone and shout about something...*anything* that sounds empowering. Standing on the soap boxes of social media, their cries are entering the ears of this generation, "We're not stuck in the past anymore! We don't have to live like our grandmas did, and we certainly don't have to live by the Bible anymore! We are FREE." They're calling it a revolution. They don't want to "judge" anyone for their "sexual preference." They want to wear lust-worthy clothes, but they don't want guys to treat them like a piece of meat. They want to beat the guys at anything and everything and show them no respect, but at the end of the day they still want to be loved and protected. They demand respect and love, but they won't give it. They want to be sassy, sexy, but still labeled as "smart." They want to give women the "right to their own bodies," and abortions are happening in the millions. They want to protect the whales, the planet, and the sea turtles, but not the unborn. Is any of this making sense?

When you stop and think about it, this "feminist" movement has nothing to do with real "Girl Power." It has nothing to do with encouraging and strengthening females to be who God created them to be. Attacking men, taking off our clothes, and buying more handbags isn't empowering to women. It's destroying us. I believe that "feminism" is just a big fat campaign of CONFUSION from the enemy. In these days, boys want to be girls. Girls want to be boys. But don't label them! Labels are "evil." Perhaps the most disturbing thing of all about the "feminist" movement is that we, God's people, are slowly believing these lies. Maybe it's because we haven't been taught, or maybe we're just slowly forgetting what God created a woman to be; beautiful, strong, modest, loving, a servant, a cheerleader of men, pure, excellent, brave, courageous, a 1 Peter 3:3 girl, a Proverbs 31 Woman, a Titus 2 lady who will care for, nurture, and raise up a new generation of royal Princesses! The world is saying, "Women should be strong, sexy, powerful, and any gender they want to be."

They are trying to destroy the "Princess" label. They don't want to be seen as soft, weak, gentle, vulnerable, or in need of saving. They frown at stay-at-home moms and see modesty, faith and purity as some kind of creepy cult. I've read some extreme stories about feminists being angry with their daughters because they gave birth. Some feminists believe that women shouldn't subject their bodies to the "un-empowering" act of giving birth. That they should be "stronger" and "smarter" than that. What in the world?!

Sisters, we have to remember who we are. As females, God created us so uniquely. We are the ones who were created to conceive, nurture a developing baby in the womb, and then give birth. We are the ones who bring new life into the earth, and then nurture that sweet little soul. We are the ones with soft hands and a gentle touch. We are the ones with a deep well of strength inside our souls. We are the ones who have the power to turn a guy into superman or destroy him forever. We have the responsibility to speak life and to protect our children and the children of this world; to know the truth, to speak the truth in love, and to faithfully cling to God's Word and His Ways. His ways are always right.

Yes, He has given us natural limits and boundaries as females, such as the fact that men are going to be stronger and better than us at some things. But why in the world do we need to freak out about it? Are we really that prideful? Let them be better at some things, and let us be better at some things, but let us remember that we are always better *together*. Not when genders compete against one another, but when they champion one another!

Being a woman is a beautiful, amazing, spectacular thing. God designed male and female, and the order of that union is so perfect. God said it was GOOD. It is not to be changed. The enemy is sowing seeds of confusion all over this world; right and wrong are being blurred together. Gender specifics are being erased. As Christians, sometimes we are afraid to speak up and live out what we know to be true. But God's Word can never be changed, and He said one man and one woman. The end. If we stray from that, we are twisting His Word and following the enemy's deception. That is *not* what we want to do.

Femininity is a God-given gift. Everything about who we are as females is to be treasured and protected. If you've been considering hopping on the crazy "feminist" train, it might be time to reevaluate. If you pause and look over your shoulder, you'll see another movement happening. It's the true femininity movement. It's the Princess Culture arising. It's a generation of Christian girls who are choosing to stand up and say, "I am valuable. I am cherished. I am treasured. I am loved. I don't need to take off my clothes to feel beautiful. I don't need to tear down men to feel powerful. I don't need to conform to the pattern of this world just to make my friends happy. I'm a Princess. I embody the spirit of true femininity because I am walking in the fullness of all God has created me to be."

Feminism is just another age-old plot with a fancy new name.

It can also be traced back to Ishtar. There are many different ways that the influences of Ishtar can be seen in our culture today. I encourage you to read over the list of problems that our world is facing and pray about what specific area the Lord wants you to bring His heavenly answers to!

-Abortion
-Human trafficking
-Sexual impurity in our culture
-Child prostitution
-Gendercide
-Suicide
-Self harm
-Body image and eating disorders
-Teen pregnancies
-Lack of holiness in the arts
-The orphan crisis
-Lack of honor toward men

Do you feel something stirring deep inside of your spirit when you hear about one of these topics? Do you long to be an example of righteousness, and partner with Jesus to make the wrongs right?

It is my prayer that as a cry for justice and restoration comes from inside us, we do not use our anger with the way things are to attack the world. People who don't know Jesus are simply deceived. Our purpose is never to throw rocks at them, condemn them, and tell them that everything they are doing is wrong. They don't know any better! As royalty, we have a higher calling than accusing and name calling. If we start throwing sticks and stones at people who do not line up with our beliefs, we are not doing what our loving King has done for us! He loves the lost. We must make sure that everything we do to put an end to evil is done through the motivation of love, not through the desire to "prove people wrong." We do *not* want to be Pharisees!

When the woman who was caught in the act of adultery was dragged before Jesus, the religious figures wanted to see her stoned and punished. They were not compassionate or even aware of the fact that there was a greater enemy who need to be attacked. Sisters, may we never, *ever* waste our energy throwing rocks at people. May we never forget about the dung pile that we used to be involved in before we knew Jesus! We have no right to judge anyone. Ever. We have been forgiven from the same unthinkable crimes!

Psalm 113:7-8 says, "He raises the poor from the dust, and lifts the needy out of the dung hill, that He may set him with princes, even the princes of His people." Setting out to change the world must be done in total humility and gentleness. It is my prayer that as Daughters of the King, we bring classy back. I see a generation of Princesses who wear garments of love, patience, kindness, and gentleness; women who sparkle with hope, joy, and beautiful dreams for the future.

When the world asks why we have chosen to live like this, like 1 Peter 3:3 ladies, we can tell them that we are on a mission to shift the culture. We want the media to follow our lead, and we will set a high standard for women. We are not leaving things up to Hollywood; we are taking matters into our own hands. We want women to be portrayed differently in the arts and entertainment industry. We want women and children to be treated as treasures not sex objects. We will tell them that we don't want to come under the disgustingly low standards of our culture, and that we are fighting for this distorted image of what a "woman" is, to change, because we must end modern day sex slavery. We want something more for ourselves, our children, and the generations to follow. And so, we are going to do something about it.

Day 27
Swift Horses and Beautiful Words

I think it is fair to say that I am slightly obsessed with words. Language is a beautiful thing. My heart is totally intrigued by the fact that stories are universal; and whether they're told through songs, books, poetry, or a conversation with your best friend, words are always the tools used to express a myriad of emotions, ideas, and self-expression.

Words are used in many different ways. Tragically they can be used as rocks, knives, and weapons of mass destruction. Lies that poison the mind and kill the spirit fly at us like arrows. So many magazines, movies, and media outlets use their words to deceive and discourage. Just ask the girl who stares at herself in the mirror and hates what she sees. Who told her that she wasn't beautiful? Talk to the broken heart. The girl who cries every day after school, cuts her wrists, and wishes to end her life because the tormenting words of death just won't stop. Who told her that she was unworthy and unloved? But words don't only have the power to bring death. They also have the power to bring LIFE.

Words can shape an entire generation; their culture, beliefs and patterns of thinking. It's funny how everyone thinks something is "normal" until one lone voice stands apart from the crowd and shows them what heaven's idea of "normal" is. God's standards are good, perfect, and pure. He desires such great and glorious things for His children. He wants us to be free. Free from the lies. Free from the poisonous candy-coated apples of deception that our culture is trying to invite us to bite into. If you take a peek through the pages of history, you can see how minds have always been molded and changed through words and ideas. For example, child labor used to be "normal." The fact that kids were working in terrible factory conditions was not a big deal. Slavery used to be "normal." Racism used to be "normal." Throughout history the American people have gone along with some heartbreaking ideas; but because of deception, nobody knew that things could be any different. Or that they *should* be any different. But the heartbeat of heaven demanded that they *had* to be different. Our culture didn't know how God felt about these subjects, therefore nothing changed until one voice decided to rise up and abolish the "norm." Throughout history, many individuals have chosen to live from heaven's perspective and set a new standard of "normal." Today our culture's idea of "normal" is an absolute nightmare.

School shootings, bullies, suicides, gang activity, eating disorders, self-harm, abuse, broken marriages, dysfunctional relationships, human trafficking, the orphan crisis, world hunger, and so many other heartbreaking issues have become "normal." In many ways, we've become numb to the condition of our culture. We've lost hope for any true change, revival, or revolution. But again, if we return to Esther's story, the same thing was happening then. Esther lived in a time when not only was her own life in jeopardy, but her entire nation had been threatened with the promise of sure destruction. A crazy conspiracy to completely annihilate ALL of the Jewish people was launched like a rocket determined to decimate its target. When the Jewish people learned of this plot, they were absolutely wrecked to the core. They were terrified and had no hope for themselves, their children, or their grandchildren. Yet Esther, an orphan girl chosen to be Queen, saw God's hand on her life and knew that He was beautifully weaving together and orchestrating every detail of her story, until the moment arrived to do what she was created to do. Stand up. Speak out. And fight for freedom for those who had no voice.

Esther had the power, favor, and calling on her life to be in the perfect position to do something about the hopeless, impossible condition of her generation. Sister, does this sound familiar? It should because this is our story! This is *your story*. This is the moment we are living in right now! I like to call it a "kairos" moment. (Kairos is a Greek word meaning "a time of favor with a good chance of success, a moment for action or decision," literally meaning "opportunity.") A "for such a time as this" moment.

What I find so totally fascinating about Esther's story is how she and Mordecai partnered with God and the pagan King Ahasuerus to change the outcome of this intended massacre. Haman, the evil mastermind behind this plot, had an exact date set on the calendar on which the Jews would be attacked. When Esther asked the King about changing this law and royal proclamation that went out, the King said that he could not change it. So they had to create a *new* law which would override the original decree. At first glance this new law didn't look like it was really going to change much. All it did was give the Jews permission to defend themselves. What was so significant about that? But this was a royal decree issued from the courts of heaven! God breathed on this piece of paper, and it gave them the courage, inspiration, and encouragement to fight back on their so called "day of doom."

Esther and Mordecai got out their royal stationary and encouraged God's people to fight. Their message was so simple, but I believe it spoke volumes to the hearts of God's children. The words rang deep in their spirits. They could hear the unspoken battle cry behind this simple piece of paper. "Pick up your swords!" Something inside of them spoke to their hearts, "Don't let the enemy destroy you and your children. Remember who you are. Remember Who you belong to! Remember Who is fighting with you and for you. Don't give up yet! It's not over! Stay strong, have courage, be of good cheer. God's got this. We are His! All you have to do is stand strong, believe, press on, and don't you dare back down."

Esther 8:10-11 says, "And he wrote in the name of King Ahasuerus, sealed it with the king's signet ring, and sent letters by couriers on horseback, riding on royal horses bred from *swift* steeds. A copy of the document was to be issued as a decree in every province and published for all people, so that the Jews would be ready on that day to avenge themselves on their enemies. The couriers who rode on royal horses went out, *hastened* and *pressed on* by the king's command..." There was such a sense of urgency to get this royal letter out to the world. This news needed to travel quickly. There was a lot of land to be covered and very little time to do it. King Ahasuerus' dominion was huge. The letter had to spread all the way from India to Ethiopia and be published in one-hundred-and-twenty-seven provinces, which included many different languages! (See Esther 8:10) The letter was sent out on swift horses. These horses were sons of the fastest steeds in the kingdom! I love the fact that royal horses were used for this task. I can only imagine how regal they must have looked, pounding forward like thunder shaking the earth, with their hooves kicking up whirlwinds of dirt flying wildly behind them. Nobody could stop them. They were on a mission. They hastened and pressed on. Everyone had to hear this new decree before it was too late. They HAD to let God's people know that things had changed. If they could share the good news quickly enough, there was no way that the enemy would win!

The letter wasn't complicated. Esther and Mordecai simply published the perspective of heaven. They told the world what God's perspective was on the matter. And that literally changed *everything*. Knowing what God thinks and says about the time in which we live is so, so vitally important! If we don't know the truth, we will be prisoners of the lies. When we look into the mirror, we will believe that we're ugly. When a voice says, "There's no way you can do this, it's impossible, you're such a failure, just give up," we will be tempted to believe it. When tragic things happen all around us, we will be tempted to put on our "sackcloth and ashes" and believe that nothing is ever going to get better. When the enemy shows up on our doorstep, pounding and clawing to get inside with such intensity, if we don't know Whose we are and what God says about us, and the fact that He told us to fight back, then we will be so tempted to give in.

Sister, this is NOT time to give up! I know it can be discouraging when we look at the culture and see how messed up everything is. You might feel like you're the only girl in your school that is choosing faith, purity, and love; making hard choices day after day. Your family life, school life, and personal life might be incredibly challenging and you feel constantly attacked, but things can change. *You can be that change*. You can be the one voice who starts a revolution. The girl who stands up and says, "This is what the world says about what's going on, but I'm not going to believe it. I'm going to rise above it and get God's perspective on the matter! I'm going to believe His royal decree, the word that has been delivered to me by His swift horses. I'm going to believe His beautiful words. His Word is true, and that's the standard I'm clinging to!"

You might feel like you're the only one, the only voice standing up for righteousness and justice. Esther felt the same way. She had to go before the king all by herself and totally risk her life on behalf of a bigger purpose. But even if all of your friends betray you, your family thinks you're crazy, and you're standing up for a cause that seems so impossible...speak anyway. Be that one voice. Ideas spread like wildfire. Words spread like a pebble on the water. One little splash causes a huge ripple effect. Every rainstorm begins with one drop. Every earth-shaking, ground-breaking revolution has a small beginning. Don't be discouraged. People who stand up for love combat the lies and dare to publish the truth that can totally shape this culture. We can deliver the beautiful truth to this world if we ride out on swift horses and press on in love!

Just like Esther did, we have a lot of land to cover. There are so many broken, terrified souls who need a paradigm shift. They need to see from heaven's perspective! But we are living in a unique time in history where one idea can be shared with hundreds, and even thousands, through a simple Tweet, a blog post, or a YouTube video. We can share this message through music, movies, media, and even with our friends at slumber parties! We don't need to send out handwritten letters (although getting something in the mail is always super classy and sweet!) and send them out on horseback. We've each been given a unique sphere of influence that we can use to share our message!

There are many areas of our culture that need to be influenced with the truth. So whether you are a writer, a storyteller, an artist, an actress, a teacher, a doctor, a mother, a missionary, or a social media guru, take advantage of the unique voice you've been given. Be a good steward and use your gifts for God's glory! We have many nations, languages, cultures, systems, and areas of this world to touch. The whole globe is spread out before us! The time in which Esther lived was so vital, but we have to realize that today we have an even bigger job than Esther did, which means this is going to take all of us, a whole generation of Esther's, all uniting for the same purpose: To ride forward on behalf of truth like a letter of love, sealed with the King's signet ring; a published, open-faced story of freedom and victory just bursting with lovely words of life and love for everyone to read.

Sister, we are the swift horses. We are the beautiful words. We are the spark of change. We are the revolution. We are the counter culture.

Day 28
Abundant Life

He breathed out the stars. He tenderly fashioned every newborn's tiny fingers. He knew what would make the ocean blue and invented brilliant colors of green to paint the countryside. Everything that we see, touch, adore, experience and long for has been sent to us from heaven. He made it all. The one who glittered moonlight reflections off the lake, created my heart and yours.

As Creator, it is his nature to create. Just like an author can't not write, and a singer can't keep herself from singing, the Creator can't help but make everything His finger touches beautiful and breathtaking. I believe that heaven is brimming with colors, brilliance, and creatures we've never seen before. The realm hidden to our natural eyes and veiled from our imaginations is more glorious than we could dream. Isn't it amazing to ponder how God designed all of this? The plummeting curves in the Grand Canyon, the tone of your skin, and the golden retriever puppy who sleeps on the foot of your bed; creation sings of God's glory daily. The leaves whisper mysteries to the wind. Everything around us quietly worships the King. The dolphins dip and dive with acrobatic leaps of joy teaching us something about our Creator. What can we learn from watching these carefree creatures? That He loves to see His creation enjoy themselves. That He, Himself, loves to play.

If we quiet our souls and examine the mysteries around us, perhaps we can learn a few things. I know these three things to be true simply from observing this world. 1) He took pleasure in planning for us. 2) He delights in diversity. 3) Our Creator is *not* boring!

Just when did we begin rehearsing the elaborate idea in our minds that God is dull and boring? Was it when Moses came down from Mt. Sinai with an icy law etched into cold stone tablets? When the blood sacrifices of bulls was demanded? When priests with long coattails and long frowns told us we must cease from all sin and from doing things we enjoy? Pleasure has become a most forbidden word. Enjoyment? Snuff it out! A holy life is a miserable life, right? Religion has backed many of us into a tight corner, a suffocating space where we trudge through a drab, fearful lifestyle of striving for an impossible standard of perfection. We view God as old and demanding, impatient and rigid because both our culture and many churches have displayed him to be so. The enemy of our souls has drafted a tricky campaign, "Vote for Satan!" His campaign posters scream, "I want you to have fun, and God does not!"

I am offering a forewarning to all who have felt this way: Your tight religious knee socks are about to get knocked off! You ready for this? God desires that you enjoy your life! More than that, He desires that you have an abundant, amazing, vibrantly-colored existence, brimming with the people you love and things you enjoy doing! How do I know this? I have traced the fingerprints back to the Potter's hand. I have found blueprints for the original design. I have dusted off and uncovered a fairytale dream authored by a big idea God. A foggy vision in the distance that lies dormant beneath the heavy chains of man-made rules. Let's return to the very beginning…

Genesis 1:1 says "In the beginning God (prepared, formed, fashioned and) created the heavens and the earth." (AMP) The highly anticipated moment had arrived. God would breathe to life and release those things locked up deep inside Him. The force of His voice would be like a mighty waterfall, calling things that were not as though they were. His creative power would bring to pass something He earnestly longed for, the beginning of a world. On Page One of a spectacular saga He would create a stage where the greatest story ever told would play out. It would be His story, and He would hold all rights to it. Written, directed, and produced by Him. The purposes tucked away in the deep chambers of His heart would be seen. He would finally create His masterpiece. After designing the glorious background set, He would form the characters. And for the leading actor, He would choose a most brilliant figure as the model and inspiration for this character,

Himself. "God said, Let Us [Father, Son, and Holy Spirit] make mankind in Our image, after Our likeness, and let them have complete authority over the fish of the sea, the birds of the air, the [tame] beasts, and over all of the earth, and over everything that creeps upon the earth." (Genesis 1:26-27 AMP)

So we see 1) He took pleasure in planning us (in verse 31 God patted Himself on the back and deemed it good, he approved it completely.) 2) No wonder God enjoys diversity…there are Three of Him! 3) Let's be honest here for a moment. Have you ever been attracted to a guy? Have you ever choked on your hamburger in the cafeteria and thought, "Now that guy is fearfully and wonderfully made!"? God is not boring. He made men attractive and knows what looks good!

After executing Exhibit A, God followed up His masterpiece with (in my opinion) the grand finale! Women were not an afterthought. Adam needed more than a beautiful love interest. Women were tenderly crafted with something deep inside their spirits that men don't have. Women possess something this world needs and craves. His masterpiece production wouldn't have been complete without Eve!

God placed Adam and Eve just where He wanted them…in a glorious paradise; a lush, beautiful garden. Not only did they have 24/7 access to an all-you-can-eat garden buffet, they were offered something spectacular… the opportunity to know God, to walk around with Him, ask how the universe was made, learn how to tend their garden, and steward the land. Do you think Adam and Eve dreaded meeting with God? Did they find him boring and life in the garden dull? Absolutely not! I don't imagine God would've been lecturing Adam and Eve all day about the perils of sin, the fires of hell and that they'd better stay in line or else! Why would He have to? There were no worries in the garden!

Adam and Eve had only one rule. One forbidden fruit. Why would God stress over it? He graciously gave them the gift of choice and knew they were capable of breaking His heart or bringing it the greatest joy. Sin had not entered the world yet. But He knew that when it did, He had a marvelous plan to save all humanity. So why would God be focused on anything other than enjoying His creation and being Himself with Adam and Eve? God must've cherished every second with His marvelous creations. Can you imagine laughing, joking, and singing playfully with God as you sit by a bubbling brook? What would it be like to pick blueberries with the Maker of them all? Adam and Eve had been given the great honor to spend their hours with the Majesty of Heaven in all his unveiled glory, and in His presence is the fullness of joy! They must've been beside themselves with giddy happiness! No cramming for exams, fretting over popularity contests, or worrying about the future. We can be sure that in the beginning Adam and Eve were carefree, joy-filled, exuberant, and living an amazing life! They knew who they belonged to, who they were loved by, and who deemed them Prince and Princess of the land. They walked with authority and high honor, with total dominion and responsibility over their entrusted piece of land. They were learning what it meant to be sons and daughters of the Most High God. Wouldn't everyday feel like the best day ever?

In this paradise, Adam didn't have to till the ground. Eve didn't have to worry about impressing Adam or gnaw at her fingers with unsettled jealousy as he flirted with another woman. IT was all good! They were simply themselves, learning what the word LIFE was all about as they dwelt daily in God's presence. Doesn't it sound something like a dream?

"No eye has seen, no ear has heard, no mind has conceived what God has prepared for those who love him" (1 Corinthians 2:9 NIV) God desires that you live a spectacular life. Like we saw in the Garden of Eden, His original intention for His creation was something we all dream about. It wasn't until sin entered the world that a cunning thief stole our *zoe* quality of life. Adam and Eve's disobedience cost the Father His Son. Adam and Eve believed the enemy's deceptive leadership campaign and cast their votes for this rulership. It seemed like a good idea at the time. Instant gratification. But what they didn't know? Voting for the enemy would cost them everything. They were driven from the Garden, cut off from intimate communication with God, the ground was cursed, and Eve became familiar with the bitterness of pain.

Sin brings punishment, and fear of punishment means we've fallen far from God's perfect love. Curses now had the legal right to rule and reign over Adam and Eve's lives, making their existence nothing more than a regret-ridden, pain-stricken, fear-filled, depressing, stale, choking existence. Maybe you know the feeling?

Sin is a slippery slope. Deadly poison is masked in candy-coated deception. It looks undeniably delicious. At the time, you think you're doing what's best. Do you remember those silly rules your Mother used to burden you with as a little girl? Don't eat too much chocolate, don't go outside after dark, and don't go to the beach without sunscreen. At the time, you thought she was being ridiculously unfair. Now, looking back at her rules, you know she did what she thought was best to protect you, out of love, right? You have now learned from painful experiences. Overdosing on chocolate gives you a stomachache, gangsters roam the streets late at night, and sunburn kills when you hop in the shower. Your mother's seemingly silly, restricting rules gave you the urge to break each one of them. You learned the hard way, suffering nightmares from watching a rated R movie, getting hurt by the boy your parents warned you to stay away from, and failing a test because you chose to party rather than study. The truth hurts doesn't it? As we grow older we begin to see that rules, when chosen and presented in the purest form, are meant to set us free, not chain us up! God's rules are given to us because He desires that we have an amazing life. Not because He wants us to be overly-sheltered, miserable church girls who don't ever have fun.

"But," I hear your mental wheels turning, "How can my life be so spectacular when the world is cursed by sin? Aren't I still going to be tied down to my fair amount of misery, pain, sickness, and punishment because the earth is cursed? After all, I am a daughter of Eve." The answer to that question is simple. Are you operating in a sin-infested lifestyle, or have you surrendered your life to Jesus and asked Him to make you new? If your answer is B, then every shadowy curse has been broken. You have been redeemed by His blood, all transgressions and guilt washed you clean, and you have been birthed into a brand new existence! You have become a new creation! A daughter for whom every written, coded curse was canceled and declared null and void!

Romans 5:17 says, "For if because of one man's trespass (lapse, offense) death reigned through that one, much more surely will those who receive [God's] overflowing grace (unmerited favor) and the free gift of righteousness [putting them into right standing with Himself] reign as kings in life through the one Man Jesus Christ (the Messiah, the Anointed One)." Isn't that spectacular?! You can reign as a king (or queen!) in this life! (Check out 1 Peter 1:9.)

That, my friend, places us right back where we were originally made to be. Christ's amazing sacrifice deletes all sin, crams the backspace button on every mistake, and blots out every curse. Suddenly, carried by His grace, we find ourselves back in the Garden. God has tailor-made a sweet destiny, a garden for each of us where we're doing what we love alongside our Creator! God wants to draw you to the garden He made for you. He has amazing things prepared for you - places to go, people to meet, and a legacy to leave.

Remember that verse, "No eye has seen and no ear has heard what God has prepared for those who love Him"? (We can dream big, but God dreams bigger!) Well girl, get ready to be excited because that was only Part One!

"Yet to us God has unveiled *and* revealed them by *and* through His Spirit, for the [Holy] Spirit searches diligently, exploring *and* examining everything, even sounding the profound and bottomless things of God [the divine counsels and things hidden and beyond man's scrutiny]." (1 Corinthians 2:10) He desires to unveil and reveal who He truly is, who you are, and what you were made for!

I can say with full assurance that I consider myself the most blessed girl ever. When I was fourteen years old, God called me into my garden. I suppose I was much like Dorothy in the Wizard of Oz, stumbling into a dream world, tripping over the threshold of a doorway, falling to find myself greeted by His strong arms. My heart was led, through a strange handful of circumstances.

"Therefore I am now going to allure her; I will lead her into the desert and speak tenderly to her. There I will give her back her vineyards, and will make the Valley of Achor a door of hope. There she will sing as in the days of her youth, as in the day she came up out of Egypt. "In that day," declares the LORD, "you will call me 'my husband'; you will no longer call me 'my master.' " (Hosea 2:14-16)

I suppose I echo Paul's words when I say: "And so here I am, preaching and writing about things that are way over my head, the inexhaustible riches and generosity of Christ. My task is to bring out in the open and make plain what God, who created all this in the first place, has been doing in secret and behind the scenes all along. Through followers of Jesus like yourselves gathered in churches, this extraordinary plan of God is becoming known and talked about even among the angels!" (Ephesians 3:8-10 MSG) God desires to share His secrets with you. Those things that have been hidden He wants to make clear. He wants to unveil and reveal His many-sided, diverse wisdom and personality to you. He wants to meet you right where you're at and call you into your garden!

Day 29
His Gardens of Glory

Look around. No two gardens cultivated by God's love and mercy are ever alike. Some people say that variety is the spice of life. In that case, God must've really flavored the earth with some yummy stuff! So tell me, how does your garden grow? With silver bells or cockle shells? Do you prefer pink flowers or blue? Some people enjoy tending to carrots and others prefer hearty potatoes. What works for you?

Your DNA is totally unique, which means you've been designed to live and thrive in a tailor-made atmosphere. Do you desire rose bushes and grape vines to be crawling up your stone garden walls or would you rather place everything in a neat and orderly fashion on the ground? Just like God placed Eve in her ideal setting and condition, God desires to do the same with you.

When you were skillfully woven together in your mother's womb, God placed seeds inside your soul. Things that make you, uniquely you! He gave you an individual personality, interests, loves, pet peeves, strengths and gifts. 1 Corinthians 12:4-10 (MSG) says, "God's various gifts are handed out everywhere; but they all originate in God's Spirit. God's various ministries are carried out everywhere; but they all originate in God's Spirit. God's various expressions of power are in action everywhere; but God himself is behind it all. Each person is given something to do that shows who God is: Everyone gets in on it, everyone benefits. All kinds of things are handed out by the Spirit, and to all kinds of people! The variety is wonderful…"

He has given you something special. He has given you something that you do really well, and He desires that you do it for His glory! In fact, He has probably given you more than one strength because God gives His gifts liberally! Take a moment to ask yourself: "What am I good at? What can I do with ease that others are sometimes surprised by? Am I good at organizing events? Do I get enjoyment out of caring for my siblings? Do I run faster than everyone at school? Is it easy for me to design websites?" What do you *enjoy* doing? What makes you feel good inside when you're engaged with the activity? Do you feel a small tingle of success when you do it well? It doesn't matter how small or silly it is, it's a gift from your Creator! A message of love from your Maker when He said, "I am a Master Mathematician, therefore I am going to make you spectacular at math. Numbers will click for you, and you'll get great enjoyment out of them…just like I do!" Or, "I am a Master Storyteller. You will love musical theater, big productions, and dreaming up scripts…just like I do!" God is Master at everything. Master Carpenter, Master Scientist, Master Guitar player, Master Party Planner, Master Shopper… He has given you a unique token that shows and displays a unique facet of His diverse personality.

Remember the parable of the talents? The Master gave each man a gift, an amount of money to steward. God has done the same with us. Instead of giving us physical money amounts, He has invested in us something of far greater value, He has invested Himself. He has shed his blood to redeem us, and therefore He wants all of us! He wants us to dedicate our whole lives for His glory. Romans 11:36 declares boldly, "For from Him and through Him and to Him are all things."

The Author has taken the effort to create a grand story for His own pleasure. Everything He designed was purposed to point to Him and His glory. I don't want you to take this lightly. Embrace this truth. You are so, so blessed. You have a life. Every breath is a priceless gift. The fact that you are here is a miracle. Your ancestors could've been killed. There are a thousand ways your great, great, great grandfather could've lost his life. A logging accident, cholera, starvation, suicide…Have you ever stopped to think about how amazing it is that God watched over and protected your linage to make sure that you would arrive safely? You could've been aborted. You could've died in the cradle. What if you never had the opportunity to breathe in this air today, open up this book, and hear this truth whisper in your spirit, *"You have been given a life...so live to your fullest potential!"*?

You didn't ask to be here, yet you are! Grace has birthed you, grace has redeemed you and given you this moment. Cherish it! Use it! Don't let it slip away! Let the lyrics of your life be written as a thank you letter to the One who has given you more than you could've ever asked for. You are a gift sent from heaven above, crafted and designed for God's pleasure. You were sent by Him as a gift to Him. The package you arrived in could've read: "To: God, From: God, Through: God."

The little pink bundle of joy that arrived from heaven gave your parents some of their happiest days. You were a delight to watch over and care for. Even if your earthly parents didn't feel this way, God sure did! And He still does! He thoroughly enjoyed watching you waddle and toddle your way through life. Every time you played with your doll house, creating stories that needed to be told from the perspective of a five-year-old, or kicked a soccer ball through the goal post, every time you designed a stunning piece of art with play-dough or organized a game of "Follow the Leader" with your neighborhood pals, God was there smiling upon you. You were operating the gifts that He gave you, those seeds that He planted in your soul, and those talents that He invested in you. You were exercising and rehearsing the way that you might someday represent God as an ambassador in this earth. Little you was pretending to be big you. You dreamed and schemed about what was ahead, dreaming about a world so much bigger than the field in your backyard. Would you grow up to be a supermodel, a teacher, or a librarian? Would you become a famous athlete or a costume designer?

Where have those childhood dreams gone? The flame that burned so brightly in your soul was tested by your parents' divorce, your friends who said your dream was totally uncool, or the teachers who said you wouldn't amount to anything. Reality stepped in and played a dictating role as it told you all the reasons why you can never be who you want to be. Did we blow them out with the candles on our thirteenth birthday cake? Somewhere, deep inside you, the quiet ember of your dreams still glows. God has guarded the flame.

The seeds He planted inside you need a safe place to sprout and grow, and blossom into full bloom! Only an expert gardener knows how to carefully cultivate his plants with TLC. Place a precious plant in the sunlight too soon and it just might wither. Shower it with too much rain and it could drown. God understands that we must be placed in our ideal conditions to thrive and allow the seeds deep inside of us to become fully matured. So where can you find those buried dreams? Those hidden talents that you've hoarded and guarded for fear of what people might say? Where can a girl find the boldness and the courage to live the life she's always dreamed about? How can she make her mark on the world and be who she was meant to be for God's high pleasure and glory? The answers all lie in one place - the secret garden of her heart.

"The Lord appeared from of old to me [Israel], saying, 'Yes, I have loved you with an everlasting love; therefore with loving-kindness have I drawn you *and* continued My faithfulness to you.' " (Jeremiah 31:3 AMP) God is always calling us to that secret garden of relationship with Him. God desires to have a close, intimate relationship with you. To be intimate with someone simply means to share yourself with them. You share your thoughts, ideas, feelings, dreams, fears, and inadequacies. To be intimate is to take off your mask and be yourself with another person.

A friend that you can be intimate with; a friendship where no games are played, the makeup is off, perfection is off limits, and being real is your only option, those are friendships worth cherishing and maintaining. Knowing that you can trust yourself fully with a person is both exhilarating and encouraging. But it also contains a certain element of danger. Can you truly trust yourself with a person? Will they whisper your deepest secrets behind your back? Will they be disappointed if you share what you've been struggling with? Will they see you in a different light and hate you for it? These fears tug at the back of our minds when we think about taking the next step in a relationship. Being intimate with another human being can be all-out frightening. The idea of spending one-on-one time with God, bearing your heart and letting Him see your soul, can also be terrifying. What if He sees how imperfect and unfit you are for His Kingdom? What if He's disappointed in the girl you really are? Thoughts like this can keep us far from our secret garden. It's all too easy to ignore His call. We claim that we're busy and have other things to do, but is it possible that fear is keeping us from spending time alone with the Maker of our souls?

While searching for this Garden romance, this great dance with God, we find ourselves looking for Him nearly everywhere...except where He dwells. We search for His perfection in guys with great hair, at the shopping mall, on our social networking sites, in movies and magazines. We even seek for His wisdom, counsel and loving touch through our pastors, youth leaders and friends. We seek His hand and not His face. We want to hear His message, but not see His eyes. We'd rather get the news through a prophet than go up the fiery mountain ourselves.

In many ways, we have wanted God involved in our lives just as long as he doesn't creep in too close. We have set boundaries on His involvement in our lives, boxed up His goodness, and with that act we have locked ourselves in cages of loneliness. We attempt to fill the void with boyfriends and best friends, but why have we not stopped and slipped away to the garden with Christ for an hour or so and find ourselves deliriously lost in His love? We have failed to search in the one place where Christ truly dwells…in our hearts.

Perhaps the reason we've been so frightened to escape from the busyness, to close our bedroom door and sit quietly before the King, is because we're not exactly comfortable with ourselves. There is so much we wish to change. Just like fear hoards and hides our dreams, it attempts to chase us into a corner of self-loathing, where we believe we will never be good enough to dance with the King.

Let's pause for a moment and slip away to another garden. The Garden of Gethsemane. The place where our Savior cried tears so distraught that they turned into blood. His soul withered in agony, feeling boxed into a dark room where he would be suffocated. Fear cornered Him on every side. He was about to enter the bloody boxing ring, to get pounded and demolished by the enemy of our souls. In the long hours before Christ's crucifixion, He called his disciples away to that secret garden. He wanted to reassure them of His steadfast love. No doubt, what was to come would shake them all. Their King would be crucified, and for three days be seemingly defeated.

Let's sneak into this vineyard and listen. Can you see them; Peter, James, and John, huddled in the moonlight, warming themselves by Christ's words? There He is, our Savior and Champion, perched on a rock. Come with me, let us hide in the shadows, incline our ears and listen. What is He saying?

"I am the true vine, and my Father is the gardener," He begins in that storytelling voice of His. Peter crosses his legs and inches closer. You look around and examine the haunting beauty of this garden in the late hour. What a prime spot to be sharing a message about grapes. "He cuts off every branch in me that bears no fruit, while every branch that does bear fruit he prunes so that it will be even more fruitful. You are already clean because of the word I have spoken to you. Remain in me, as I also remain in you. No branch can bear fruit by itself; it must remain in the vine. Neither can you bear fruit unless you remain in me."

Suddenly you shiver as your imagination plays tricks on you. Did you hear the thundering sounds of steel-shod, Roman footsteps in the distance? You cautiously eye Judas who looks over his shoulder ignoring the words of Christ. He is waiting for the perfect moment to signal the ambush.

"I am the vine; you are the branches. If you remain in me and I in you, you will bear much fruit; apart from me you can do nothing. If you do not remain in me, you are like a branch that is thrown away and withers; such branches are picked up, thrown into the fire and burned. If you remain in me and my words remain in you, ask whatever you wish, and it will be done for you. This is to my Father's glory, that you bear much fruit, showing yourselves to be my disciples. **As the Father has loved me, so have I loved you. Now remain in my love.**" (John 15:1-9)

The forecast of His eternal love has been set in motion. But nobody knows except you and me, hiding in the shadows. We know how far Christ would go to prove his words faithful. **As the Father has loved me, so have I loved you...**

Knowing that you are loved changes everything. Perfect love casts out all fear! You're never afraid to be yourself when you know that someone loves you *for you*. But when you're just getting to know someone, you're not sure if you can trust them yet. So how can you be totally confident that Christ will accept you as you are, will not judge you, or despise you for your imperfections as a human might? How can you open up with Him, bear your soul, and be intimate if you're struggling to trust Him?

Let's look at a man in the Bible who was totally confident in Jesus' love for him! John 13:23 (KJV) says, "Now there was leaning on Jesus' bosom one of his disciples, whom Jesus loved." During the last supper, this disciple (who in the book of John is dubbed three times as "the one Jesus loved") made himself comfortable and took the liberty to rest upon God. He leaned in close and knew that he wouldn't be turned away or refused. Don't you long to sit in your Papa's lap? Don't you long to lean your head against His chest and experience His love once again? Don't let the fear of rejection keep you from drawing near. He will never turn you away or despise you!

I find it amusing that John was the author of this book but never stated his name. Instead He chose to paint his true identity to the readers. He confidently stated the one true fact about himself that would never change: he was the one Jesus loved. At the end of the book of John, he reveals that *he* was the disciple whom Jesus loved. He wasn't being egotistical or bragging about their special intimate friendship; He was simply stating the unwavering truth! John had full confidence in the Father's love and so can you. You are the daughter whom Jesus dearly loves!

"Be still and rest in the Lord, wait for Him and patiently lean yourself upon Him...." (Psalm 37:7) Just like John, you can in full confidence lean yourself upon Him, knowing that you will not be turned away. You have not been given a spirit of fear but a spirit of adoption, which is a spirit of trust.

Intimacy with God can only happen when we choose to be our complete, real, and true self with God; hiding nothing, but bringing everything about ourselves into the light. The good, the bad, and the ugly! Are you willing to take the risk? Let me tell you, it is a risk worth taking!

The Lord longs for us to respond to the invitation. He has tried everything to capture our attention and enrapture our hearts. He has sent love letters to your doorstep, written your name on the palm of His hand, sent text messages, left voicemails, knocked on the door and tossed pebbles at your window. Can you hear Him calling? Can you hear the invitation?

"Behold, I stand at the door and knock; if anyone hears *and* listens to *and* heeds My voice and opens the door, I will come in to him and will eat with him, and he [will eat] with Me." (Revelation 3:20) Will you let Him in for a quiet afternoon of tea and scones? What about a morning coffee date?

"And when Jesus reached the place, He looked up and said to him, 'Zacchaeus, hurry and come down; for I must stay at your house today.' " (Luke 19:5) Christ desires to hang out with you today! He wants to tell you a story, sing you a song, heal your scars, remove your worries, and make you laugh. He longs to set your heart at ease, put your mind at rest, and light you on fire with His all-consuming love.

"Then Jesus said, "Come to me, all of you who are weary and carry heavy burdens, and I will give you rest." (Matthew 11:28 NLT) Remember, you didn't ask for His love. You didn't strive for His attention. You didn't ask for this life. You didn't seek an invitation. You didn't choose Him, but He chose you! He held His hands out to you and gave you everything when you deserved nothing! He has invited you to experience something that very few humans ever get to…an abundant, amazing, epic life. Will you respond to His invitation?

Day 30
Connecting with Your Creator

Imagine that you're an alien from outer space and you've never seen a blender before in your life. It's a strange shape, sits on an odd pedestal, and if you press the buttons on the base it makes a crazy loud noise! Whatever could it possibly be made for? An accessory for your computer? Something to plug your iPod into? How might an alien discover the blender's created purpose? Well, he has two choices:

A) Read the owner's manual.
B) Contact the creator.

Isn't it the same way for us? How can we possibly know what we're made for it we don't get in touch with the One who made us? Mom can say you would make a fantastic school teacher, Dad can say you should be an athlete, and Grandma might say you should join the mission field; but how can you possibly know your divine purpose?

Connecting with your Creator feels like a flawless kiss. It just feels *right*. In a rush of revelation, everything suddenly makes sense. Just like a blender could never provide power for an iPod nor work as a printer for your PC, you will never work right until you're plugged in and connected with your Creator and your divine purpose. Okay, you'll survive if you become a teacher just like your parents expected you to. But if your passion lies in engine mechanics you will never truly thrive. Don't you want to know who you are and what you're made for? Contact the One who made you.

"Okay, so if I click with God and figure out what I'm 'destined to do' does that mean my life will be perfect? No more headaches, heartaches or singing the blues?"

Eh, no. Please don't misunderstand what I'm saying. Connecting with your Creator and having an intimate relationship with Christ is not a cure-all. There is no magic prayer that will erase all your problems and instantly transport you to the life you've always dreamed about. You won't wake up the next morning driving a Ferrari and dating Harry Styles!

God is a fantastic storyteller, and He knows that "perfect" stories are dull. They have to have a plot. A successful cinema must include epic challenges, heartache, tears, perseverance and a powerful ending! God guarantees that there will be drama, trials, and tests. But the beautiful thing about having an intimate relationship with God is that you'll have someone faithful to see you through it all. He will promise to you your happily ever after if you continue clinging to Him! He has promised that the righteous will triumph and be more than conquerors! You don't have to get beat up in this life like a cursed victim but you sure have to fight, and cling to your faith! The journey to know Christ is exactly that…a journey, a trail of tears, triumphs, and greatest joys.

"Be still *and* rest in the Lord; wait for Him *and* patiently lean yourself upon Him; fret not yourself because of him who prospers in his way, because of the man who brings wicked devices to pass. Cease from anger and forsake wrath; fret not yourself—it tends only to evildoing. For evildoers shall be cut off, but those who wait *and* hope *and* look for the Lord [in the end] shall inherit the earth. For yet a little while, and the evildoers will be no more; though you look with care where they used to be, they will not be found. But the meek [in the end] shall inherit the earth and shall delight themselves in the abundance of peace." (Psalm 37:7-11 AMP) Evil might be running rampant on the earth today, getting away with injustice and all sorts of disgusting lawlessness, but we have the promise. If we lean ourselves upon Him and cling to Him, we will delight ourselves in the abundance of peace. And in the end, when it is all said and done, we will inherit the earth as kings and queens! Check out Philippians 4:6-7 and Colossians 3:15 to see the New Testament backing up these Old Testament promises!

You say, "Wait a minute. I'm a little confused. You said that in Christ we are set free from the curse, but the enemy still runs crazy and rules the world. So how are we supposed to be victorious as 'kings and queens' when we're still under the enemy's rulership? Do we have to wait until heaven to be real queens?"

Okay, let's review. God is the supreme, omnipresent, lofty, ultimate power. Absolutely nothing, no power or authority or king or evil spirit can ever top or trump Him. Ever. When He created the earth, He gave man dominion over it. Adam and Eve forfeited their rulership power over to the enemy. Keep in mind that Christ never lost *His* authority! God was never in submission to the enemy. He is still the ultimate authority; when Christ conquered the enemy, He retrieved man's rulership authority and handed it back to us. Now it is a power struggle. A war. The enemy tries to make us think that he is in control. We are to assert our authority in the realm or garden of influence and dominion that God has specifically placed us in.

"This is what the Sovereign LORD, the Holy One of Israel, says: 'Only in returning to me and resting in me will you be saved. In quietness and confidence is your strength.' " (Isaiah 30:15) So how does a girl spend time with her Creator? It's a strange concept. For most of us, "God time" doesn't go any further than reading a chapter in Matthew and tossing up a few rehearsed prayers. As God's girls, many of us have not had much practice in spending time with God, just like we would a friend.

But how would you feel if it was the same old routine every time you met with your friend? What if she only spent five minutes a day with you, telling you the same rehearsed lines every day? Psh, she wouldn't be much of a friend! Sometimes I wonder if God's heart aches a little at the lack of time we spend with Him.

What love message is that sending? For most of us, the idea of "spending time with God" is a little awkward.

"Be still before the LORD and wait patiently for him..." (Psalm 37:7) How do you start your day? Do you grab a Pop Tart, straighten your hair, and hop on the bus? Do you spend a few moments in the morning texting your friends or chatting with your parents at the breakfast table?

What about God? How does He fit in your schedule? If you would like to make more of an effort to spend time with God, why not have some morning coffee (or tea) dates? Grab a beverage and maybe some breakfast and sneak away into your bedroom for a few moments. Sit out on your back porch. Get somewhere with Him for a few moments every day, then do what King David did...sit down and have a conversation with Him!

But wait...how are we supposed to have a conversation with a God we cannot see? Shouldn't I have just said, "pray and let God know how you're feeling about things"? Why would I use the word *conversation* if God never responds? The amazing thing about spending time with God is that God is totally active. His Spirit wants to communicate with you! It's not like you're trying to put on a show for Him. You're simply saying, "Hey God, I'm here, let's hang out, I want to get to know you better."

But how can God communicate with us? Here's a quick crash course on how this works. Please know that God is so uncontainable and He can do whatever He wants whenever He wants. He isn't a magic puppet or a vending machine in which you can pop in a prayer and expect everything to happen just how you expected. I'm just sharing with you what has been real in my life and how you can connect with God. If you make yourself available to Him, He will do the rest!

Many people believe the only way God speaks to us is through the Bible. But that's not what Jesus said. When He was on the earth He said, "I have much more to say to you, more than you can now bear. But when he, the Spirit of truth, comes, he will guide you into all the truth. He will not speak on his own; he will speak only what he hears, and he will tell you what is yet to come." (John 16:12-13) Jesus said, "I'm not done talking yet! When I leave there is more I want to say to *you*. And I will use my Delivery Man to do so!"

The Lord talked a lot about sending His Spirit of Truth. This Spirit is also known as the Holy Spirit. He is part of the Godhead Trinity; the Father, Son and Holy Spirit. They are all connected and work as One. I love having the Spirit of Truth. Deception is a frightening thing, and it's so good to see with a clean heart and clear eyes!

Jesus told his followers that it would be better for us after He left to be in heaven; then He could send His Holy Spirit. Before this, Jesus as a man could only be in one place at one time; but now, Holy Spirit can be everywhere on this earth at once! In Acts 2, after Jesus ascended to heaven and sat down at the right hand of God the Father, He poured out His Holy Spirit (Spirit of Truth) upon His followers. If you read this chapter you can learn about all the crazy stuff that happened that day. The folks in town were really worried as God shook things up, but Peter explained it all.

"Peter replied, 'Repent and be baptized, every one of you, in the name of Jesus Christ for the forgiveness of your sins. And you will receive the gift of the Holy Spirit. The promise is for you and your children and for all who are far off—for all whom the Lord our God will call.'" (Acts 2:38-39) It was clear. God wanted everyone to have His Holy Spirit. All we have to do is repent, believe in Christ, and *receive* His free gift!

When we receive the Holy Spirit, God's Spirit of Truth actually comes to dwell inside us. The Holy Spirit brings us God's heart, His truth, His wisdom, His guidance, and His secrets! Jesus said the Spirit of Truth would only speak what He heard the Father speak.

So how in the world are we supposed to hear the Holy Spirit speak to us? I, for one, have never heard God's thundering voice shake my bedroom. I have never heard anything audible from heaven. Some people claim to hear a voice outside their head, but I have never had that experience. So how does God speak to me? Through my heart. His Holy Spirit actually communicates with my spirit.

What is your spirit? That's the inner you, the part of you that is eternal and will never die, long after your body has given up. Your spirit will continue living. The Bible says your spirit lets you know what you're thinking. It clues you in on what's happening around you and what's floating through your head. Only your spirit and God's Spirit know the true you, your inner self.

"For who knows a person's thoughts except their own spirit within them? In the same way no one knows the thoughts of God except the Spirit of God." (1 Corinthians 2:11) Isn't that amazing?! God wants to take HIS thoughts, send them through the Holy Spirit who is like a transmitter sending the secret code from heaven, and place them in YOUR spirit to see what you will do with it!

So many girls get frustrated because they want to hear from God, but they don't realize that what God is saying comes through their spirit. So it actually sounds JUST like them! It might sound like that voice you always argue with in your head. Why? Because the Holy Spirit has to speak to and through your spirit, and when your spirit clues you in on something, it sounds just like you!

This is where a girl can start to freak out. We've all argued with ourselves in our head before. And just like God drops nuggets of information into our spirits, so does the enemy. He attacks our minds with lies. Our choices are influenced by people around us, what we've been taught, and how we've grown up. So how are we supposed to distinguish the difference between all these thoughts? How are we supposed to know what is from God, what's from the devil, and what's just silly old me?

1 John 4:1 says, "Dear friends, do not believe every spirit, but test the spirits to see whether they are from God..." Don't believe everything that pops into your head! Don't believe everything that tells you, "Ohh I think this might be God talking to me." We are to test the spirits, and this can also be called *discerning* spirits. The Lord wants us to be so sensitive to the spiritual realm around us that we don't always take things at face value, so that we're aware of what's happening behind the scenes. He wants us to know what is of darkness and what is of the Light. He doesn't want His daughters to be deceived! Read Romans 8. I'm not fabricating this. God wants us to be more focused on the spiritual than the natural. He wants our inner selves to be purified, honed, trained, and tuned into His heart.

So how can a girl get to that point, where she can discern the spirits and know when God is talking and when it's just her imagination? This totally takes training. It takes flooding your mind with the Word of God. It takes spending hours and hours soaking in His presence, asking Him to speak and teach! Romans 12:2 tells us to be transformed so that we CAN reach that place...the place where our hearts are so sensitive to God's leading that we always know how He's thinking and feeling.

Just like you would get to know a friend, it takes time to become close with God. God's ultimate dream for us is that we will be so sensitive to His Spirit, to His light and guiding, that all we have to do is look into His eyes and know what He is saying.

"I will instruct you and teach you in the way you should go, I will guide you with my eye. Do not be like the horse or the mule, which have no understanding, which must be harnessed with bit and bridle, else they will not come near you." (Psalm 32:8-9) The Lord doesn't want us to be like stubborn mules who will only move if we are shoved! In the Old Testament, God was dealing with a whole lot of stubborn people. His Holy Spirit had to be contained in a box and carried around with His people through the desert.

They wouldn't obey the cold, stone law because their hearts were frozen stiff.

God desires for our hearts to be cracked and broken, and sensitive to His heart. He wants us to have deep compassion for those around us and to be moved by a crazy love. Compassion caused Christ to leave His throne and suffer the cross. The Lord desires that we have that same compassion to get out of our comfort zones and reach a hurting world. He wants us to feel what He feels and see what He sees. He desires that we know Him so well that with the look of His eye He can lead us.

Have I reached this place of absolute oneness with God? No way! I'm only twenty-two! I'm just learning this stuff, just like you! I am on a journey to get closer to my King. I don't know everything yet. And I won't know everything this side of eternity. All I know is that God wants me, I want Him, and together we can do something beautiful in this world.

Is the same true for you? Do you desire to know Him in this way? Do you desire for your heart to communicate with Him, to remain in His love and become One with Christ? Set time aside today to ask for that kind of radical friendship with God. Read John 15. It's an amazing place to start.

Day 31
Undercover Princess Arising

Throughout this journey we've talked a lot about the importance of spending time with our King. But there are only a few more pages left in this book, and after you close the back cover it's going to be up to *you* to keep that daily connection with God going! Don't abandon your morning coffee meetings! We've learned many secrets of royalty together, but God has so much more that He wants to reveal to you on your own!

I want to encourage and cheer you on as much as possible, so just in case you're not totally inspired already here is a long list of reason why spending time with God is absolutely the best thing ever!

-You can learn to be alone without being lonely. Learning to be still, quieting your heart, calming your racing mind, and sitting in a quiet room is something so many people never learn to do. They fear being alone because they don't like who they are. Spending time will teach you that you don't need constant company or friendships to be happy. You have His companionship!

- You will get to know yourself better. Knowing and being comfortable with you is vital before being successful in any other human relationship. It's important to learn to be a friend to yourself before you can effectively be a great friend to others! ("Love others as you love yourself...")

-Your mind will be renewed and transformed. You will think about yourself and those around you in a positive, healthy way. Changing your thoughts changes your life! "As a man thinks in his heart, so is he..."

-You will learn to have healthy, inspiring, beautiful relationships with the girls and guys that you know! God can help you understand others just as much as He can help you understand yourself. He can show you how guys think, why girls are insecure and touchy about certain topics, and how to communicate better with those you love.

-You will become more honest with yourself. Spending time with God is like looking in a mirror. He is faithful to show you where you're really at. You won't deceive yourself by thinking you're any worse, or any better than you thought you were! In His light, we see light. (Psalm 36:9)

-He is the best relationship mentor, dating guide, and marriage counselor ever. Because He created the essence of relationships, He knows what makes them work and what makes them crash and burn. He is eager to show you how to be successful in your relationships and to find, cultivate, and treasure friendships that glorify Him! You will also become an irresistible catch for the guys! ;)

-Your mind will spend less time thinking about yourself and more time thinking about others! Who you hang out with is who you become. Spending time with Jesus will make you a more thoughtful, caring, sweet, spectacular person!

-You'll learn not to worry so much. Learning to trust the One who is in ultimate control is so refreshing! He has already written out every day of your life even before one of them came to be. He promises to work out everything in your life for your good, and His glory!

-You'll learn to conquer fear, move forward when you're terrified, try new things, meet new people, become strong and very courageous!

-You will begin to see what's happening behind the scenes. You'll learn to fight against mental strongholds, evil spirits and "every perception that sets itself up against the true knowledge of God." (AKA destructive lies) (2 Corinthians 4-5)

-Your mind will be set free from the lies of the enemy. He can speak no truth, and he loves to implant roadside bombs on our dreams. "When he lies, he speaks his native language, for he is a liar and the father of lies." (John 8:44) Knowing the truth will help you see with clear eyes, and love and appreciate yourself for who you really are!

~*~

I love making lists, so here's another list of ways that you can spend time with God! These are some ideas to get the juices flowing. "God time" does not have to be boring. Just like when you chill with your friends, you can provide activities and the environment for fun and communication!

-Read a different version of your Bible. Mix things up with a little bit of funky wording from the Message Paraphrase!

-Take a bike ride. I love bike riding with God. Breathing in His creation, telling Him how I feel about life, and asking Him to change my mind and heart to His!

-Pray the scriptures. Look up some of the amazing, powerful prayers in God's Word and start declaring them over you, your friends, and your family!

-Sing the Psalms. God loves to hear you sing. Sing a new song to the Lord and make it up as you go along!

-Sing with your favorite worship C.D. Who says you have to wait to get to church to have a praise and worship experience? Exalt God in your bedroom!

-Read Ephesians 1 every day for a week. I DARE YOU. It will radically change your mind. Devour it in every translation possible. Try to memorize the whole chapter. Think about it constantly. Let those words sink deep into your heart.

-Start a Bible Study. Get your girlfriends together and choose a chapter or two to read and then talk about. Have a small prayer time and talk about real issues that you all face. Not only does this build stronger friendships, but also gives God an opportunity to teach you!

-Pray about a topic you never have before.

-Sit quietly before God and ask Him to teach you something. Practice feeling His peace and hearing His voice.

-Make a list of reasons why you're thankful.

-Read all of Proverbs.

-Journal a prayer to the Lord in letter format.

-Close your eyes and imagine a scripture as you read it. Try to visualize everything you read.

-Have a TGIF date night with Him. Watch a movie and pop some popcorn, and ask Him to watch it with you. It might sound silly, but I love watching movies with God! I always ask, "Holy Spirit, what do you want to teach me while I watch this movie?" You'd be amazed at everything He shows us if only we take the time to invite Him into moments like that!

~*~

As we close out this amazing journey that we've been on together, I want to leave you with the final chapter to our story...

The whole idea was intimidating. Senior year. No two words made the Princess feel such a terrifying mix of anticipation and terror. But there she was, standing in the hallowed halls of Cross Creek High School, plaid pink book bag draped casually over her shoulder, notebook clutched tightly to her chest. From the outside, Her Royal Majesty looked like any other student on the first day, standing tall by her locker; cool, calm and under control. But inside she was shaking like a leaf.

Dear God, she tossed up a silent prayer toward heaven, *please give me strength. I feel like a nervous knobby-kneed colt. Help me get through this day without blowing my cover.* The

Prince had sent her out into the real world. Royal Wedding preparations were underway, but she must complete this task before they could finally be joined as one in marriage. She had to face the real world. The battlefield was intense, but these high school hallways brought the word scary up to a whole new level. She had traded in her petticoats for a pair of denim blue jeans. And now the moment had arrived. It was her time to change the world.

"No matter what," The Prince told her before sending her out with a soft kiss on her heart, "don't forget who you are. Never forget that I am with you and watching out for you. If you need me, just call My name and I'll be there."

The Princess took a daring step forward as she pushed through the crowded, perilous halls of high school. Her Converse-clad toes continued as her presence passed the girls' restroom, unaware of the conversation that was taking place inside. The Princess' arrival had already been noticed. The girls were discussing this new character, eager to discover who she was and where she was from. She had tried her very best to keep her royal identity under wraps and desired to blend in like a chameleon. She had made it half-way through her first day without being discovered (or so she thought). But when you're the light of the world, it's nearly impossible for the darkness not to notice.

As the Princess pushed through the double doors into the high school cafeteria, the room was bustling with activity. Little old lunch ladies stood behind the kitchen counter, scooping unidentified goop onto the hungry students' plates. The gray-haired ladies smiled politely and reminded the growing teens to eat their vegetables.

Just like a swarm of bees, hundreds of 11th and 12th

graders flocked to their favorite tables in a stampede to get the best seats. Those seats resided by the windows, at the front of the cafeteria, going on down the line, the very worst being the two tables by the trashcans. The Princess glanced around the room nervously, after receiving the lunch on her tray, searching for an empty seat. She considered a spot by the window, but those tables were quickly filling up. She watched a student enter the cafeteria and parade to the table. The long distance from the doors to the favorite tables served as a runway for this supermodel, who looked more like Barbie than she did a real girl. Long slim legs carried her petite body across the room. She was tall, blonde, and had the complexion of a cover girl. The designer clothes that fit fashionably snug around her body looked expensive. She had seen this girl in three of her classes and recalled that she went by the name Annabelle.

The girl smiled when she saw the Princess, and invited her to the table. "Hey, come sit with us!"

The Princess silently weighed her options and decided to join the friendly crew. She placed her tray on their table and lowered herself onto the bench.

"I'm Annabelle," the girl held out a perfectly manicured hand and a warm smile, "what's your name again?"

The Princess shared the name that the King told her to use on this particular mission, and she was quickly introduced to all the faces around the table. The conversation which carried on around her met her ears, but she couldn't recall a word they said. Her eyes had drifted over to the tables by the trashcans where a student was sitting all alone, wearing a dark-grey hoodie while dirty, black hair brushed over his eyes. He stared intently at the food on his tray, but he didn't touch it. She watched him to see if someone was going to join the young man, but no one did. Her heart flinched with a sting of compassion.

Annabelle noticed The Princess' distracted gazed and said, "He always sits by the trashcans. Styling the same grey hoodie and dark black jeans every day. He never changes his clothes. He smells like a wreck. The guy knows nothing about hygiene and like never showers. His hair is greasy, and dandruffy, and," Annabelle shuddered, as if it made her greatly uncomfortable just to look at him, "he grosses me out."

The Princess turned to look at Annabelle, "Does anyone ever talk to him?"

Anna shrugged, "There are all sorts of rumors about him, but nobody really knows the truth. His appearance is enough to scare us all off, and the way he just stares into space with those dark grey eyes is just *not* normal. He never says a word. Even when other kids tease him, he just stares at them until they walk away. He's never talked. Most of us don't think he can; he's such a retard."

"I still say he's a vampire," another young man threw in his two cents worth. His comment was not welcome. Annabelle waved her hand as if she was swatting an annoying fly away.

The Princess felt her heart ache for him. He truly was an outcast. He was a living prisoner of the Worthlessness Camp. She wanted to stand up, walk over there, and speak to him. She wanted to share the good news of the King, who could set him free from all his inner demons. But she remained glued to her seat. *What would the other kids think of me?* she thought. *Surely they would label me as a weirdo!* So instead, she turned her attention to the food which lay on her tray and began eating the tasteless meal.

~*~

In the weeks that followed, Annabelle proved to be a friend to the Princess. And though her secret identity was still under wraps, she enjoyed spending time with Anna. The girls went shopping together several times, once to the football game, and on another day Annabelle and a group of friends all went out to dinner. They stormed the local *Lobster House* and each ordered the Seafood Buffet. Their table was full of company.

As they each dived into the delicacies on their plates, Annabelle spoke excitedly about the upcoming school dance. "We will all go dress shopping on Thursday," she told them. "I know of a fantastic place where we can get ball gowns on sale. Then Friday night you can all come over, and we'll get pedicures and manicures and get totally dolled up!"

Everyone joined in with excited chatter, except for Anna's boyfriend, who was zeroed in on his plate, stuffing handfuls of shrimp into his mouth; and Amy who picked shyly around with a fork on hers. The Princess had noticed her insecure behavior earlier, when it came to food. In the cafeteria at school, Amy would only play with her food, eat a few bites, and then throw the rest away. This happened repeatedly, and the Princess thought it was only because the food was undesirable. But the Princess now saw her friend in a new light, realizing how thin and pale she looked. Almost sickly.

Amy then stood up and excused herself to the restroom. The Princess suddenly realized what was happening. The same pattern with Amy day after day was making itself blatantly known…play with her food, eat several bites, escape to the restroom…She sighed heavily as her heart was burdened for another. Amy and food were not friends. The girl was acting anorexic. The Princess didn't know what to do. Should she say something? Had the others noticed too? She looked at Anna who continued chatting happily. *No, the* Princess shook her head, *I must be overreacting. Nobody else seems to be worried about her. Besides, Amy probably has things under control.*

~*~

The deafening crack of a gunshot echoed through the hall, followed by the sound of hair-raising screams. The fear-filled students dropped to the ground, covering their heads with their hands. The Princess' knees buckled along with the rest of them. "Jesus!" she cried out, "Protect us!" Every student cowering in fear had fallen to their knees, making way for a man to come parading down the hall. But he was scarcely a man. She immediately recognized the grey hoodie, and the little boy who hid inside it. With a gun at his side he took careful steps, and every high schooler feared for their life.

But the Princess was not worried about hers. She knew the promise of Heaven's protection was all around her. Only, she feared for the one with the gun.

He took several steps closer, and Princess looked straight into his pain-stricken eyes. They were glossed over with layer after layer of hurt, pain, and apathy; his beautiful eyes were frozen like ice. The Princess took a deep breath and slowly rose to her feet. Feeling empowered by the Holy Spirit within her she spoke, "Please put the gun away."

"Don't move!" He shouted at her, hand shaking, as he aimed at the innocent. He held the power to take a life right in the palm of his hand, and with one swift pull of the trigger destruction and death would be set loose.

"I've seen you sitting alone," she spoke slowly in a calm voice, "and I should've talked to you before this. I've never been so sure of anything in my whole life, and it's that you are loved by a King, who sees you valuable and worth his life!"

"Shut up!" he shouted at her, "You don't know anything about me or my life. And I don't know this 'king' you speak of, but I'm sure he doesn't care either. I've been going to this school for four years and nobody cares that I even exist. So from this moment on, I won't be a problem any longer." The boy locked his finger on the trigger, and aimed...

~*~

How does this story end? Did he end up pulling the trigger? Did he find love and restoration in the King's family or did it all end in tragedy? Did Amy find freedom from her eating disorder? Was the Princess brave enough to share the reality of the Kingdom with those at her school?

My dear sister, *this* is when I hand the pen over to you.

What kind of ending will you choose to write?

Will the kids in your school find their true worth and value in Jesus Christ?

Will you minister to the broken and afraid?

Or will you ignore the outcasts and the misfits and allow the enemy to steal another soul?

I believe that you will write a most beautiful ending to this story. The Author trusts you enough to co-author with Him. He has faith that you will make the right choices and so do I! I've put my pen down, and now it is time to pick up yours.

We have been on a magnificent journey together. All the way from the terrible Worthlessness Camp, into the courts of the Kingdom, dancing with our precious Savior and King! And now He is sending us out into the world.

He is sending us to our public schools, college campuses, jobs, and families. Each of these mission fields is a raging battleground. As undercover Princesses, we will each go our separate ways and infiltrate this world with the Truth of the Kingdom!

We will seek out the lost and let them know what priceless treasures they are. We will point them to the cross and introduce them to the One whose love is endless and all consuming. We won't hinder those around us, but offer a hand of help. We will be the first to show up, the first to give, and the first to stand up for injustice. We will speak, even when our voices are shaking. We will stand, even when our knees are about to give way. We will fight, even when we are exhausted. We will believe, when it appears that all hope is gone. We will give value to the things that the world despises, and we will despise the things that the world holds onto so dearly. We will be ambassadors, and bring the Kingdom of Heaven wherever we go!

We won't be perfect, but we will continue pressing on. When we fall and wipe out on the pavement below, our sisters in Christ will be beside us to help us up, tend to our skinned knees, and cheer us on.

"You can do it, you can do it! You can do all things through Christ! He is in you! You are unstoppable!" You'll hear the voice shouting from beside you. "Don't give up!"

We will use our hands and our hearts for God's glory, dreaming up heavenly answers for this broken and discombobulated world. We will give to the hopeless, care for the fatherless, defend the defenseless, and celebrate the forgotten.

We are Princesses.

Royalty is inscribed on our hearts.

Righteousness is coursing through our veins.

Royal garments embrace us and cover all our past shame.

A crown of beauty is shining brilliantly on our heads.

Our swords are raised high.

We are running forward in our combat boots,

with a battle cry on our lips.

Sisters, this is our hour.

The pen is in your fingers.

Write on.

Love from your sister in Christ,
~Livy

ROYAL DECLARATIONS

Written by Natalie Swoveland for the *Unfading Royalty* Conference.

The word of God is powerful. When we boldly declare the reality of our royal identity in Christ, things begin to change! Use these Royal Declarations to speak over yourself, and allow the truth of God's Word to transform your mind!

-I am a child of the Most High God (Galatians 3:26, 1 John 3:2)

-I am chosen, and I am royalty (1 Peter 2:9)

-I am a citizen of the Kingdom of Heaven (Ephesians 2:19, Philippians 3:20)

-I am adopted, and God is my Daddy (Romans 8:15)

-I walk in freedom, because I know the truth (John 8:32)

-I walk as a child of the Light (1 Thessalonians 5:5)

-I am free from darkness (Ephesians 5:8)

-I am free from the lies of the past, and I believe the truth about myself (John 8:36)

-I am free from the chains of the dungeon, God has set me in a large place (Psalm 18:19)

-I am loved unconditionally and nothing can separate me from God's love (Romans 8:38-39)

-I am accepted (Ephesians 1:6)

-I am wanted (Ephesians 1:3-5)

-I am God's masterpiece (Psalms 139:14)

-I was created with a purpose (Jeremiah 29:11)

-I am the head and not the tale, above only and not beneath (Deuteronomy 28:12-13)

-God's favor surrounds me like a shield (Psalm 5:12)

-I have been crowned with beauty and glory, I am a priceless jewel in the hands of God (Is 62:3)

-I am the apple of God's eye (Psalm 17:8)

-I am protected and I walk in safety (Psalm 91, Psalm 4:8)

-I am hidden in Christ (Colossians 3:3)

-I rest in perfect peace (Isaiah 26:3)

-I do not fear (1 Timothy 1:7, 1 John 4:18, Psalm 34:4, Hebrews 13:6)

-I rest in perfect peace (Isaiah 26:3)

-I walk in boldness because I know who I am in Christ (2 Corinthians 3:12)

-I can walk in miracles like Jesus did because His spirit lives inside of me (John 14:12)

-I have resurrection power living inside of me (Romans 8:11)

-I have authority over darkness and over all the power of the enemy (Luke 10:19-20)

-I throw out toxic thinking, taking every thought captive and making it line up with truth (2 Corinthians 10:3-5)

-I think like the royal princess that I am, and put on the mind of Christ (Philippians 2:5-11)

-I am free from the curse of death and I walk in new life (Psalm 117:18, 2 Corinthians 5:17)

-I am anointed to set the captives free (Isaiah 61:1-3)

GET CONNECTED:
THERE'S MORE TO EXPLORE!

Connect with us on Twitter!
@FoReVeR_ShineOn
(Don't forget Facebook and Instagram too!)
www.facebook.com/ForeverShineOn
Instagram: @crownofbeautymagazine

Write to Us!
 Need advice? Got something to share? What do you think
of *Secrets of Royalty*?
Send us a message! Email:
crownofbeautymagazine@yahoo.com

Join our Free Email Subscribers List!
Visit www.crownofbeautymagazine.com to sign up for our
"can't miss" subscribers list! You'll be the first to know
when brand new books, articles, magazine issues,
giveaways, workshops, events and other exciting updates are
released!

Get Crown of Beauty Magazine in Your Mailbox!
Have you heard? The latest issue of Crown of Beauty
Magazine is available in print! Visit our website to order
your copy!

Can't Get Enough of Crown of Beauty?

Check out our book, *Beauty, Boys and Ball Gowns*.

Beauty, Boys, and Ball Gowns covers popular and useful topics regarding boys, true beauty, changing the world, and who we are as daughters of the Most High King.

Immerse yourself in the truth of God's Word while enjoying this fun and unique "teen magazine" format. Featuring advice from Christian artists, authors, and supermodels (Including Moriah Peters, Kari Jobe, the Duggar sisters, Kylie Bisutti and others!), it's a must have for any teen girl who desires to walk in the fullness of who God has created her to be! Find it on our site! <3

www.crownofbeautymagazine.com

Made in the USA
San Bernardino, CA
26 November 2017